Huckstepp

John Dale is the author of *Dark Angel* and *The Dogs Are Barking*. His web site is www.johndale.net.

Huckstepp

A dangerous life

JOHN DALE

This edition published in 2001
First published in 2000

Allen & Unwin
83 Alexander Street
Crows Nest NSW 2065
Australia
Phone: (61 2) 8425 0100
Fax: (61 2) 9906 2218
E-mail: info@allenandunwin.com
Web: www.allenandunwin.com

National Library of Australia
Cataloguing-in-Publication entry:

Dale, John, 1953– .
Huckstepp: a dangerous life.

ISBN 1 86508 488 3.

1. Huckstepp, Sallie-Anne, d. 1986. 2. Huckstepp, Sallie-Anne, d. 1986—Fiction. 3. Murder victims—New South Wales—Sydney—Biography. 4. Murder victims—New South Wales—Sydney—Fiction. I. Title.

364.152099441

Set in Garamond by Midland Typesetters, Maryborough, Victoria
Printed by McPherson's Printing Group

10 9 8 7 6 5 4 3

To hide something means to leave behind traces.

—WALTER BENJAMIN

Contents

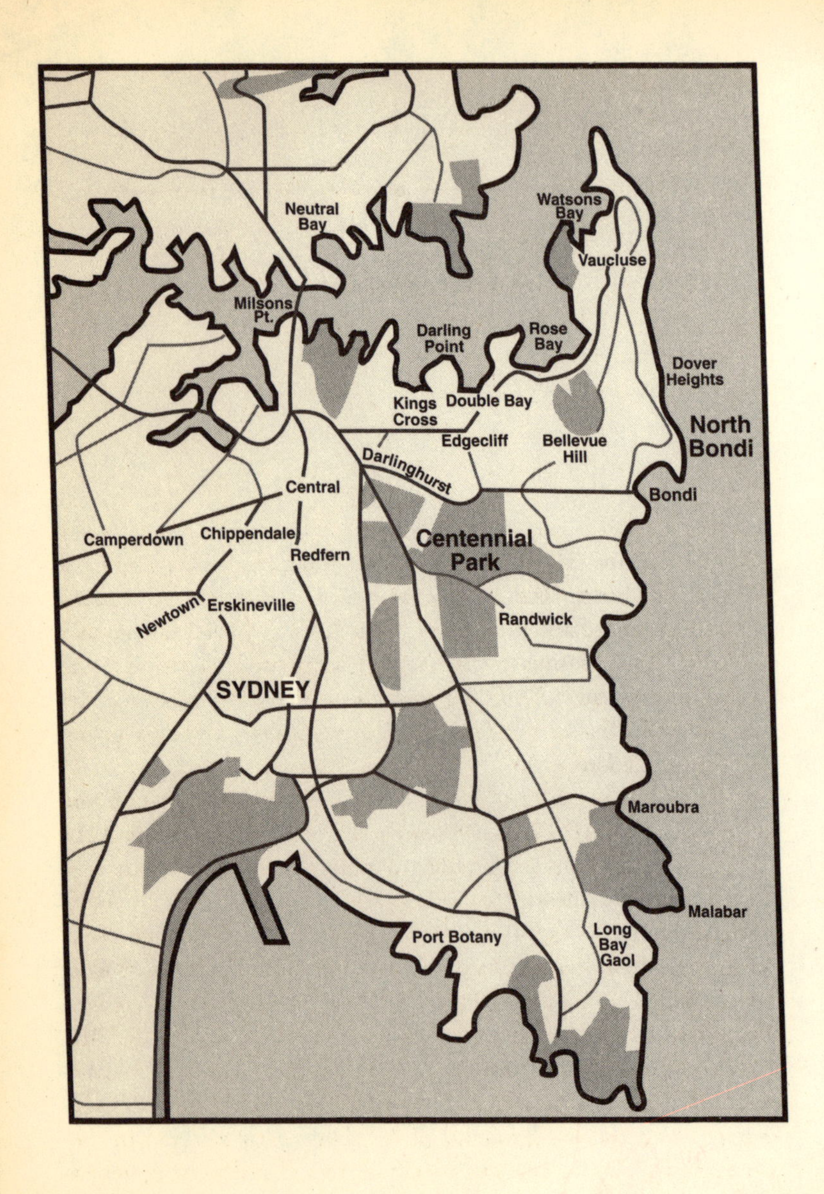
Neutral Bay
Watsons Bay
Vaucluse
Milsons Pt.
Darling Point
Rose Bay
Dover Heights
Kings Cross
Double Bay
North Bondi
Edgecliff
Bellevue Hill
Darlinghurst
Central
Bondi
Camperdown
Chippendale
Centennial Park
Redfern
Randwick
Newtown
Erskineville
SYDNEY
Maroubra
Malabar
Port Botany
Long Bay Gaol

1

The phone call

On the last day of her life, Sallie-Anne Huckstepp arrived home at 4 p.m. and sat by the window of her two-bedroom flat directly above a heater shop in Edgecliff. The flat was small, cottage-like, with white walls and cream carpet. Sallie-Anne stared out the window at the dark clouds massing over the city and rubbed at her forearm. The fracture didn't seem to be healing and was giving her a great deal of pain.

She had changed into the camisole that she wore around the house, her flatmate, Gwendoline Beecroft, was telling me, recalling the details of that grim Thursday in February.

'It was really pretty. This little apricot camisole with lace. Sallie used to walk around in that with shorts on. It looked like she'd settled in. "Let's have a quiet night," she said. "I'm expecting a telephone call at five to eleven." She wasn't going out. I cooked dinner and about nine o'clock went down to the Cock 'n' Bull for a bottle of wine. I was only gone about ten minutes; when I came back Sallie was doing her nails. She was really calm. Scott McCrae popped in to pick up a suitcase of his clothes that he'd left in the dining room. He did not stay. I went off to bed and woke up when the phone rang. It was 10.55. Sallie-Anne was in the shower. I got up and answered it.

'A man's voice said, "Is Sallie-Anne there?" Sallie had come out of the shower with a towel wrapped around her. I handed her the phone and went back to bed. I was lying there when she came into my room and flicked on the light. "It's Wozza," she said. "At least I haven't got to go to Ashfield this time."

'She became flustered. She started running around like crazy. She got changed into her blue top and jeans and went out the door and then she came racing back up the stairs. The way she ran up the staircase really frightened me. I jumped out of bed and went to the door. Sallie called out, "Gwen, it's me, Sallie!" Her mood had changed from being totally relaxed to being really frantic. And she just brushed past me and ran to the bedroom. "What are you looking for?" I said. "What's wrong?"

'"My keys," she said, "I've forgotten my bloody keys." She was going through her big brown carrybag.

'I said, "Is everything okay?"

'She rushed into the lounge and turned over the cushions on the sofa where she slept. She was panicky. "I'll be back in five, ten minutes," she said—the way people do. Then she flew out the door. I didn't hear the car pull out or anything. I went over to the front window. I stood there for a few minutes just in case I saw anything, but there was nothing, not a car or anything. I returned to bed. I thought she must know what she's doing. I didn't think anything was wrong. I didn't think it was that unusual to go out at eleven o'clock. I mean some people don't go clubbing until two or three.'

On a blank sheet of paper, Gwen Beecroft carefully drew a map of the interior of the Edgecliff Road apartment she and Sallie had shared. 'My bedroom was overlooking the street,' Gwen explained to me across her kitchen table in Christchurch, where I had finally tracked her down on the tenth anniversary of Sallie-Anne's murder. Gwen Beecroft was the last person to see Sallie alive and I wanted to find out exactly what she knew.

'It was basically a warm room,' Gwen said, 'got a lot of sun. Nyran, my son, was using the other bedroom. This guy Scott McCrae brought Sallie around to my flat. I was moving out. "Can you put my friend up?" he says. I told him I was moving out.

"Maybe she could take the flat over," Scott said. "It might suit both of you." I knew nothing about her. She was just this lovely little blond lady. Tanned. She was just really nice. I thought she was lovely. I'd never heard of Sallie-Anne Huckstepp before. I was going through a hard time then. Breaking up with the father of my son. Kevin was in a band. And a lot of the people I knew from Mi-Sex, I found out Sallie knew. So she stayed and as time went on she began to tell me about her life.

'She showed me photos of Kalgoorlie, the old gaolhouse where she worked as a prostitute. She told me she knew a lot of Sydney criminals. She'd started using heroin through her husband, Bryan. It was funny, she had regrets, but she didn't seem unhappy about her past. She was upset about the corruption, the ruthlessness of certain New South Wales police. She used to get worked up about the cops. The way they got hold of your life and manipulated you, she said. A couple of weeks after she moved in I had a dinner party and Sallie had too much to drink. She started swearing like a gutter rat and there were people from the medical profession there. She was saying "F" this and "F" that and I had to tell her to cut it out. She was behaving rather tacky.

'Then she started getting these phone calls about every second day and she'd say, "Oh that's Warren Richards." She called him "Wozza". At first she seemed happy to get the calls. She told me that Warren Richards fancied her but she wasn't interested in him, she didn't explain why. The last two or three weeks things changed. She owed him money. She owed him a lot of money and was trying to pay it off through dealing. On the Tuesday morning of the week she died she had to go and see him in Ashfield. She was really hesitant to go and she said, "Oh God I wish you could come with me!"

' "Why, what's going on?" I could see something was wrong, and then she said, "No, no, I don't want to drag you into it." She was scared. Really scared of Richards. She was being harassed. In the last two weeks I felt it in the air. My house took on a bad atmosphere. There was a lot of mould in my bathroom and it just grew. The mould grew in my shoes and bags and things. I remember having to throw out all these clothes. Then I caught her hitting up between her toes in the bathroom. She was sitting on the loo with her legs up on the vanity. I told her I wanted her out. I said my life's stressful enough without that. She started crying; she said she had nowhere else to go.'

Underneath her map Gwen wrote in pencil, 'I hope you can understand this drawing'. She sketched in the furniture. Arrows led from the entrance up the staircase to the hallway. 'Everything had got chaotic.' Gwen marked a large cross in the corner of the living room. 'When Sallie was home, she crashed *here* on the couch beside the phone, but if I wasn't there she used my bed. Sallie just had a couple of bags of clothing which she kept under the window in my room. She had a couple of nice dresses for when she went out with Pete. Usually she wore jeans and a top, or a blouse and skirt. When my Australian friends heard that I was living with Sallie-Anne Huckstepp, they said, "Gwen—you've really gone down hill!"'

I wondered aloud why Gwen had let Sallie-Anne stay on in her flat. What was in it for her?

'I'd been in a bad marriage,' Gwen said. 'I had guilt playing on my mind. I think I was emotionally ill at that stage.'

Before I spoke to Gwen Beecroft I had been told that she was an unreliable witness. A senior Homicide detective said there were things Beecroft knew about this murder that she wasn't revealing.

'What am I supposed to know?' Gwen said. 'I told the police everything. Sallie loved the criminal lifestyle. She was in too deep to get out. The sort of guys she knew. Guys like Warren Richards. She told me how Richards used to boast he'd killed people. How he sold babies. She told me about Roger Rogerson and Neddy Smith and how they murdered Warren Lanfranchi. She was going out with this young Federal policeman called Peter Smith. They were going to go up the coast, go north you see and open up a gym. He was into bodybuilding. I thought they were very much in love.'

'Was there anyone else in your flat on that Thursday night?' I asked her. In an exclusive newspaper article an unidentified man in his early forties had claimed to have visited Sallie-Anne just after

8 p.m. He told the reporter how Sallie kept a journal and a tape of corrupt New South Wales police. He said that Sallie was very excited and that something was 'Set to go'.

Gwen Beecroft pressed a hand to her temple. 'All these people have told me since that they were there at my flat, but they weren't! If there were any other visitors I can't remember them.' She was nursing her baby daughter on her knee and trying not to shout. 'My mind had become too stressed out. I was dealing with so much after Sallie's murder. I was scared of the police and everyone involved in the case. I stayed on three weeks in that flat and then I got out. I couldn't stand it.' Gwen Beecroft had gone back to New Zealand to start her life afresh. To put some distance between herself and her memories of the harbour city.

'The day Sallie-Anne died was a quiet day. I walked my son down to the Woollahra school early and when I got home,' Gwen told me in a calm, hypnotic voice, rocking her daughter in her arms. 'Sallie was up and about. She would leave around 10.30 a.m. There were only a couple of times she told me where she was going. One time she had a meeting with Detective Scullion. She was meeting Scullion quite regularly. Another time she went to some garage where her furniture was stored. She always had somewhere to go. She did her own thing.

'I remember the night Sallie died was one of the rare occasions that she ever had dinner with my son and I. She sat on the sofa eating and leafing through magazines. I turned the lounge room lights down. I was tired and just wanted to relax. I asked Sallie if she wanted a coffee, she said, yes, she was still on the sofa with her magazines. I mean she never used to do much in the flat. She never cooked. I did all the cooking, I like cooking. Sallie just used to paint her nails, or sit on that sofa cutting up magazines to wrap her heroin in. It was very warm and humid, one of those tropical Sydney nights. Sallie was looking out the window and rubbing her arm. I remember her saying she thought it was going to storm.'

Gwen lifted Grace into the bassinet. I had checked the weather for Thursday, 6 February 1986. The humidity in Sydney was 73 per cent and the temperature at 8 p.m., 21.8°C.

'There was mould coming up the walls in my bedroom,' Gwen whispered. 'The walls were so damp in there. I woke up on the Friday morning and Sallie had not returned. At 9.30 a.m. the phone rang. I picked it up, but no-one answered. It rang again. There was still no answer. I made a coffee and decided to go out to the shops. When I came back Sallie had still not returned. I thought she was with her boyfriend. I was tired. I went to bed and the phone woke me up about one o'clock. It was Peter Smith ringing from Newcastle. He told me the news. I walked around the flat dazed. I had to lie down, it made me feel weird.'

A friend of Gwen's, Roz Nelson, told police three years after the murder that around 9.00 a.m. on the Friday she'd received a telephone call from a distraught Gwen Beecroft informing her that Sallie-Anne Huckstepp had been murdered. Immediately Roz Nelson drove over to the well-to-do suburb of Edgecliff arriving at the upstairs flat, 'definitely no later than 9.30 a.m.'. Nelson told the coroner that Beecroft was frightened that police would find drugs belonging to Sallie-Anne. Nelson also revealed that she had been at Sallie's flat on the Thursday night and had made plans with the other two women to go to a Mosman gymnasium the next morning at ten o'clock.

But Gwen Beecroft denied any memory of those events. She carried the bassinet into the bedroom and came back through to the kitchen to set the facts straight. 'I think that Sallie knew she was going to die. She was really scared of Warren Richards and she was scared of Dave Kelleher, her former boyfriend, who was in gaol. Dave Kelleher used to bash her around. She told me how she used to lie in bed with Kelleher and she used to try and get out from underneath him. She used to try and lift his arm up from around her while he slept. To sneak out of the house and have a hit and go and deal to get some money of her own.

'She was buying her gear from Warren Richards and Richards was a friend of Kelleher's and Sallie had no choice but to deal with him. She used to talk about Warren's red Porsche—it had a black panel on the back. In the last two weeks her attitude towards Wozza suddenly changed. She became very scared of him. She was short of money. She had to find $600. She asked me for a loan of one hundred, but I couldn't give it to her. I was living on two hundred a week and I had my son to think of. I never expected that she was going to end up dead.'

I glanced down at the magazine photograph of Sallie-Anne that Gwen had shown me shortly after I had arrived on her doorstep. It was the only photograph Gwen had kept of her former flatmate. Slightly built, Sallie is striding down a city street in a pair of high-heels. Her honey-blond hair is brushed back off her forehead, she has heavily mascaraed eyes and gapped white teeth. The sleeves of her tight-fitting sweater are pushed back to her elbows, the slit in her skirt reveals muscular legs. In her left hand she carries a briefcase and, tucked under her arm, a leather folder. Delighted, she is smiling at the camera. The caption underneath reads, '*Sallie-Anne Huckstepp*: A Natural Writer'.

On the Friday, only hours after Sallie's body had been discovered, Gwen Beecroft was at home with her son. 'It was getting on for 2.30 in the afternoon,' she told me, 'when there was a knock at the door. I'd got out of the shower. I was dressed in my bathrobe with a white towel wrapped around my head and three detectives burst into my lounge room. Detective Scullion and two others from Maroubra police. One of them, a short stocky detective said, "What happened last night?"

'I told him that Sallie got a phone call from a guy called Warren and she didn't come home. The first thing Scullion wanted to know was if Sallie had ever mentioned his name. He said, "Do you know who I am?"

'I said, "Yes I do. I've heard of you." They were very aggressive. They wanted to know if Sallie had any diaries or tapes. The three of them were looking around the flat, they went over by the piano where Sallie-Anne used to cut up her magazines. The short stocky detective said, "Look at these—are you dealing?"

'I didn't reply, I was too scared.

'The short stocky cop said to me, "Get dressed Snow White! You're coming with us."

'They followed me into my bedroom. They searched my place

without a warrant and they found 5 grams of coke and $1000 in my purse that my ex-husband had given me to return to New Zealand. I told Detective Scullion that money was for my airfare.

'"Don't worry about it," Scullion said, "You'll get it back."

'They took me and Nyran down to Maroubra Station. My head was spinning. I couldn't think right. Why were they harassing me? They took all of Sallie's belongings with them. They asked me again if she had any tapes. I didn't think it was going to be that heavy. They charged me and every time I asked for my money Scullion said, "You give me proof that the $1000 isn't drug money and you'll get it back."

'When they questioned me they had me in tears. They wanted me to lie. That's more our way of thinking, they'd say. They were putting things into my head, they kept saying to me "Are you sure X didn't happen. You didn't see Y?" And I'd say no, "I told you what happened. Sallie got a phone call from a guy she said was Warren. No-one else."

'It was a very bad time in my life,' Gwen Beecroft spoke softly. 'I was dumped on so badly I felt I was never going to come out of it. After a few months I was called to the coroner's chamber, I told them I was very suspicious of Detective Scullion because of the way I never had my $1000 returned, I told my ex-husband, Kevin, what had happened, he said he was prepared to stand up in court for me about the money, that money was for my tickets out of Sydney. I needed to get out. The lawyer, the female lawyer I spoke to at the coroner's chambers, asked me if I'd like to go home, I broke down and said yes. I felt my life was on the line because of what happened to Sallie.'

'What about the inquest?' I interrupted.

Gwen Beecroft shook her head. 'They never ask you the right questions. My parents paid for my airfare so I left in a hurry afterwards. I just couldn't deal with it. I was scared of the police and everyone else involved in the case. I really felt I was going to end up dead.'

It was getting dark outside and the temperature had dropped

suddenly. I thought of that warm humid evening on 6 February, exactly ten years ago.

'That's all I can tell you,' Gwen Beecroft said finally. 'It messed up my whole life. My family never forgave me for getting involved with her. Sallie-Anne was very much into herself those last few weeks, she seemed preoccupied, but she never gave me any real details of what was going on. Hanging out with criminals and crooked police seemed to give her a buzz. Sallie liked the fast lane. I don't think she had any regrets at all,' Gwen said. 'I think she was a bit of a ratbag. It was just the way she was.'

•

When I arrived back in Sydney that evening there was a message on my answer machine. 'I'm the Roz Nelson that used to know Sallie-Anne,' a well-spoken female voice said. 'I'll ring you tonight.' Several times I'd tried to contact Roz Nelson, but she'd left all the old addresses, changing towns north, along the coast. A prominent Kings Cross activist at the time of Sallie's death, Ms Nelson had helped form the Australian Prostitutes' Collective. Three years after that brutal Thursday she'd been persuaded by a male friend to come forward and tell her story to police.

Roz Nelson was articulate, wary of talking over the phone to me at first, and very convincing.

'Oh yes,' she said, 'I was there that night Sallie died. I remember it clearly. I drove around to Edgecliff Road in the early evening about six o'clock and stayed on to about nine. I came over on my bike, I had a Kawasaki 750 then. I remember Gwen Beecroft was there and her young son and Sallie. I used to go around and help Gwen with her washing or take the boy to the park. Gwen didn't have many friends in Sydney, only Sallie who was staying with her temporarily. When I first met Sallie at Edgecliff she was in hiding. She'd only recently left this house in Botany. She didn't feel safe. Sallie was very cautious when she was in that flat. If there was ever a knock at the door Gwen would go and answer it.

'I remember Sallie was trying to dry out. We'd all scored some coke that night and we were sitting around having a glass of wine. Sallie had broken her arm in a car accident just after Christmas and it'd only come out of plaster a few days. I remember sitting on the sofa and looking at her arm. It was wasting and she asked me if she'd taken the plaster off too soon. I told her she should have physio. Her arm looked really sore and weak. I remember her saying she'd started to get back into writing. We made an arrangement, the three of us, to go to the gym next morning. I drove home to Coogee about nine.

'The next morning I got a phone call from Gwen. It was about 8.30 or nine o'clock. When I picked up the phone, Gwen said, "Sallie's gone! Sallie's gone!"

'"What do you mean she's gone?" I said.

'"She's dead!"

'"How do you know?" I said.

'"It was on the news. The cops are going to be here any minute." Gwen was terrified. She thought they'd find Sallie's stash. I told my flatmate, Mark Costello, what had happened, then I came beetling over to help Gwen. I got there definitely no later than 9.30 a.m. and Gwen and I searched the flat for syringes, any sort of drugs. I saw Sallie's diary lying near the sofa. It was white with a little red heart on the front. I knew Sallie kept the names of police in it so I copied all the names and addresses from the diary. I felt in danger and I just had this idea that whoever killed Sallie, his name would probably be inside the diary. I dashed off to the city and gave the copy to my solicitor. I said to him if anything happens to me, make sure this is made public. I thought I should ring Gwen from the solicitor's office so at least the police would know that someone from outside had been in contact with her. I had no idea whether they were good cops or bad cops.

'When I phoned in her son answered. "Is Mummy okay?" I asked. "Is Mummy okay?" "Yes," he said. Gwen came on. She sounded really shaken. I tried speaking to her. I was concerned. I tried talking to her in code. "Give me some information." She said three detectives were there. "Who are they?" I said. She said they wanted to take her to Maroubra Police Station. I couldn't understand why they wanted to take her there. She said one of the detectives was Scullion. I remember Sallie saying the night before she had a meeting with "Scully" the next day. His name was in the diary along with the names of all these Darlinghurst detectives. I hung up. I was terrified. I didn't know who'd killed her—whether it was Darlinghurst detectives or Dave Kelleher's mates. I became increasingly paranoid. I was watching my back at all times. I had no confidence in the police. I had no confidence in the judiciary. And then I just got out: I went bush. I thought they would get me next!'

Roz Nelson put down the phone suddenly.

I could hear children yelling in the background then Roz came back on the line and started to tell me about her change of name and the new life she'd made for herself thousands of kilometres away from the harbour city.

'I had an admiration for Sallie,' Roz revealed. 'I'd admired her from afar ever since she went public over the Lanfranchi killing. I'd met her husband Bryan in the Sovereign Hotel years before. Sallie was very warm, vivacious. Very strong. She stood up for herself. She was in hiding. I think she knew she was going to go at some time. There was the feeling that her days were up. Later when I moved into a house on the corner of Moore Park Road, close to Centennial Park, I used to have nightmares about Sallie's body floating in the pond with those huge eels that live in there. You see I identified with Sallie quite a lot. Being a prostitute. She was like my shadow in a strange kind of way.'

•

The call from Roz Nelson seemed to jolt Gwen Beecroft's memory. She was in bed trying to beat off the flu when I rang Christchurch the following night. 'Yes,' she told me. 'I've got a funny feeling that Roz did come around at some stage, but she's lying about the phone call. I remember sitting on the floor and Roz teaching me some sort of code. The police were there. But that was later. It wasn't on the Friday morning. I don't understand why Roz wants to get involved in all this. She was just a visitor. Sallie spent no time with her. She's lying about the drugs, I didn't ask her to help me search the flat. Why would I? I don't know why Roz's doing this. Anyway, it couldn't have been that early. I took Nyran to school and soon as I got home I got those two phone calls where no-one answered. Then I had the call from Peter Smith. I just feel that it was about one o'clock because the sun was pouring into the front room. But it could've been earlier. I don't know.

'All I remember was that he rang. I didn't even know he was in Newcastle. I heard the phone ringing and I went over and picked it up. It was weird, but even before I answered I knew that it was bad news. I just had this feeling, the way you do. I held the receiver up to my ear.

'"I've rung to tell you," he said. "Sallie's been murdered."'

2

Darlinghurst Road

'Sallie would take anything,' one of her close friends told me when we met in my borrowed apartment. Situated on Darlinghurst Road, the place has no views of its own, except for a dark treeless courtyard, but the walls of the living room are lined from floor to ceiling with the owner's books. After ten years away I have come back to Sydney to try to piece together the story of Sallie-Anne's murder.

'She used to carry around a medicine cabinet,' the friend said. 'Serepax was a favourite, Benzedrine, Mandrax, Valium. Pills were a big thing with her. Pills were like lollies, rattling around in her handbag. One of the interesting things about Sallie, she had all this chaos in her life and she'd be functioning on that level and then she'd get really frantic about paying a parking fine and run off to pay it. She was full of contradictions. She used to flick between roles: junkie, mother, flirt. She was funny, aggravating, attractive and talented. But so many of her traits and behaviour were those of an addicted woman.'

•

Darlinghurst Road has long been the place in Sydney to buy drugs and sex. It was here that Sallie-Anne Huckstepp, between the ages of nineteen and twenty, accumulated 27 convictions for prostitution.

The bulk of her 'pinches' occurred in the early hours of the morning when the rest of the city was sleeping.

She was first apprehended for loitering on Darlinghurst Road at 1.20 a.m. on Christmas Eve, 1973, twelve days after her nineteenth birthday. The arresting officer noted on his charge sheet that Sallie was 'Seen to stop a number of men and speak to them. Admitted she was there for the purpose of prostitution. Nothing to say.'

The only unusual detail was her address in Bellevue Hill, one of Sydney's most exclusive Eastern Suburbs. She described her occupation as 'domestic'. At 1.45 a.m. she was released and, an hour before dawn, police picked her up again.

For the next eighteen months she was apprehended with monotonous regularity. On 30 January, after her arrest by the notorious 21st Division, she failed to appear at Central Petty Sessions the following morning to answer a charge of 'Stopping Men for Immoral Purposes'. The Stipendiary Magistrate was on the verge of forfeiting her bail when Sallie-Anne appeared, flustered and out of breath. 'My baby is not well, your Worship,' she said. 'Please, I could not have come earlier.'

A fine of $80 or sixteen days hard labour was imposed; the defendant asked for time to pay.

On 11 March, a Vice Squad officer noted on his charge sheet that Sallie was seen to be 'Offering French Love' to young men on Darlinghurst Road. This time her fine was $100.

'In those days,' Sallie told the journalist, Elisabeth Wynhausen, eight years later when she was in hiding for her life, 'the Vice Squad used to take care of us—if there was any trouble with a mug, the Vice Squad would come to the rescue.' The police in Kings Cross regarded her 'as one of the VIPs'. She was sitting in a saloon bar in the Blue Mountains west of Sydney with a contract out on her life and her honey-blond hair tucked up under a woollen hat in a perfunctory attempt at disguise. She was certain that if she went to gaol, she wouldn't come out alive.

'We paid a weekly bribe to the 21st Division, as well as the weekly $40 to the Vice Squad,' Sallie said. 'The price for the 21st Division was $60. Not all detectives in 21st took money, though, just a small group of senior detectives. The younger guys definitely didn't know.'

Sallie was convinced that the Kings Cross police were personally interested in her welfare. She claimed she was arrested relatively infrequently—once a month on Darlinghurst Road, instead of the usual once a week.

'I became used to paying them. I saw the police I made regular payments to as "mates"; I'd have a joke and a laugh with them, and never considered them a threat.'

Sallie sipped from her double bourbon and Coke. 'One of the Kings Cross detectives told me I had the best arse in the business,' she boasted.

In reply, Elisabeth Wynhausen wrote: 'The face, somewhat ravaged by the use of heroin, barbiturates and booze, still shows that Huckstepp is a persuasive nymphet. Her full mouth is arranged in a pout. Her eyes are the intense blue that generally fades in adulthood. Although only 5ft 3in tall, she has the broad shoulders and muscular calves of a natural athlete.'

'Paying the police in Sydney became such a common occurrence that I never thought about the morality of it,' Sallie said. When she later moved briefly to Auckland to work in a massage parlour she was astonished to find she didn't have to pay a 'vice tax'. 'I couldn't believe it. There were actually straight cops in New Zealand. It used to blow me right out!'

The yellowing charge sheets on her court papers attest to the litany of convictions accrued on Darlinghurst Road. At 3.10 a.m. on 8 April 1974, she was arrested by Detective Punch who scribbled in his duty book: 'Seen to be speaking to men on Darlinghurst Road. Admitted loitering for immoral purposes. History: Well known. Defendant: Nothing to say.'

The procedure was always the same. Fifteen minutes after she was apprehended by the Vice Squad or 21st Division she would be driven the short distance down Darlinghurst Road to Darlinghurst Police Station, a red brick and sandstone building tucked in behind the Supreme Court complex. At the station Sallie would be formally charged and would have to sign a recognisance to appear at ten o'clock in the 'forenoon' at Central Petty Sessions. Bail was always $100 cash and a $1 fee. If she did not appear a warrant would be issued for her arrest and her recognisance forfeited. The court fine was $80 so naturally she chose to pay whenever she could. Alongside her name are the names of hundreds of others arrested on Darlinghurst Road for drunkenness, vagrancy, begging, indecent language and prostitution.

'In a sense,' Sallie-Anne later wrote in *Penthouse*, 'I was being encouraged to remain a junkie and keep prostituting myself in order to line police pockets. I have made hundreds of payments to detectives. As a prostitute and heroin addict, I had direct contact with bent police and it was most unusual to find a detective who would refuse to take money.'

Sometimes the police would pull her up on Darlinghurst Road, search her shoulder bag, and find nothing, but knowing her to be an addict they threatened to plant drugs on her. Not a threat to be taken lightly, as she discovered when she refused to pay.

On 29 May 1974 at 9.10 p.m., two days after she'd been discharged from Prince of Wales Hospital, Sallie and two other girls were sitting in the Lido Cocktail Bar in Roslyn Street, Kings Cross when two Consorting Squad detectives entered. One of the detective senior constables explained what happened next. 'On the table was two handbags. I noticed some quick movement and Huckstepp grabbed the red handbag and put it on the seat.

'I walked across to her and said, "Who owns this?"

'She said, "I do."

'I said to her, "Do you use heroin?"

'She said, "I used to, but I haven't used for twelve months."

'I said to her, "Pull up your sleeve and show us your arm." She did this and I saw large bruises and fresh puncture marks on the inside of her elbows. "How do you explain these marks?"

'She said, "I've been sick and they gave them to me in hospital."

'"I suspect you are a drug user," I said, "and I'm now going to search your handbag." Then I went through her bag and placed all the articles on the bar table. It contained the usual female cosmetics and a capsule containing a brown substance wrapped in tissue paper. "This looks like heroin," I said, "Whose is it?"

'She said, "I don't want to say, but it's not mine. I don't use it."

'I said, "You will have to come with me to the CIB. You are going to be charged with possession of heroin."'

'No no,' Sallie told her probation officer seven months later. 'What really happened, see, was those two jacks charged me with possession when I'd dried out and wasn't using. I was told that if I paid $500 I'd get a bond and all charges would be dropped. I was making about $3000 a week. I'd only recently paid $12 000 to the police to get my husband, Bryan, out on bail so I refused to pay. I was sick to death of paying the police.'

'The offender absolutely maintains her innocence,' her probation officer, Judy Johnston, wrote in her pre-sentence report. 'Additional information regarding Sallie's background is now available:

> Sallie is a married woman aged 20. She is separated from her husband and although they are friends it is unlikely they will be reconciled. There is a child, Sascha, aged 2, who is being cared for by Bryan Huckstepp's mother. Sallie's parents separated when she was young and she and her sister were looked after by her father. It seems that Sallie accepted much of the responsibility for running the house. She has not seen her mother since her parents' separation and has no contact with her father. Although a bright student, Sallie left school at the age of 15, due to the family situation. She worked in several pharmacies, but quickly found excitement on Darlinghurst Road where she worked in a discotheque. It appears that Sallie has been seriously involved in drug use for several years and has been addicted to heroin. She also appears to have had a long history of psychiatric illness and has in the past made several suicide attempts. In recent years Sallie has worked mainly as a prostitute. However, it is believed that she no longer intends to follow this occupation. Sallie-Anne is an intelligent young woman who has reached a turning point in her life. She is aware that the next few months are going to be difficult and a further period of supervision may assist her to lead a more socially acceptable way of life.'

'I think if we had met outside the formal system we would have been friends,' Judy Johnston said twenty years later. 'Sallie taught me a tremendous amount about lifestyles of which I had no experience. She talked a lot about what her clients wanted her to do. From when she asked them to put on a condom to when they withdrew from her body. She saw prostitution as a business and tried to rationalise it in that way, but basically she hated it. She had a cynical view of our criminal justice system. She saw how the police operated. She was highly articulate and could present a good case as well as any duty solicitor.'

After twice failing to appear before the Magistrate Sallie pleaded guilty and was convicted on the charge of possessing morphine. 'That ended up costing me five times the amount of the bribe those two jacks asked me for,' Sallie told her probation officer.

'Sallie was someone who touched me,' Judy said. 'Someone I admired. She was a highly intelligent person. She had a tremendous strength of character at one level, but she'd never developed emotionally. I admired her capacity to think things through, her sense of humour, but I despaired over her lifestyle. She started ringing me at home. She told me she had a housekeeper. She had no money coming in and she had a housekeeper. How can you afford it? I asked and then I said, no, don't tell me. Sallie played out these parts. One was the intellectual, one was the comedian and one was the tragic character. In the end she could never discard the fantasy of being the gangster's moll, the Mrs Big of the underworld. She often talked about going straight but she liked what heroin gave her, the way it pumped her adrenalin. I remember her telling me in Central Local Court, "Judy," she said, "the underworld excites me as much as heroin did the first few times I used it."'

•

On 8 April 1975, Sallie was charged with conspiracy to defraud. A flatmate had stolen a Commonwealth Bank stamp from McMahons Point Post Office and Sallie and her de-facto, David Oliver, a house painter, had attempted to open a false bank account in Edgecliff in the name of Surry and David Scott.

Sallie planned to use the stolen stamp to deposit and withdraw money from the false account to buy heroin. According to police the scam was cleverly thought out, but clumsily executed. Bank staff became suspicious. Sallie's photograph was captured on security camera. Wearing flared jeans and a striped blue top, her long hair pulled back in a pony tail, she glances nervously around the bank interior while her de-facto holds her two-year-old daughter. When staff tried to delay their departure, Sallie and Oliver fled. Hours later she was arrested by Federal Police at 'a run down slum-like premises' in Edgecliff.

Placed on a 'good behaviour bond' for three years, Sallie was directed by the court as a condition of her bond to undertake treatment at the private hospital, Chelmsford, in Pennant Hills where the psychiatrist, Dr H. Bailey, had a phenomenal success rate in unhooking young people from narcotic addiction.

Oliver's parents kindly offered to pay for the cost of her treatment. Six weeks later the psychiatrist wrote to the court:

DR. HARRY R. BAILEY
M.B., B.S., M.A.N.Z.C.P., D.P.M. (SYD.), M.R.C.PSYCH. (LOND.)
TELEPHONE: 221-1322

Park House
187 Macquarie Street
Sydney 2000

27.8.75.

This is to certify that Mrs Sallie Huckstepp has been under my professional care for treatment of narcotic drug addiction.

Mrs Huckstepp was admitted to Chelmsford Private Hospital, Pennant Hills on 10.7.75 and she was discharged on 3.8.75. On her discharge she no longer needed to take Heroin and she was well motivated for the future.

I would be grateful if the Court would take this factor into consideration when assessing Mrs Huckstepp's case.

Harry R. Bailey
MB BS DPM MANZCP MRCPsych.

David Oliver had described himself on the phone as thin, grey-haired and wearing a white shirt, but the Hall Street cafe in Bondi was filled with men fitting that description. I went up to the wrong person.

'Over here!' Oliver called. He was rolling a White Ox and sipping black coffee. Recently he'd settled out of court with the medical insurers for the treatment he'd undergone 21 years earlier at Chelmsford Hospital.

'When I met Sallie it was a beautiful romance conceived in heaven,' Oliver said. 'We met in the psychiatric unit of St Vincent's hospital on a methadone program. Sallie moved in with me and Sascha was with the grandparents and then she came down from the central coast. We both had solid habits. Most days there were drugs. We'd use as much as we could get.

'Sallie was working and as part of her deal with the police, she'd cop a pinch every week. She was paying four squads about 40 or 50 bucks each. I was with Sallie for about a year. She could be anything on the continuum from a sweet girl to a real bitch. She had some pretty snarly conversations with my parents and they had a pre-judgmental view of her. They thought she was a terrible influence. Sallie was very bitter about her father. She was taking a lot of barbs before Chelmsford. We gave them a real bash.'

'Can you tell me about Chelmsford?'

'A nightmare. Bailey was a maniac. I asked him, "What do you do here, Doctor?" And he said, "We work on the *addiction centre* of the brain." He claimed a 94 per cent success rate. There was no empirical evidence that it worked. They put me in the sedation room. Fed me barbiturates and Sustagen through a nasal tube. I was being given 2400 milligrams of Tuinal, a combination of two barbituric derivatives, amylobarbitone sodium and quinalbarbitone sodium. A massive amount of drugs. When you are in a coma state they give you electric shock treatment.

'I can remember being pulled out of therapy because I had pneumonia. I woke up, my wrists were strapped. I tried to escape and I had no peripheral balance, I was that physically weak I collapsed. I was under Deep Sleep for sixteen days. Having been so deep in a coma for so long I had epileptic seizures, *grand mal*, from withdrawal from the barbiturates.'

•

Sallie's probation officer received a phone call from Chelmsford. 'Get me out, please,' Sallie said. 'They're killing me.' When Judy Johnston drove out to the hospital, she found Sallie heavily sedated. 'Her eyes were sunk into her face,' Judy said, 'she had these big black circles and she had high cheekbones anyway. Her whole face was hollowed out. It was human experimentation.'

Sallie had a remarkable tolerance for heroin and barbiturates, according to her younger sister, Debra, but after Dr Bailey's electric shock treatment, Sallie nearly died. 'She was down to four and a half stones (30 kilograms),' Debra told me. 'She couldn't talk, she couldn't walk, she couldn't think properly, she couldn't do anything. They'd given her fourteen shock treatments over fifteen days. She used to crawl around on the floor. She used to dribble. She had epileptic fits from the barbiturates Bailey had given her. She used to get these black depressions and stay in bed for days and days.'

Sallie's flatmate, Helen F, saw her the afternoon she got out of Chelmsford. 'My God!' Helen said, 'I couldn't believe how thin Sal was. She was like something out of a concentration camp. Then Sallie told us what they'd done to her. She'd come off heroin, but she had a huge barbiturate habit. I don't think she ever really recovered from Chelmsford. Sallie was bright and it didn't dull her brightness, but you could see the light in her eyes had gone. It was like the shine had been taken off her. Sal had such a vivacious face, she was a very attractive woman. But it knocked something out of her. She was quiet. She laughed about what had happened, the way she'd come out with a worse drug habit than when she'd gone in. Sallie always had a black sense of humour.'

•

For the next ten years Sallie remained a heavy user of heroin. She injected herself between her toes when she didn't want people to know she was using and in the back of her hands. According to one underworld dealer she injected herself in her mouth. 'Once hooked,' Sallie told friends, 'you're either stoned or ill.' She also injected 'nebbies', a dangerous business.

Barbiturates provide an emotional lift in the short term, but in the long term they heighten anxiety and depression and sleeplessness. Medical researchers have found that addiction to barbiturates is far more serious than morphine addiction. Coming off barbiturates is extremely difficult. Within twelve to 24 hours, symptoms may include fever, seizures and *delirium tremens*. Death may occur. In the 1970s in Australia, drug companies and the medical profession saw barbiturates as an easy antidote for sleeplessness and readily over-prescribed them.

Five years after Sallie-Anne was 'satisfactorily unhooked' by Dr Harry Bailey, she checked into Langton Clinic in Surry Hills to detox. Ever since her cure at Chelmsford she had been injecting 5–6 grams of heroin daily. The nursing notes record her stay:

> Day 1: Patient extremely restless, difficult to convince that she must stay in room. Unsteady on her feet. Valium 10 mgs given 9 p.m. and 4 a.m. Sallie unable to give spec of urine. Menstruating at moment. Quantity of tablets removed from uterus 10.30 p.m., 4 Serepax, 8 Codeine. Told to settle down as she would not be having any medication for some time. Sallie constantly observed. Sleeping well throughout the night. Awake 3 a.m. restless and demanding a.m. medication. Settled down at 5.50 a.m. sleeping.
>
> Day 2: Complained of abdomen cramps, leg pains.
>
> Day 3: Said feet terrible—pain all over. Doloxene II given. Patient hysterical at lunchtime. More medication given.
>
> Day 4: Better mood today. Patient noticed she had pubic lice. Doloxene given.
>
> Day 7: Patient discharged.

Follow Up Record

Oct 20, 1980: Attended Clinic. Wants desperately to come off heroin. Behaviour inappropriate to someone seeking help despite begging and superficial tears. Minced off upstairs when asked to wait outside my door. Main problem is current boyfriend, Kym, who is pathologically jealous. Sallie wants to leave him, but unable to do so. Kym due in court for breaking and entering this year, prob 2 yr gaol. Kym deals and controls her through heroin. Family—Father cold. Married 3rd time in QLD.

•

When asked to describe herself in her own words, Sallie wrote on the hospital file in her distinctive handwriting:

My looks were mysterious, sensual. I was stunning.
I'm intelligent, but I don't use my brain.
I ran away from home at 14 because of my father.
I want to stop using, but I can't handle the W/D alone.
I'm a survivor and I'll bounce back.

•

'You take drugs when something else in your life is missing,' Sallie told Michael Willesee in a 1982 TV interview. She was sixteen when her boyfriend and future husband, Bryan, asked her to become a prostitute. 'I felt I owed him,' she explained. He was a heroin addict and needed the money to leave Sydney for a while. After she started working at the Cross she too became an addict and that meant she had to supply both of them.

'My strongest memory of those days,' Sallie said, 'was parading up and down Darlinghurst Road. It took me a long time to come to grips with the fact that I was a prostitute.'

When she ran into friends from the Eastern Suburbs Jewish community and former classmates from Dover Heights High, Sallie used to hide, but after a while she would say hello and keep on working.

'When I first started working as a prostitute, I was very eager. I wanted to make money and make plenty of it. I used to come in at eight or nine o'clock at night and work 'til three or four in the morning.'

As Sallie's habit got worse, she started supplementing her heroin habit with barbiturates.

'I was shooting 15–20 Nembutal a day and I started getting later and later. I'd get in about eleven or twelve and then I'd come in at one and I was working through to eight or nine o'clock in the morning. People would be on their way to work and I'd still be standing there on Darlinghurst Road.

'I became very hard, I mean I really . . . I . . . hated myself and I hated being a junkie. I knew I was really slipping, I was going downhill very rapidly. And I hated my clients. I was very rough. I wasn't very nice at all. I mean I wouldn't let them touch me, if they had been drinking I wouldn't let them breathe on me. If they didn't get dressed quick enough I used to just take their clothes and put them out in the corridor. I mean I was really a nasty little girl.

'Most of the men I felt nothing for. I used to cut off, switch off with them. Often I had knives pulled on me, guns. But we had a very good system with what they call sitters, guys that look after you in case of trouble who would be up in a minute. I was very aggressive anyway and I just used to attack them first which took them by surprise. I didn't, I didn't like the Cross, I didn't hang around up there. I just came to work and I left.'

One evening Sallie was working above the Lido and a young, well-built client paid her for half an hour. When his time was up he wouldn't leave. He hadn't yet ejaculated and he demanded an extra fifteen minutes. Sallie called security and the young man was tossed out. An hour later he came back with a double-bladed axe and the sitters took off. He ran up the stairs and started axing in her door. Police arrived and the young man escaped through a back entrance. Years later Sallie would tell Warren Lanfranchi about this madman she met in the Cross and he burst into laughter and said, 'That was me, Sal, that was me!'

•

The corner of Macleay Street and Darlinghurst Road was one of Sallie-Anne's favourite spots. She worked the arcade near the Bourbon and Beefsteak Bar, and she would also stand and solicit outside the chemist shop on Darlinghurst Road. Her first full-time job was in a chemist shop.

'In those days,' her sister, Debra, said, 'it was tough on the streets. You had to fight for your spot. Sallie hated working as a prostitute. I think because she was such a sexual woman and when she fell in love she really gave of herself completely and then to do it like that for money, and to know she was as beautiful as she could be and being in the Jewish community, I mean Jewish families would walk through the Cross, I know we did when we were young—my father, Sallie and me—have dinner at Bill and Toni's, then we'd go for a stroll through the Cross, we'd look at the working girls, and laugh and snigger, and then Sallie found herself there.'

The Kings Cross area is the heart of Sydney's sex industry, partly because of the proximity of the Garden Island naval depot, partly because the Cross has provided an escape from suburban conformity since the 1920s. Today there are more than 30 brothels in the Kings Cross area and underage male prostitutes still work outside the sandstone wall of the old Darlinghurst Gaol. Prostitution is now legal in New South Wales provided the workers don't solicit near a church, school or residential area. Police try to restrict the trade to designated areas, but it spills over onto the Burton-Street side where teenage girls lean against the spiked iron lace of the terrraces. The suburb of Darlinghurst still retains faint echoes of its roiling past. Migrants, addicts and sex workers mingle in its narrow backstreets with the more solid shapes of designers, gallery directors and stylish art students. A red Porsche reverses into a space beside a rusted FC Holden with Tasmanian plates; a radio blares out a horse race from a boarding-house window a few doors up from one of the city's most exclusive Italian restaurants. There is a saying that in Darlinghurst everyone finds their right level, and it was here that I first saw Sallie-Anne Huckstepp.

•

I was working the lounge bar in a run-down hotel in Stanley Street when she came in with two men who looked like they pumped weights for a living. She was loud and happy and a little high and the dark roots were showing through her honey-blond hair. Her party sat over near the jukebox and The Pretender's 'Brass in Pocket' was playing, or at least that's how my memory has arranged it.

I had the impression she was much more observant than the men she was with and that she was possibly afraid of one of them. She was self-conscious, looking around the dimly-lit, red-carpeted lounge to see if anyone was watching her. It was not that Sallie was beautiful, or that she dressed with any great style or that she had a figure to die for, it was just that she gave off a certain vibrancy.

I'd hit rock bottom in my own life, although I didn't know it, and I found myself washed up in Darlinghurst working in a hotel frequented by drug-dealers, punks, towies, drunks and prostitutes. It is a cliché to say that Sallie-Anne turned heads, but she was not unaware of her looks, and when she was on her way out through the tiny bottle shop in her white cotton dress, sandwiched between the two hard men who could've been police or drug-dealers, or both, she smiled warmly while her companions looked right through me. I felt then that Sallie was an actress, rehearsing for some kind of role, that she needed an audience to appreciate her moves, and that I had been selected purely by chance.

Detectives often dropped in to the lounge around nightfall, big bulky men in ill-fitting suits from some of the city's hard-hitting squads, and I was under instructions from upstairs that their drinks were free. They rarely stayed long, just drank their neat spirits chased down with draught beer and took in the faces, looking around, drinking, looking around. Darlinghurst was known as Goldenhurst then because the pickings from prostitutes and drug-dealers were so profitable. Everyone knew what went on, but Sallie-Anne was the first one to come out with it publicly.

Sometimes I think about Sallie that hot autumn evening with

the jukebox playing in the corner and the pavement cooling outside. She was smoking St Moritz cigarettes and drinking double bourbons and Coke; beach-tanned, muscular, flashing her white gapped teeth. I wish I had said something to her now, exchanged a few words. I know I could not have warned her, for I had no knowledge of what was about to happen. No idea of who she was. For a while I kept an eye out for Sallie-Anne when I worked the night shift, but I never saw her in Darlinghurst again.

•

Three months later, at 4.45 p.m. on 15 July 1981, accompanied by her father, Jack Krivoshow, and her Legal Aid solicitor, she strode into Police Headquarters in College Street and sat down in an interview room. Two senior New South Wales detectives were waiting for her.

'I am Detective Inspector Ralph and this is Detective Reith,' the older man said. 'We are attached to the Police Internal Affairs Branch. I would like you first to look at a seven-page document received by the Commissioner of Police from the Office of the Attorney General. Is the information you have sworn in this document true and correct?'

'Yes it is,' Sallie said.

'Because there are a number of serious allegations here, I would like to ask you some further questions. Would you give me your full name and address?'

'I don't have a fixed address right at the moment,' Sallie said. 'I can be contacted through the Redfern Legal Centre.'

'What are you prepared to tell me about your background?'

'I will tell you everything,' Sallie said. 'I have the following criminal record: I have 31 convictions for prostitution. I have a conspiracy to defraud conviction which occurred shortly after I left Harry Bailey's tender care at "Chelmsford". I then had two further marijuana convictions. A heroin conviction when I was loaded up by Detectives Peter and Tomich at the Lido bar. I have a further "use" charge in which Detectives Peter George and Jungblut were involved. In both the latter offences significant sums of money were paid to police to effect the outcome.

'While operating as a prostitute I made regular payments to members of the Vice Squad over ten years. I have been involved in a number of transactions which I referred to in my statement which have involved substantial payment to members of the Drug Squad and other detectives relating to drug matters. I believe that the New South Wales Drug Squad and the Armed Hold-Up Squad are both totally corrupt and that they feed on the very activities which they are supposed to stop.

'My name is Sallie-Anne Huckstepp.'

3

Centennial Park

It was 8.45 on the morning of 7 February 1986, when a jogger came into the ranger's office behind the kiosk in Centennial Park and said that he'd seen a body floating in Busby's Pond. 'The jogger took off, didn't want to have anything to do with it,' Brian Calbert explained.

'I got into my ute and drove over and sure enough two-thirds across Busby's Pond I seen the body of a woman floating face down near the Robertson Road entrance. She had long blond hair. There was a heap of police from the Tactical Response Group already training in the park. I went straight up to this sergeant sitting in his car and said, "You'd better put out a call, there's a body over here." I then radioed for a row boat. I rowed out across the pond with a couple of uniformed constables and towed in the body of a female person head first, the two police with me dragged her out and placed her face down on the sandy bank. Police were coming from everywhere, there must've been 30 of them. I'd never seen so many police. When the detectives rolled her over on her back, one of them said, "That's Huckstepp!"

'She was wearing blue jeans and a pink skivvy top, the top was rolled up all the way to be resting above her breasts. From my recollection,' Brian Calbert continued, 'the detectives were bent over examining her throat for marks or somethin'. I was there a fair while. It would've taken me about fifteen minutes to have the boat brought down and ten minutes to row out. She was lying on the bank for about an hour near that big old willow tree.'

Photographs of the crime scene show a circle of grim-faced police standing around the body, some wearing raincoats, all looking down at Sallie-Anne. Early rigor mortis has set in and her hands sit upright. There are marks on her throat as if a necklace had been torn away from the skin. Her blond hair is matted with silt, her breasts wrinkled from immersion in the pond. She is wearing white Adidas sneakers and the top button of her jeans is undone. In death she appears shrunken, smaller. Her eyes are wide open, her long eyelashes smeared with dirt. When police roll her over to examine her back, white froth bubbles out of her nose and mouth.

Behind Sallie, the lily-covered pond is bordered with native paperbarks, Phoenix palms, a big old willow. The steep grassy banks are green from summer rain. Native eels disturb the surface of the water. Ibises and great black cormorants roost in the trees. With its reed-fringed shore and little nesting islands, Busby's Pond is an idyllic place.

•

At 10.30 a.m. on Friday, 7 February, Detective Sergeant James (Jimmy) Waddell of the Eastern Suburbs District arrived at Busby's Pond after receiving a call on his police radio. As the most senior officer present, Detective Waddell took control of the investigation. He commandeered the Tactical Response Group's truck—it contained a mobile telephone—and used it as his command post.

'Although I had never met Huckstepp I recognised her immediately from the media,' Detective Waddell said. 'She was wearing jeans and a white sloppy joe. I arranged to seal off the crime scene, contacted scientific officers and organised TRG and other police to search the banks of the lake. I also briefed the search party to search for any handbag, clothing or marks where the deceased may have been dragged into the water.'

Julia Soares, a young woman visiting her boyfriend who worked in the park, handed the driver of the TRG vehicle a New South Wales Police identification badge, consisting of a four-digit serial number, she found lying in the soil on the far side of the pond. 'I picked it up and the number was 86 something,' the twenty-year-old said. 'I walked over to some police and handed it to a uniform bloke. "Are you interested in this?" I said and gave it to him.'

The policeman told her that the badge had fallen off a New South Wales policeman who had been retrieving the body. He said to Julia Soares, 'You're a nice young lady!' and she walked away.

That evening Constable Bradley Conner, a motorcyclist from 'A' District who had assisted in the search, discovered that his collar number 8326 was missing. He admitted, 'It often got caught up in my jacket.'

Two investigative journalists, Wendy Bacon and Geraldine Brooks, were suspicious of how a New South Wales Police badge had turned up on the shore opposite where the retrieval was taking place and queried its loss in the *National Times* in an article entitled 'The Murky Case of Sallie-Anne'. 'The killing of a "bad woman" such as Huckstepp,' they wrote, 'seems to have been shrugged off as though it is somehow acceptable for a loose-living junkie to die violently in the dark precincts of a public park.' Their reporting of the lost badge was to play a significant role years later in the investigation.

Police divers described the spot where Sallie was found as 'thick as bean soup'. The depth of the lily-covered pond ranged from 30 centimetres around the edges, where layers of coarse sand, silt and sediment were packed in hard, to several metres out in the middle. 'The further you went in, the softer it became,' one of the divers explained. 'We did extensive searches, but found nothing.'

Large numbers of police were still arriving at Busby's Pond on the morning of 7 February, including Detective Senior Sergeant Geoffrey Prentice from the Homicide Squad and the Government Medical Officer, Dr Sergio Staraj, who examined the body and pronounced 'life to be extinct'.

Detective Sergeant Prentice explained what happened: 'We got called out to see the body in the lake. So we raced out there. It was raining and I walked over. She's lying there on the ground covered up. I pulled a blanket off her, looked at me offsider and I said, "Mate, you know who this is?"

'He said, "Nuh."

'I said, "We got a problem here for the next twenty years. It's Sallie Huckstepp." I said, "Oh mate, mate ..." And the whole thing just flashed in front of me. All the drama with Rogerson. I knew then it was going to be a notorious case, because of the players involved.'

At 12.30 p.m., Detective Senior Constable Clinton Nicol of the Scientific Investigation Section arrived at the park and was briefed on the situation. He examined the body of a deceased female lying on her back dressed in a pair of Smiths jeans, a white jumper and sandshoes.

'I saw that the top clasp of her jeans was open and the jumper was rolled up to the top of her chest,' Detective Nicol wrote in his report. 'I saw that she had on her right hand a gold ring and a gold bracelet and on the left hand a gold ring, a gold chain and a gold watch that had stopped at eleven o'clock and the date was showing the 24th. I made an examination of the deceased and saw a number of abrasions on the cheeks, right side of the chin and lips and several dark marks or lines running across the upper throat region directly below the chin.'

With Dr Staraj, the Medical Officer, they turned Sallie over and made an examination of her back, taking note of the vertical scratches to her shoulder blades and to her middle back, the bulk of which had scabbing. Detective Nicol then proceeded to the north-western corner of the pond near a storm-water outlet. There were several areas along the bank where the one-metre-high reeds had been disturbed and parted into a V-shape. He made a thorough examination of the dirt roadway which ran along the western edge of the pond at the top of the grassed bank.

'I saw that in the dirt were several distinct tyre impressions,' Detective Nicol wrote. 'There had been heavy rain overnight and I felt with my finger that the ground surrounding the impressions was damp while the tread indentations had no water in them.'

Constable Nicholls of the Mapping and Photogrammetry Unit arrived at the scene at 12.45 p.m. 'I was taken to the body of a Caucasian female on the northern bank of the duck pond,' Constable Nicholls stated. 'I took photographs of the deceased and saw two 3–5 millimetre circular superficial scratches to the face, one to the lower lip, the other to the right cheek. There were a number of narrow lines running across her upper throat region. There was no mulch or weeds in her mouth, but extensive foam around her lips.' Constable Nicholls handed all the film he had taken to Detective Nicol and a plastic bag he had found in the reeds containing a portion of what appeared to be human hair.

The wind was blowing in a westerly direction across the pond, recorded at 16 kilometres an hour from Observatory Hill, and police were concerned about the possibility of the wind or a current having shifted the body from its original position. The ranger, Brian Calbert, told police that the pond didn't have a current although he did say that sometimes articles were pushed out from the culvert after it had been raining. He described the spot where he'd first seen Ms Huckstepp's body as being 'probably 20 or 30 metres out from that big old weeping willow tree.' When he first saw her she was not moving.

Paul Robinson, a General Hand in Centennial Park and boyfriend of Ms Soares (she had in fact given police her sister's name) who had found the New South Wales Police badge, described the injuries to the body when Sallie was dragged from the water. 'She had marks on her side which appeared to be bruises, a cut under the left eye, a fat bottom lip and her hands were clenched.'

Despite strangulation marks on Sallie-Anne's neck, abrasions on the right-hand side of her chin and extensive scratch marks on her face and back, the initial police response was to entertain the possibility of suicide. Only hours after Sallie's body had been discovered, a senior New South Wales Police officer told the reporters and photographers arriving at the park that there were no obvious signs of violence on her body—despite the fact that bruises often take several days to show.

'We have no idea of what caused this woman's death,' Detective Inspector Gordon Spink said. 'It may be a straight overdose, but we can't prove anything yet. We have known of her for some time.'

Inspector Spink stated that police had no idea where the woman was living before she died or who her close friends were. He added that rain in Centennial Park in the early hours of the morning may have destroyed any evidence of footprints or a struggle.

Detective Sergeant Jim Waddell, who remained at Centennial Park until 1 p.m. on the Friday, discounted the scenario of Ms Huckstepp being forcibly injected with a lethal dose of heroin. 'She was extremely fit and well and would have put up a hell of a fight if anyone had tried to put anything in her,' he told reporters arriving on the scene.

Some two hours before the body of Sallie-Anne was discovered on the morning of 7 February, a second jogger, Andrew Gibbons, had found a black leather wallet beside a clump of Melaleuca trees inside the fence near the horse track. About 30 centimetres away a packet of St Moritz cigarettes and a lighter, a leather pouch of keys and a small blue comb were lying on top of the long grass.

'I picked up the wallet and looked inside and saw about 50 cents and a Commonwealth passbook,' Mr Gibbons said in his statement. 'I looked around but there was no-one who could have dropped it, so I took it home.' On Saturday morning he read in the newspaper about the death of Sallie-Anne Huckstepp, checked the name in the passbook and found it was the same. Immediately he rang Paddington Police Station who contacted Detective Sergeant Waddell. Waddell then drove over to Paddington and inspected what he described as 'some property belonging to Huckstepp'. Waddell then went with Detective Carter to Centennial Park and organised a further search of the area between Busby's Pond and where Gibbons had located her property 'a stone's throw from the pond'.

By now Sallie's white 1973 Ford Cortina, registration GNJ 641, had been discovered parked in Martin Road, near the junction of Lang and Robertson Roads, outside the wrought-iron gates of the park. It was towed back to Maroubra Police Station and fingerprinted.

Sallie-Anne's prints were found on the inside of the Cortina's rear window and an unidentified palm print on the outside of the boot. The palm print could not be matched.

Uniformed police had already searched the vicinity thoroughly but three days later the Police Rescue Unit were called in to conduct a 'line search' from the entrance gate in Martin Road, to the area surrounding the pond. It was a two-and-a-half-hour search 'in very close proximity', one of the men explained. Nothing was found.

•

At 1.45 p.m. on that Friday the body was removed by government contractors from where it had been lying 2 metres away from a wooden picnic table. A final photograph of Sallie-Anne in Centennial Park shows her lying on her back on the bank with her breasts exposed, her jeans unbuttoned, her eyes closed and foam protruding from her nose and lips. Silt from the bottom of the pond is smeared across her ears and face. At 2.40 p.m., she was officially identified by her sister and her father at the City Morgue.

The following day a small column on page 3 of the *Sydney Morning Herald* disclosed that police were investigating the death of a well-known prostitute, heroin addict and former girlfriend of the heroin dealer, Warren Lanfranchi, who had been shot dead by police five years earlier. There was no firm evidence at all, police stated, to suggest that Miss Huckstepp had been murdered and her body dumped.

'We are trying to find friends who might have been with her before her death,' a police spokesman told the *Daily Telegraph*, 'but we can't find her address.'

When Teresa Whitehouse heard the news on 2UE over breakfast that the body of a young woman had been found in Centennial Park, she contacted police. She and her husband, she said, were in the habit of walking their dogs around Centennial Park.

'On Thursday, 6 February between 10.40 and 10.45 p.m.,' Teresa Whitehouse said, 'I was in Alison Road near the Glensynd Motel when I saw a motorbike travelling down Alison Road from the Randwick direction towards us. It turned right and drove onto the private bus road and then crossed the little pedestrian bridge which leads into Centennial Park. There were two persons on the motorbike, the driver I am unable to describe. The pillion passenger had no helmet on, he had shoulder-length hair, a white sleeveless top and a pair of dark long pants.'

Her husband, William Whitehouse, was more interested in the motorbike which he described as an older-style 'easy rider' motorcycle. 'Possibly a Yamaha,' Mr Whitehouse said, 'with low-handled bars.' When the bike crossed the footbridge it followed the direction to the right and then proceeded along the cycle track towards the centre of the park.

The Whitehouses stood with their two dogs on Alison Road and watched the bike's red tail-light disappear into the darkness.

•

The drive from 141 Edgecliff Road, Edgecliff, to Centennial Park at 11 p.m. on a Thursday night takes approximately five minutes. Although pedestrian and bicycle access is possible at various points around the circular spiked iron fence that encloses the park, all eight vehicular gates are locked at 8.30 p.m.

The park remains unlit at night, except for gas lights which illuminate the main entrance, and although the park is classified as a safe area, rangers recommend that any female coming in after dark should carry a mobile phone and be accompanied by a friend.

Gwen Beecroft was certain that Sallie-Anne left her flat at 10.55 p.m. Two other witnesses said that Sallie often met her dealer in Centennial Park. When Sallie-Anne's body was found next morning the gold Michel Herbelin watch on her left wrist had stopped at exactly 10.59.

'She had beautiful gold jewellery on her,' her sister, Debra Krivoshow, told police. 'If she'd been with real junkies, there's no way they would have left the jewellery on her. Sallie had such a resistance to dope. I'd never seen her overdose in her life. She knew a lot of business about a lot of people. She knew too much.'

4

Furs and informers

Ten weeks before her death, Sallie-Anne met Glenn Michael Stone at the 77 Club in Kings Cross. It was Friday, 29 November 1985, and Stone had just won $1000 on Lotto.

'I noticed this girl who was very attractive and well-dressed,' Stone said. 'She looked pretty classy and during the night we got closer and closer and we ended up going to have some coffee. She dropped me off home, gave me her number and asked me to ring her. So I rang her the next day and we had lunch at the Cosmopolitan. I didn't know who she was, but I saw a couple of scars on her hands that looked like old track marks, and I thought hmmm, maybe she's not quite what she appears.'

When Sallie mentioned that her ex-boyfriend was Warren Lanfranchi, Stone realised who she was, but it didn't matter. He was breaking up with his wife and he was interested in her.

'She stayed the night at my place,' Glenn Stone said, 'and then she was living in a cheap motel in Bondi and she had to get out of there, so she moved in with me. We stayed there for a few days but Sallie didn't get on with the people I was living with, so we moved to Botany. Sallie was doing a bit of small-time dealing. She had a huge rock that she was minding, a heroin rock. Apparently this belonged to a guy called Dave Kelleher who was in gaol, and she was supposed to be doing something for him with it. She had a couple of girls working for her and then they got arrested and she lost her money and her dope and she was pretty stuck, but she still had this rock.'

'What would you think of me if I had to kill somebody?' Sallie asked one morning.

'Well, I don't know,' Stone said, 'I don't really care, it wouldn't change my opinion of you.' He didn't know whether she was just sounding him out, or whether it was her intention to give somebody an overdose, for this rock was pretty pure.

'Whether that was a fantasy of hers, or whatever, who knows,' Stone told me over the phone from the Northern Territory where he was recuperating from a .308 bullet wound to his leg. 'She had lots of fantasies.

'Sallie used the rock for herself. She knew she shouldn't have, but with a huge habit she kept chipping away at it until it was all gone. She wanted to stop using. And she tried and it would last a couple of days but then she'd do some Nembutals or Serepax, whatever she could get. She also had a ring that her ex-boyfriend, Kelleher, had given her worth about $20 000 but she lost that. She told me she lost it at a newsagent when she went to buy Kelleher some stick books, but I reckon she hocked it.

'Sallie was terrified if Kelleher found out,' Glenn Stone said, 'he'd give her a bashing. Several times she told me she was frightened that Kelleher was going to knock her, because he was a very jealous man and he wouldn't have liked her going out with other men. She also said Kelleher was selling $12 million of heroin a year. She would go and visit him in Long Bay, but then she had a car accident and couldn't see him for a while. She was still doing a bit of business, but something usually went wrong. She didn't like to distribute the gear herself on the streets. The people she had working for her weren't very trustworthy and she was being ripped off. She used to race around the streets trying to smarten her girls up. Then they disappeared and she couldn't find them. So she arranged to meet this guy Warren Richards.

'Richards was one of the few people who would deal with her.

He gave her credit. Sometimes she would give him jewellery as security. She needed him, because nobody else would do business with her at that stage. I drove her to meet him a few times. She used to meet him at only two places: Ashfield station and Centennial Park. I dropped her off once when she was going to meet Richards, I dropped her right outside the Robertson Street entrance. Right next to where her body was found.'

'Did you ever meet Richards?' I asked.

'I spoke to him once on the phone,' Glenn Stone said, 'when I phoned him for her when she was in hospital. I asked him on the phone, "Can I get drugs for Sallie?" but he said, "No. Not like that." '

'Were you present when she received drugs?'

'I was never there when she got drugs, she was always late. I went with her once to Ashfield station where she was supposed to get heroin from Warren.'

'Why did you go with her?'

'Because it was my car.'

'What happened?'

'She missed him. Most times she was unsuccessful. After Christmas she was on the way to Ashfield to meet Richards again and she'd taken my car and she'd zapped off and then she came back about half an hour later because she'd forgotten her wallet. So she raced in, picked up the wallet and she only had twenty minutes and Richards wouldn't wait for her and she knew that, so she tried to race there. On the way she turned the car over a few times in Cleveland Street and ended up in hospital with a badly broken arm. She was in there for a week or so.'

When Stone first met Sallie she had no money. 'She'd get her pension which would be about $700 for the month,' Stone said, 'and she'd go down to Double Bay and buy a pair of shoes for $300 and a designer dress for $400. She'd buy all these clothes, have her hair done for $100 and then go—"What do I do now?" "Don't worry about it," I'd say to her. "You look great."

'She was sick of dealing, that's why she didn't mind spending the money on clothes. Subconsciously it was a way of avoiding that. The next day she'd wake up to the reality that she'd just blown everything. The first few weeks of our relationship were fine and then she met this Federal cop and something started going on there and Sallie began disappearing for days or nights. I wasn't altogether happy about it but I was very much attracted to her, so I hung around for a while. Sallie had a lot of sex appeal and was quite sensual. She was very turned on by muscles and big men. She was still living with me then and she didn't really have anywhere to go. I thought I'd try and help her if she really wanted to get off dope. I mean I didn't really expect a lot.'

Not long after this Sallie went to live with Gwen Beecroft in Edgecliff. She left most of her clothes at Botany and only took a few things with her. Stone didn't see her much, but he spoke to her on the telephone every second day.

'When was the last time you saw Huckstepp alive?' Homicide police asked him in a recorded interview.

'I can't remember,' Stone said. 'I remember talking to her on the Tuesday before she died.'

'Do you know why she was murdered?'

'Because she was strutting around with a Federal Police officer and someone was worried that she would talk.'

•

Three days after Sallie-Anne met Glenn Stone in the 77 Club, Federal Police from the Major Crime Squad, Eastern Region, raided the Alice Motel in Bondi. They were searching for Steven Edward Murray who had been brought down from Queensland to give evidence in a Federal drug case. As fears were held for his safety, Murray had been afforded Witness Protection and placed in a safe house in Rushcutters Bay. During a changeover of the Federal Police shift, Murray ended up with the keys to the safe house and, having completed his evidence, he absconded with an iron, a toaster, an electric jug and two furs described as being:

(1) Mink Cape stole, fully stranded palomino fur with detachable mink tail, cream silk lining. Value $500.
(1) Golden Fox stole (large collar approximately 40 inches by 10 inches), fastening each end with beige lining, no label. Value $500.

The furs belonged to Assistant Commissioner McCabe's wife, though one can only speculate what they were doing locked in a wardrobe in the front bedroom of a Federal safe house. Sent to find Mrs McCabe's furs, Constables Turner and Muir arrived at the Alice Motel on a tip-off and went to room 18. The door was opened by Sallie-Anne. Behind her Steven Edward Murray was removing a syringe from his leg. A spoon on the floor contained a clear liquid. Turner and Muir arrested Murray and conveyed him to Regional Headquarters where Murray refused to reveal the location of the furs. An hour later, Constable Muir received a phone call from a woman who identified herself as Sallie Huckstepp.

'I want to meet with you tomorrow,' Sallie-Anne said, 'so we can talk.'

'Where?' Terry Muir said.

'The Regent Hotel at five o'clock.'

Muir reported to Chief Inspector Newell who instructed him to meet with Huckstepp 'and try and get those furs back'. Wired up, Muir and Turner met with her the following day at the Regent in George Street, but they were unaware that Sallie was also taping them. Muir pretended that he and Turner were corrupt because that would be the best way to get her to deal with them. Accustomed to dealing with corrupt police, Sallie offered the two Feds $15 000 if they would obtain the 'brief of evidence' relating to Dave Kelleher—who had been arrested by the Joint Task Force on a major drug importation charge. In return she would try to help find the furs. To make the ploy more believable, Constable Muir told her, 'I know someone that can gain access to the brief of evidence for you.'

'Who?' Sallie said.

'He's a Detective Sergeant.'

The next day Muir spoke to Constable Peter Mark Parker Smith, a junior officer, who agreed to act in the deception. With Turner assigned to other duties, Smith requisitioned a Nagra tape recorder and, accompanied by Muir, wore it to a meeting with Sallie at 10.30 a.m. on 5 December at the Whale car wash in Bondi. In return for a copy of the brief of evidence on Kelleher, Sallie agreed to talk to Steven Murray—now in Long Bay Gaol—about the theft of the furs, but she refused to discuss anything else. 'I don't fizzgig,' Sallie said.

As agreed, Constable Smith did most of the talking. Tall, with cropped dark hair and a bodybuilder's physique, Smith impressed Sallie from the start. He was 22 years of age and exuded confidence.

'We flattered her,' Smith said later. 'Both Terry and I flattered her. Because the object was to get her to assist us as much as possible, we considered it advantageous for her to like us.'

[Police Tape Starts]
Muir: How ya going, Sal?
Huckstepp: Alright.
Muir: This's Peter.
Huckstepp: Where do you fit in?
Smith: I'm the boss.
Huckstepp: Are you the do-er or the do-ee?
Smith: I'm the do-er never the do-ee.
Huckstepp: So what are you going to do for me, Peter?
Smith: Well if you let us know what you know, we'll let you know what we know. How's that sound?
Huckstepp: I'll find out where the furs are, right, when you give me the information on Dave . . .
Smith: Yeh.
Huckstepp: Then I'll tell you where the furs are.
Muir: Well, do you know where they are?
Huckstepp: Not yet.
Muir: This is from higher up. If we get the furs back, both charges are dropped against Murray.
Huckstepp: I'm not doing this for free, I'm doing this because

I want Dave out of gaol. You get me photocopies of the brief, everything.

[Long Pause]

Smith: Want to get onto a nice bloke?

Hucksteрр: What do you mean a nice bloke, a copper?

Smith: Yeh, a nice copper like Terence or myself, nice, friendly, honest—

Huckstepp: Straight down the line.

Smith: That's right.

Huckstepp: What copper would have me . . . most police are terrified of me.

Muir: (Laughter) What a career woman you'd be eh!

Smith: Tell you what, we'll look after you, if you can get us these furs, don't you worry about that.

Huckstepp: The only thing I'm worried about is you guys pulling a double cross on me.

Smith: Us!

Muir: Mate, don't worry about that, we want those furs real bad. A lot of problems can arise if we don't get them back.

[The group arrive at the Long Bay Gaol complex, but can't see Steven Edward Murray until after 1.30 p.m.]

Huckstepp: Why don't we go and have something to eat.

Smith: She's got it all worked out, Terry. I thought I was supposed to be the boss here.

Huckstepp: No, I'm the boss! (Laughs)

Smith: You're the boss are you, you've got more stripes than I have?

Huckstepp: Probably more experience.

Smith: How many years have you been at it?

Huckstepp: Sixteen.

Smith: Well you've been at it twice as long as I have. So how old are you?

Huckstepp: 31 this month.

Smith: That's not old. What are we doing for your birthday?

Muir: Yeh, where you taking us, Sal?

Huckstepp: Where I am taking you!

Smith: Yeh.

Huckstepp: I thought you might be able to get me tickets to Tina Turner.
Muir: Depends on how good a girl you are.
Smith: We can get you in anywhere you like. We can get you tickets to Dire Straits.
Huckstepp: That's too young for me (Laughs) only a couple of years older than I am. If you can get me some tickets to Tina Turner, for December 12 . . .

[Cannot decipher. Lots of overtalking about star signs]

Smith: Are you trying to say you don't want to know us out in public, we should have worn jeans?
Huckstepp: I don't want to be seen with two coppers. I have an extremely good name. Every criminal in Sydney knows me.
Muir: Like Ned Smith.
Smith: He's a bad bastard.
Huckstepp: Yeh, he sets up all his friends. I'll knock him one day.
Smith: What are you going to do?
Huckstepp: Take him out into the country, to a farm house, and I'm going to chop off his fingers one by one, then I'm going to get one of those glass, you know those very fine glass tubes you get from the laboratory?
Smith: Yeh.
Huckstepp: Put it down the eye of his cock, get a hammer and smash it.
Smith: Friendly little thing aren't you?
Muir: Very nice.
(Laughing)
Huckstepp: Fair enough. Ned set Warren up, took him there, he knew Rogerson was going to knock him. He oughta be in the police force. Wearing pips on his shoulders.
Smith: (Laughs) That's nice.
Muir: There's no rush, Sal, when you've finished making yourself beautiful.
Huckstepp: I've finished now.
Smith: Can't improve on perfection, is that right?
Huckstepp: Oh, I wouldn't put it that way.

Muir: He did.
Smith: She's beautiful, isn't she?

At the gaol hospital, Smith and Muir sat down with Sallie and, in front of 30 prisoners, began questioning Steven Edward Murray. No attempt was made to conduct the interview in a private office of the gaol. The other prisoners listened in to the conversation. Peter Smith took to his new promotion with relish:

Smith: I'm the fucking boss here right. You fuck us around, and we'll fuck you right up! Now I've had a gut full of this. We want our furs back.
Murray: Listen, I never took your rotten coats.
Smith: Well you know who did.
Murray: What about them warrants you got out on me?
Smith: You tell us and you're laughing.
Huckstepp: Tell em, Steve.
Smith: Listen. We've got to know where they went, it's just a matter of squeezing the right people. Tell me.
Murray: I'm telling ya, you'll never get em back.
Smith: Why not?
Murray: Cause the bloke who got rid of them manages a pawnbrokers right, got fucking outlets everywhere.

'The three of them,' Murray said later, 'visited me about five times during my sentence. By the three, I mean the two detectives and Sallie.'

When Dave Kelleher heard the news that she was in the gaol complex he put the word out: 'What's she doing with those Federal coppers?'

On Friday, 6 December, Smith and Muir again took Sallie out to Long Bay where she spoke to Murray and got a message through to Dave Kelleher informing him of her plan to get the police brief. Smith and Muir waited for her in the car park.

'What took you so long?' Smith said.

'The screws were fucking me around.' Sallie looked over her shoulder. 'I hope no-one sees me here with you jacks.'

The next morning Sallie rang Smith and arranged to meet the policemen at the Tea Gardens Hotel in Bondi Junction, where she used to work as a barmaid. Sallie insisted on patting down the two young Federal Police officers for listening devices. 'Turn around and put your hands on the wall,' she said.

'Ah come off it, Sal!'

'I mean it. Spread them.' Sallie ran her hands over their hips and ribcages.

Smith and Muir had not the faintest idea that she was also taping their conversation.

'How's it going with Dave's brief?' Sallie asked.

'It's a big brief,' Muir said. 'We don't know how long it's going to take.'

'Dave's told me to up it to $200 000 for the brief and the tapes.'

'What tapes?'

'The tapes of Dave at his city office.'

'I don't know if I can get the tapes.'

'Either get them or destroy them.'

'We've got to go,' Smith said.

'What about the dinner you blokes promised me?'

'What dinner?'

'I don't remember any dinner,' Smith said.

'You blokes promised to take me to dinner.'

'Sorry Sal, but we've got to go.'

'I got dressed up like this for nothing. Don't you blokes ever stick to your word.'

'It can't be helped,' Smith said.

'Peter, why don't you take me out for a drink?'

'No, I've got to go, I have to drop Terry at Central.'

'How about I meet you there?' Sallie said.

'Well, alright.'

'The deal now is the brief and *you*.'

'What do you mean?'

Sallie turned to Muir. 'Is he a bit slow or something?'

'Just a bit,' Muir said.

'I think I know what you mean,' Smith said.
'Well, when do I get a fuck?'

•

Upon arrival at Central, Muir put through a call to Federal Police Communications and arranged for Smith to be paged later that evening. Sallie went to the Orient Hotel in The Rocks with Smith and, at 11.00 p.m. as pre-arranged, he received an urgent call to return to Regional Headquarters.

'Sorry Sal, got to go.'

'But what about tonight?' she said.

'Something important's come up.'

'What time will you be finished?'

'I don't know, probably all night.'

'Shit. Am I ever going to get you alone?'

•

On Monday, 9 December, Smith and Muir informed Detective Inspector Newell of the offer they had received from Kelleher, but said nothing of the sexual offer from Sallie. 'Keep negotiating,' Newell told them.

Two days later Sallie phoned Smith, 'How about you blokes take me out to dinner tonight?'

'Have you found those furs for us yet?'

'Do you know a State cop called "Scully", he's at Darlinghurst. He's worked up the Cross for years, he's a friend of mine.'

'And?'

'He's going to have a look around. He'll ring me if he comes up with anything.'

Muir and Smith drove out to Botany where Sallie was staying with Glenn Stone. Inside the lounge room on the coffee table was a black Sony pearlcorder with a tape in it. Muir removed the tape and secreted it in his pocket, while Smith draped a coat over the recorder to conceal that the tape was missing. They drove Sallie to the Balkan Restaurant in Oxford Street, ordered a meal and Sallie got up from the table. 'Where you going?' Constable Smith said.

Sallie laughed. 'I'm going to the toilet, is that alright?'

Thirty minutes later she returned, her eyes glazed. 'Oh, the meal's here.'

'You've fixed yourself in there,' Smith said, 'haven't you?'

'I had to, I thought I was going to throw up.'

'Don't ever do that to us again!'

During the meal Muir left the table on the pretext that he had received a call and drove back to headquarters to listen to the tape. Part of the conversation involved a New South Wales Drug Squad Detective pleading with Sallie to be kept on the payroll after he'd locked up one of her runners. 'I had to do it,' the senior constable says. 'That came from higher up.'

When Peter Smith heard the tape he said to Muir, 'There's enough in that to put him away.'

•

On Thursday, 12 December, Sallie rang Smith and Muir at Federal Police Headquarters. 'Do you blokes want to take me out for my birthday?'

'Why should we?' Muir said.

'Because it's my birthday.'

'I suppose we should then.'

Smith and Muir picked Sallie up from Botany and drove to a Japanese restaurant in Little Hay Street. During the meal, Smith said, 'Trying to get these furs back is costing us a fortune.'

'Yeah, you oughta be taking us out Sal. You have plenty of money.'

'I can't touch it.'

'What do you mean?' Smith said.

'I can't tell you. Dave would kill me if he knew I was with you jacks.'

'How's Kelleher going to find out?'

'He's got contacts everywhere.'

'Are you going to tell us or not?'

'Dave always knew he was going to get caught so he buried a lot of money and heroin. I helped him wrap it.'

Smith leaned forward. 'Where's it buried?'

'I can't tell you that.'

'What did you wrap it in?'

'Glad wrap.'

'It'll still get wet.'

'No it won't. I wrapped it personally.'

Smith looked at Muir; Muir looked at Smith. 'How much is there?'

'About thirteen million,' Sallie said.

Immediately following the meal Smith and Muir sped back to Regional Headquarters and reported to Inspector Newell who now advised that they should attempt to locate the money and drugs as well as the furs. On Tuesday, 17 December, Sallie met them at Hungry Jack's in George Street. Sallie was now suspicious and started to seriously doubt that these two could deliver.

Sallie: If you don't get the brief, we're all in a lot of shit.
Smith: Why?
Sallie: Just get the brief.
Smith: Are you threatening me?
Sallie: I've told you too much already.
Smith: Listen, you either tell us what this is all about or we'll walk out that door.
Sallie: Then you'd be a fool, Peter.
[Smith and Muir start to get up from the table.]
Sallie: There's a tape.
Smith: What sort of tape?
Sallie: The first time I met you and Tez.
Smith: You taped us!
Sallie: I was supposed to make three copies and a transcript of it and give it to Dave's mum, but I couldn't do it to you.
Smith: Well, what are we going to do?
Sallie: If Dave finds out I've told you, he'll knock me.

Muir and Smith returned to headquarters and together hatched a plan to stage a fake raid on Dave Kelleher's mother to whom Sallie was supposed to deliver the tapes.

At 11 p.m. on Friday, 20 December, when Smith left Regional Headquarters in Redfern, Sallie was waiting outside in a taxi. She waved at him.

'You're not going to get out of it this time, Peter,' she said. 'Get in.'

Smith got in and the taxi proceeded to the West End Hotel in the city where Sallie and her Federal policeman spent their first night together.

On Monday morning Smith instructed Sallie to go home and make up some 'bodgie transcripts'.

'She had to have a meet with the Feds next to the Cricket Ground,' Glenn Stone said. 'It was about Kelleher and she was supposed to have these transcripts. Sallie got the typewriter out and copied all this shit out of *Penthouse*.'

'If this doesn't work and Dave finds out,' Sallie said to Stone, 'I'm dead.'

At 4 p.m. that afternoon Smith and three Federal constables went to the car park at the Hordern Pavilion and waited. A white Sigma Scorpion pulled up with Kelleher's mother at the wheel and then Sallie climbed out of a black taxi. The police pounced.

'Hello Sal, hello Mrs Kelleher. What are you doing here?'

'Nothing.'

'Terry, get on the radio and call the surveillance off the old girl. What have you got in your bag, Sal?'

'Nothing.'

'Give us a look then.' Smith grabbed her handbag and pulled out three cassette tapes and a number of pieces of paper with type on them. 'What are these?'

'I don't know,' Sallie said.

'How about we go to headquarters and have a little chat about it.'

•

Whether Betty Kelleher was convinced by this amateurish performance is unknown, but Sallie's relationship with Constable Peter Mark Parker Smith continued to grow.

At the Centrepoint coffee shop, Smith offered to help her get off heroin. Sallie had been trying to kick heroin seriously and Smith was looking for a female partner to compete with in a mixed pairs' bodybuilding competition. Smith thought Sallie had 'fairly good genetics for the weights' and asked her, 'You still interested in bodybuilding?'

'Yes,' Sallie said, 'I really want to get into it.'

'How much gear are you using these days?'

'I've been really trying, I haven't had a taste for two days.'

'If you want me to train you, well you'll have to get off the gear *and* give up smoking or it's waste of time.'

'Will you train me if I give up smoking later? I can't do both at once.'

'Alright, you got a deal, but there's one thing.'

'What?'

'If I train you and I tell you to do something or an exercise in a certain way you do it.'

'Okay, Peter,' she said. 'You're the boss.'

•

While Sallie was living with Glenn Stone in Botany she introduced her twelve-year-old daughter, Sascha, to Smith and told her that he was her new boyfriend. Sallie said he was a policeman and that he had a really high position in his job. One night Sallie rang her daughter, who was staying with her, and asked Sascha to bury some tapes in the backyard.

'She'd made these tapes of the Federal Police,' Glenn Stone said. 'I listened to them but they were such poor quality that they were inaudible.' He helped Sascha wrap two cassette tapes in plastic and bury them in the backyard of 17 Ermington Street. Later, when Glenn tried to dig them up, he couldn't find the spot.

'I sort of looked after Sascha for a couple of days,' Glenn Stone said. 'She was staying at Botany while Sallie was running around with the Feds. Sascha used to watch all these Freddie Kruger videos. They scared the shit out of me. Then Bryan (Sallie's ex-husband) had an argument with Sallie, gave her a bit of slap, a black eye. So I rang him and had a word.'

At 11 p.m. on Christmas Day, Constable Smith received a message from headquarters telling him to contact the 'blond lady' urgently. Smith telephoned Sallie who was crying.

'What's wrong?'

'I've been attacked,' she said. 'Can you come over?'

'Sal, it's pretty late.'

'Please, Peter. I'm here on my own, I don't know who else to ring.'

Smith drove to Botany and found Sallie-Anne with a number of small open wounds to her face and a bump on the top of her head. Her ex-husband had attacked her, she said, and threatened her with a carving knife.

'Why?'

'Bryan's on methadone. And he'd been drinking and he wanted to know if I had any dope. I told him I was trying to get off it and he just snapped and started hitting me, in front of Sascha.'

But Scott McCrae, a close friend of Sallie's, remembered it differently: 'They'd had this terrible argument over Christmas dinner about ripping Kelleher off. Sallie wanted to dig $10 000 up and go to Greece. Bryan said she was mad, that Kelleher might harm Sascha. Sallie was drinking. She was a pretty ugly drunk at the best of times. She got in a fight with Bryan and she hit him and then he hit her. Bryan told her to get out and Sallie said, "Come on Sascha, let's go."

'"No," Sascha said. "No, I'm not going with you."

'Sallie-Anne left on her own. She was deeply hurt.'

That night was the last time Sascha saw her mother alive.

•

Three days after the fight with her ex-husband, Sallie rolled Glenn Stone's car in Cleveland Street on the way to a meeting with Warren Richards. According to Scott McCrae: 'That's when she started dealing with Richards. Sallie was frantically trying to accumulate money so that she could buy a lifestyle and get her daughter back.' At the Royal Prince Alfred Hospital a surgical plate with six screws was inserted in her badly broken wrist. That same day Smith and another Federal constable visited Sallie at the hospital. While Smith was there a beefy New South Wales policeman arrived and Sallie introduced him. 'This is Scully,' she said.

Detective Neville Scullion nodded curtly at the two young Federal Police.

'There seemed to be a constant flow of big men in suits to her bedside,' one of her fellow patients revealed. The visitor she was happiest to see was Constable Peter Smith who visited her on a number of occasions over the next week. Sallie told hospital staff and other patients that she was in love with him, that she 'had never had such kindness from a man'.

On Christmas Eve Constable Smith had given her a gold wrist bracelet. The bracelet was 21 centimetres long, nine-carat gold with box-links, and had a circular clasp loop with a catch on it. Sallie never took it off. She was still wearing it when she was pulled out of Busby's Pond.

•

Although Constable Smith would later claim that he had no intention of a long-term relationship, that 'she was someone I was only using to get information from' and that 'I intended arresting Huckstepp eventually', he continued meeting her throughout January, booking them into motels along the Pacific Highway on different nights under false names, paying the motel bill and leaving around six o'clock each morning to drive to Regional Headquarters in Redfern.

Sallie told her new flatmate, Gwen Beecroft, that Smith wanted to leave the police force. 'They were going away together,' Gwen said, 'up north, to open up a gym.'

'I can't believe it, I've fallen in love with a Federal copper!' Sallie confided to Scott McCrae.

'Poor Sal,' another friend said. 'She always got diddled by cops.'

On Thursday, 16 January, pressure came down the line. Smith and Muir received instructions from their new detective inspector: 'Go out and get those furs back at all costs.' Smith chose not to mention to his senior officer that he was having an affair with an informant. 'Do what you've got to do!' his superior said.

Again Smith took Sallie out to Long Bay Gaol to interview Steven Edward Murray and as a result of information obtained they tracked down the missing iron, toaster and electric jug. Five Federal Police officers raided the Bellevue Hill home of a Kings Cross pawnbroker with Sallie in handcuffs—(Smith and Muir's idea)—but found nothing. They searched the flat of a friend of Murray's, William Lockrey, without a warrant.

'Four Commonwealth police and Sallie-Anne came to my place,' Lockrey said. 'They threatened me for an hour and a half about the furs. When I told them that I didn't know nothin about the bust one of the Feds threatened to bash me and that's when Sallie-Anne stepped in: "For Christ's sake tell them where they are," she says. I said to her, "You think I done the bust, don't you?" Sallie answered, "Yes." and I said, "Well I didn't." After that they left, but they kept coming back.'

A New South Wales detective investigating Sallie's murder told me ten years later: 'There musta been something else in those furs for the Feds to go to all that trouble.'

'Like what?'

'Like drugs,' he said. 'Fucking Peter Smith swanning around the Cross with Sallie Huckstepp on his arm—how stupid was that?'

Five days before her death, on 1 February, Smith took Sallie to Jensens nightclub at Avalon Beach, then they went to the Bourbon and Beefsteak in Kings Cross—a bar frequented by drug dealers and the New South Wales Drug Squad—where they stayed drinking until seven in the morning. At one stage a group of large men entered the downstairs bar. Sallie was nervous and tried to hide behind Smith.

'Those blokes are friends of Dave's.'

'So?' Smith said.

'So I sure hope they don't tell Dave they saw me here with you.'

Although Smith claimed to have been attempting 'to wind their relationship down,' he met Sallie at a Mosman gym on Monday, 3 February, and they dined at an intimate Italian restaurant in Abercrombie Street, Redfern. After going to an automatic teller machine in the city, Smith booked them into the Coronation Motel on the Pacific Highway. At 7.30 a.m. the next day she dropped him off at Regional Headquarters in her white Cortina.

It was the last time Constable Smith saw Sallie alive.

'I rang her on the Wednesday, 5 February, and again at 1.30 that afternoon,' Smith said. 'I told her I had to drive up to Newcastle on a National Crime Authority operation.'

'Take care, Peter,' Sallie said, 'won't you.'

Smith did. He went straight to room 605 in the Manly International Hotel where he stayed the night with a young woman he'd met two weeks earlier in Newcastle—Deborah Lee Travis.

On Thursday, 6 February, Smith drove to Newcastle, arriving at 17 Oliver Street at 5 p.m. where he shared a meal with Debbie Lee Travis, watched *Conan the Barbarian* together on video and went to bed around 11 p.m.

At noon the next day his detective sergeant called him into his office in Newcastle and told him the news. 'I do not recall Smith making an audible reply but he reacted in a manner in which I believe to be an exaggerated emotion,' Detective Sergeant Ward said. 'You have to get back to Sydney, Peter,' I told him. 'The New South Wales Police want to interview you.'

•

I traced Peter Mark Parker Smith through the electoral roll to a large rambling house in Pymble. Two years and six months after Sallie's murder, with his career in tatters, he'd left the Australian Federal Police and was working as a security consultant. Barrel-chested, with cropped black hair and narrow dark eyes, it was hard to fathom why so many women were attracted to him. On the phone Smith told me he was going to think over whether he should talk. He expressed a strong feeling that he'd come out of this 'whole business badly', that he wanted to 'put Huckstepp out of his mind', that he had a wife and kids now.

He sounded nervous.

The next day he left a message on my machine: 'Listen, I'm not interested in going into this anymore. So that's it, thanks.'

According to Deborah Travis's statement, Smith left her bed at five o'clock on the Friday morning that Sallie's body was found.

'Peter was a charming boy, well-dressed, articulate, effervescent,' Debbie told me over the phone. 'He was gung-ho, working undercover with the Federal Police. I was a country girl and here was this nice guy in a glamour job in a city not known for educated, articulate young men. He didn't tell me about his involvement with Sallie, he didn't tell me about his wife. It's not that he lied. He just didn't own up. I was totally innocent. Yes, I was attracted to him.

'It ended his career, his marriage,' Debbie Travis said. 'He was shafted to uniform, sent out to patrol the airport. Afterwards I asked myself a lot of questions about Peter, but he couldn't have been involved in her death, could he?'

I didn't think so. Smith was only after the furs and in many ways he was used by his superiors just as he used Sallie.

'Neither Smith nor Muir really appreciated the gravity of their actions and certainly not the ramifications which, to them at least, must be regarded as taking a tragic turn,' Chief Inspector Wells wrote in a confidential Federal Police report to his Commander. 'New South Wales Police have stated that they believe Huckstepp was coldly using Smith for her own purposes. I am personally of the opinion some doubt exists regarding this theory.'

Retired Detective Sergeant Prentice of the New South Wales Homicide Squad put it more bluntly: 'Peter Smith was a bloke in the Federal Police, at that stage the experience of the Federal Police was very limited. He only had two years in the job, they brought him out from the airport and hooked him up with another guy who had no experience either. They grabbed Sallie Huckstepp and marched her around the Cross, stood over blokes, all this mad stuff straight out of gangster comics. They just got in over their heads and then Peter Smith falls in love with her. He was taking her everywhere and rooting her silly.

'What you've got then, exemplifies the whole AFP scenario. Two young galoots who have no idea of what they are doing being run by a foolish person who has some grandiose plans of getting himself some kudos. I blame their inspector. He had no brains either. Smith and Muir were running riot, they never took any notes, they were given the use of cars and support, they spent fourteen hours making statements and got eleven hours overtime. Every turn of events exposes them for gross incompetence. There's proper procedures when you work for the police and they didn't do anything at all. No doubt in my mind it was her association with Smith and Muir that got her knocked.'

'Do you think there could've been something more to the furs?' I asked.

'I know where the furs went,' Geoff Prentice said. 'They sold them to a pawnbroker's joint in the Cross. They were never recovered. I often thought they might've had listening devices sewn in 'em.'

'In the furs?'

'Yeah, bugging their own safe house. But why would anyone hang 'em in furs eh, the crooks'd find 'em first go. Then I thought it might've been heroin or money sewn into the jackets, or—what about this?'

'What?' I leaned forward.

'Could've been McCabe who owned that unit and picked up those furs and he's hung 'em there.'

I remembered Smith's words on the tape: 'A lot of problems can arise if we don't get them back.'

'It was always a big secret,' Geoff Prentice said, 'you could never get sense out of the Feds of what the real story was with them furs. We could never work it out. But why put two idiots on it, I dunno. It was a ballsup by the AFP from the start.'

•

When New South Wales Police interviewed Peter Mark Parker Smith six days after Sallie's murder, they asked him: 'Other than Dave Kelleher in Long Bay can you think of any persons who would wish Huckstepp dead?'

'Only two,' Smith said. 'One is Neddy Smith; the other is Roger Rogerson.'

'What reason did Sallie give you these two might want her dead?'

'With Neddy I believe it was a long-running feud. She alleged he bashed and raped her. She was afraid of him, but she also thought he was a fool. Rogerson—because of the Lanfranchi investigation, what she said about him on "60 Minutes". She told me that he tried to kill her once before with a hot needle, but due to a mix-up some other girl got killed instead.'

'Do you know a person by the name of Warren Richards?'

'I know that he is a drug dealer and a friend of Kelleher's. He's heavily into karate.'

'Did Sallie ever speak of Richards?'

'No.'

'Did she tell you where she bought her drugs?'

'No,' Smith said. 'We'd sort of made an agreement that when we were together we wouldn't discuss what she'd done or what I did. Anyway Sallie never considered herself an informant.'

Sallie's friend, Scott McCrae, agreed. 'Sallie was giving information, but what kind of information. It was basically what they already knew,' McCrae said. 'She originally got involved with the Feds because of the furs. To get Dave Kelleher out of gaol. She didn't like informers.'

'It is a common police ploy,' Dave Kelleher stated in court, 'to claim that a person is an informant in order to cover up a corrupt relationship. The police tried to label Sallie as an informer to get out of why they were having any dealings with her.'

'Sallie would've told police anything they wanted to hear as long as it wasn't the truth,' her sister Debra said. 'She was never an informer. That's why Dave Kelleher respected her. Sallie was staunch. If she got caught with something she wore the blue. She never gave police information, she never helped them. She had a very good reputation.'

•

Detective Con Moores, who was transferred to Kings Cross in 1984, got to know 'the Daily Double' (as Sallie and Debra were known around the Cross) extremely well.

'After some months working in the KC area,' Moores told the coroner. 'I found that Sallie would approach me in the street while I was making patrol. I became friends with her. I found Sallie to be a friendly person who liked to talk to police at any opportunity and I believe that this was used by her to find out as much as she could about the activities of police in the area.'

Moores also claimed that Sallie was an informant of his. However, he did not keep a register of informants. Nor did he use codenames for them. 'Sallie was a person you could speak to,' Moores said, 'and obtain information from, but she certainly wasn't a paid informant.'

The only police officer who maintained that Sallie was a 'real informant' was Detective Neville John Scullion. The name 'Scully' and his telephone number, along with the names of six other Darlinghurst detectives were found in Sallie's blue and pink address book. According to close friends she met Scullion regularly in the months before her death. When questioned about his involvement with her at the inquest, Scullion replied that he used Huckstepp as an informant over the five years that he knew her and that he obtained information which led to a number of arrests. In return for this information, he provided her with the details of any warrants out against her.

'So in exchange for information which was readily available from any police station, she provided you with information over many years?' Andrew Haesler, counsel for the Huckstepp family, asked at the inquest.

'Yes, that's correct,' Scullion said.

'And you offered her nothing in return?'

'That's correct.'

'No protection?'

'She never asked for protection.'

'And yet she was happy to provide you with this information for free?'

'Yes she was.'

Scullion denied that their relationship went beyond the straight policeman–informant relationship.

'Did you have any fondness for her?'

'No, I did not.'

When asked if his visit to see Sallie in hospital after her car accident was a social visit, Scullion denied that too. Within hours of her body being found, Scullion offered his assistance to investigating police. Two days after her murder, Scullion drove Sallie's sister, Debra, out to a storage shed in St Peters that Sallie had rented. 'Scullion thought if he took me out there he'd get in,' Debra said, 'he wanted to see if she had left any documents or diaries.'

Although Scullion denied having any 'business relationship' with Sallie, Glenn Stone claimed that Scullion and Sallie 'were looking to take over a club together in the Cross called Bruno's'. It had a licensee then and Sallie planned to take it over with Scullion as the muscle. 'I met Scully about ten times,' Stone said. 'Sallie and Scullion were pretty good friends.'

'The day after her death,' Scott McCrae told me from New Zealand, 'Neville Scullion and a detective from Maroubra went around to the flat and arrested Gwen on some bullshit charge. They were shitting themselves that Sallie had kept information on them.'

After a two-year hunt I'd managed to track down Scott McCrae with the help of a senior Federal Police officer. Apart from Gwen Beecroft, Scott McCrae was the last person to see Sallie alive.

'The night she died,' Scott said, 'I'd left my job at Fairfax and I went around to Edgecliff to pick up some clothes about twenty to eleven and I told Sallie that I'd quit work and she said, "You're just a fucking idiot, Scott." She really gave it to me. She said that if only she had a straight job. She'd give anything to be clean. She was terribly depressed about her daughter. They'd had this fight and she'd taken off. Sallie didn't know where she'd gone. She fell apart when she didn't have access to Sascha. Scullion was involved with her; apparently he was trying to find Sascha for her, he was acting as a go-between. That night I asked her to find out about the nightclub, to ring Scullion. I was a cleanskin and Sallie thought she could use my name to take over the club's licence. She was meeting Scully the next day.'

'Did she have a relationship with him?' I asked.

'Sallie would have had some kind of relationship. There were six or seven detectives that she'd had relationships with.'

Scott had known Sallie since shortly after the murder of Lanfranchi. Five years later he ran into her again in a Japanese restaurant in Chinatown, the night she was there with Peter Smith and Terry Muir.

'Sallie looked really presentable and she seemed very keen to talk to me,' Scott said. 'She gave me her mobile phone number and we connected. I teamed up with her, not in a relationship. She was living out at Botany in a house full of transient waiters, and she wanted to get out of there. I introduced Sallie to Gwen Beecroft. Gwen was someone I knew. She's a nut, an absolute nut. Gwen was someone who'd been living in Sydney for seven years and she had no idea who Sallie was. She'd never heard of Roger Rogerson. She lived in her own little world. Sallie thought that Gwen was really sweet.

'After Sallie was in hospital she went for four or five days without a hit which is a long time if you're a junkie. She ran out of gear and she got pretty crook and then she got a delivery from a Federal policeman—[*Name deleted*] brought her out some smack—and that's when I really started to believe that Sallie's stories weren't exaggerated. She had a go at withdrawing. She tried to clean up. I think that she'd decided that it was just too hard, that she was too battleworn. So rather than thinking about giving up drugs, she got back into dealing. Sallie always equated stability with financial security. She was a really good operator. She started off dealing very small amounts and was quickly turning over a couple of grand a week. I stayed at Edgecliff for about three or four weeks and during this time I spoke to Warren Richards on the phone a couple of times for Sallie—"I'm here now," he'd say. "Tell her to come around."

'He had her running like, it was an incredible timetable. He'd ring and sort of say be there X Y Z time and if she wasn't there he'd just disappear. Sallie would go off and come back exhausted. He was getting her out from Edgecliff to Ashfield and places like that. She showed signs of being frightened to go and meet him alone. She would become preoccupied and fidgety, abusive. In the last week and a half she started making references to, "he can't know that I'm using" and this sort of thing.'

On a number of occasions, when Sallie would return from these meetings with Richards, Scott McCrae watched her take out a plastic bag containing about 5 grams of heroin. She would then take out her black clutch bag, in which she kept her needles, spoon and belt. She would mix the heroin and inject it into the back of her hands.

'The last night I saw her I could tell she was withdrawing,' Scott McCrae said. 'She was fidgety, sniffling and quite agitated. I didn't stay long, I picked up my clothes and left as I had a taxi waiting downstairs, I know the time was a quarter to eleven, because I checked in order to monitor my taxi fare. Hanging around with Sallie was a bit like a fantasy world and then when she died it became very real and very scary.'

'How do you mean?'

'Basically at the time we didn't know what was going on. We didn't know who to trust. We were scared we might be next. Within weeks of her dying,' Scott McCrae said, 'I was in a room with some people who were using and I turned to one of them and I said, "Give me some of that."

'I'd seen what the needle had done to Sallie, but I didn't care. When you are a junkie you risk death for pleasure. I ended up being locked up. I didn't get free of it for another six years.'

'And Sallie, is there anything more you remember?'

'Sallie was a fascinating character. She had so many neglected needs. She had so many twisted emotions. Her father had taught her and Debbie that making money was it. That material satisfaction was everything. Sex, food, alcohol, all that superficial grasping stuff. But with Sallie there was a very strong emotional side. She fell apart when she didn't have access to Sascha. She loved her daughter. Whatever Sallie's unfulfilled childhood needs were, I don't know, but I used to see her as this little girl running around looking for people to approve her.'

•

A former friend and addict, Jenny Bain, described Sallie's last weeks: 'She was running too hot. She was driving around the Cross with the Federal Police, two car loads of Federal Police, looking for these bloody furs. She's full of Serepax and the coppers are all pumping her and treating her like a princess. After a couple of weeks it gets in your head, the power of it all. You give Sallie-Anne a little excitement and attention and she'd thrive.'

When Peter Smith was asked, shortly after her death, if Sallie-Anne was killed because she was an informant of his, he replied, 'It may not be the entire reason but, yes, that's my opinion.'

'Sallie was only involved with us in relation to the furs,' Muir, the senior of the two officers, stated at the inquest. 'She wasn't giving information about anything else.' He denied that they took risks with her, that their conduct had contributed to her death. 'She chose to take those risks,' Muir said.

'But you willingly let her?' Counsel for the Huckstepp family asked him. 'You took no steps personally to see that she was protected.'

'We tried to keep it confidential.'

'You don't think associates of hers in the criminal element at the Cross knew that you and Smith were police officers?'

'Well they may have, yes, but we weren't getting around in suits all the time.'

'It never occurred to you that you were placing her in considerable danger?'

'No, she was in no danger at all,' Muir said.

5

Post-mortem

The business end of the Institute of Forensic Medicine is hidden away in a narrow leafy street in the inner suburb of Glebe. Police cars arrive day and night in the reserved spaces outside the brick and concrete building. It was here at 2.30 p.m. on 7 February 1986, that Dr Sergio Staraj, the Government Medical Officer, began what would prove to be the first of two post-mortem examinations on Sallie-Anne Huckstepp.

'The body was that of an adult female Caucasian of early middle age,' Dr Staraj wrote, 'weighing 57 kilos and measuring 161 cm in length and in a good state of nutrition. White froth was present between the lips. A number of recent parchment abrasions were present on the lower face overlying the right mandible and the lower left cheek. A dark purple bruise was noted on the left lateral margin of the inner lower lip and a poorly defined dusky red bruise on the adjacent external skin. Situated on the front of the neck, below the chin and running parallel to the neck creases, were three linear bruises, the longest measuring 4 cm and the smallest 1.5 cm. Numerous recent vertical scrape abrasions were present on the back predominantly on the right side. Old linear venipuncture marks noted on the dorsa of both feet. Two old surgical scars were noted on the right arm, the larger measuring 9 cm and the smaller 3 cm.

There was wrinkling of the foot and hand pads. Fine barely discernible petechial haemorrhages were noted over the conjunctivae and over the malar surfaces. There was no major trauma over the body surface.'

Dr Staraj opened the three cavities of the body and upon examination found:

> The tongue, mouth and teeth appeared normal; apart from the bruising. There was no foreign matter present in either mouth, pharynx or major airways.
>
> The lungs were well expanded and congested.
>
> The liver was congested.
>
> The stomach contained one litre of partly digested food in a fluid state.
>
> The brain, heart and reproductive organs were normal.
>
> The bladder was empty.
>
> There was no evidence of trauma about the external genitalia.

In order to record the presence or absence of any bruising to the underlying tissues of the neck and the underlying muscles and neck structure, Dr Staraj made an incision from chin to sternum. Blood was not drained prior to the incision and the incision method carried out produced no evidence of trauma. Dr Staraj concluded that sufficient force therefore had not been used to cause deeper bruising.

When questioned what the frothing on the lips and in the airways indicated, Dr Staraj replied that it was considered to be good evidence of death by drowning. Frothing occurs due to the inhalation of water mixing with blood from the lungs. The liquid part of the blood like the white of a beaten egg comes up through the air passages and into the mouth. The fine petechial haemorrhaging in the conjunctivae, Dr Staraj explained, was the result of the rupture of very fine blood vessels, the capillaries, which is often found in cases of asphyxia especially due to suffocation or strangulation. Staraj also found venipuncture marks in the ankles of the deceased, the veins of her forearm and the backs of her hands, although none of these marks had been made in the preceding 24 hours.

Due to her criminal history, New South Wales detectives were of the opinion that the deceased had died of an overdose, perhaps forcefully injected by another person, but Dr Staraj could not reach a final conclusion on Friday afternoon. He removed hair and fingernail samples from the body as well as blood and bile samples for chemical analysis and sent them to the Department of Analytical Laboratories in Lidcombe for further testing.

'In my opinion,' Dr Staraj wrote, 'death has taken place about 15 hours previously—around 11.30 p.m. on February 6—with a margin of error of several hours either way.' He placed no value on the fact that Sallie-Anne's watch had stopped at eleven o'clock.

Three days later, a further external examination of the body was made in an attempt to find recent puncture marks on her legs and ankles consistent with the use of heroin. Police were still looking to find evidence of an overdose.

On 14 February, Assistant Commissioner Ross Nixon spoke to Dr Thomas Howard Godfrey Oettle—a prominent forensic pathologist—about the Huckstepp murder. Senior New South Wales Police were concerned about 'media speculation' and 'inconsistencies as to the direct cause of death'. Detective Sergeant Geoff Prentice of the Homicide Squad explained what happened next:

'I went down to the Division of Forensic Medicine and we were waiting for a medical report and we couldn't get one for ten days. So I complained about it and I saw Gus Oettle who was head of forensic. Now the other fellow was renowned in our circles as being incompetent. I said, this is just hopeless, so Gus said he'd have a look at her. Gus Oettle went down and conducted another PM for us. Staraj did the first one and then a coupla days later old Dr Brighton came in who'd been retired. He was an expert on strangulation and he had a look at her, he could see the little blood vessels in her eyes and then the bruising showed up around the throat.

'It was Assistant Commissioner Nixon who rang Gus Oettle—

they knew each other from when Nixon worked in ballistics—but it was me who went through the back door. I was talking to Gus Oettle about her and he says to me, this sheila here, she's a prime suspect for HIV positive or hepatitis C or E. He says the best thing is to go get this bloke Peter Smith and tell him to have a test straightaway, but I couldn't get hold of Smith. Someone had pumped his head full of this crazy business that the New South Wales Police were going to load him with the murder.'

•

On 15 February, Dr Godfrey Oettle personally examined the body of Sallie-Anne Huckstepp and on the following day, with the assistance of Dr Staraj, Dr Oettle conducted an external autopsy. The fine petechiae had become much more prominent and the neck abrasions had darkened. Finger-tip bruising was now evident on the right side of the chin and the left side of her neck. Markings on the right side of the deceased's throat were consistent with a thumb print. It appeared to Dr Oettle that there had been an attempt at manual strangulation. Small marks inflicted around the neck were caused by someone holding her around the throat and pulling on a necklace, but it was the imprint of someone's hand grabbing her around the throat that had caused the major trauma. The abrasions on the right side of her chin on the edge of the mandible were also consistent with manual strangulation.

A small amount of morphine was detected in the liver, blood and bile of the deceased, but neither pathologist was able to indicate the precise time at which the drug was ingested. There was also bruising underneath the jaw more consistent with a ligature being used, and a large amount of bruising on the lower lip and inside the mouth. Dr Oettle believed that the injuries to her neck were caused by a succession of applications of force, one of which was by means of a thumb, the other by a ligature. He stated that two sets of pressure were applied to the throat, both consistent with asphyxial haemorrhages and leading to unconsciousness.

The doctor added that heroin is a cerebral depressant and diminishes the ability to resist attack. In addition, as there was only about three feet of water in the pond, if Ms Huckstepp had been conscious, he would have expected her, a woman of some physical fitness, to be able to walk. The marks on her back were consistent with being dragged into the water. An area on her lower back that was redder was also consistent with a foot being applied to her back. The bruising inside the mouth, according to Dr Oettle, was consistent with a blow to the face.

With the result of the blood chloride tests (used in cases of suspected drowning), Doctors Oettle and Staraj were of the opinion that the deceased had drowned and subsequently issued the following cause of death thirteen days after the murder, on 19 February: 'That Sallie-Anne Huckstepp died as a result of drowning due to asphyxia by manual strangulation and associated narcotic intake (morphine).'

Surprisingly, no mention was made in the report of the fact that Sallie had fractured her right arm just five weeks previously and it had only recently come out of plaster, though a broken wrist was surely a factor in her reduced ability to fend off an attacker.

Fingernail clippings were also removed at the second autopsy from the deceased's left and right hand and packaged and labelled. Dr Oettle explained that fingernail clippings were taken as a matter of course in all victims of strangulation. Tissue was excised from the left and right ankle, left and right foot and from her inner lip.

'At 3 p.m. on February 7,' Detective Senior Constable Clinton Nicol from the East Sydney Crime Scene Unit stated, 'I attended the first post-mortem examination on the body of the deceased person HUCKSTEPP at the City Morgue. I received a pair of blue jeans, a white sloppy joe jumper, a pair of white sandshoes and a pair of pink coloured panties. I also received a sealed jar containing a sample of head hair removed from the deceased by Dr Staraj. These items I conveyed to the Sydney Crime Scene Unit in Surry Hills and placed in the Crime Scene Unit Exhibit Room.

'On the 14/2/86 I completed a P377 Exhibit Examination Form listing 3 items for examination: (1) One plastic jar containing hair fibres recovered on Centennial Park Lake. (2) Bag containing pink panties worn by the deceased removed at the Post Mortem. (3) Jar containing head hair labelled Sallie-Anne Huckstepp and removed by Dr Staraj on 7/2/86.

'On Sunday 16/2/86 while rostered on a rest day I was recalled to duty to attend a further Post Mortem on the body of the deceased person Huckstepp. I attended the City Morgue in Glebe at 10 a.m. and had a conversation with Dr Staraj and Dr Oettle. I received from them a jar containing fingernails from the left hand of Huckstepp and a jar containing fingernails from the right hand of Huckstepp. I added these 2 items to the P377 Exhibit Examination Form. I then removed the five items from the Sydney Crime Scene Unit Exhibition Room and attended the Division of Forensic medicine at Glebe.'

SCIENTIFIC INVESTIGATION SECTION

Deceased: Sallie Anne Huckstepp

Suspicious Death

Due to the unusual circumstances of the death and the fact that at this stage no cause has been found it is desired to have these 5 items examined to ascertain if the hair found in a plastic bag near the body is human and possibly be compared to a hair sample removed from the body of the deceased at the PM by Dr Staraj. Could the panties be examined to ascertain if the victim has any seminal stains in order to establish if the victim had met a sexual relation prior to her death.

C Nicol

Det Const 1st Class

Crime Scene Unit, February 20

The Commissioner of Police

Division of Forensic Medicine
42–50 Parramata Rd, Glebe

Re: <u>Suspicious Death of Sallie-Anne Huckstepp</u>

I, Gaynor Maria Clancy
hereby certify as follows

(1) I am employed as a Forensic Biologist by the Department of Health, New South Wales. My scientific qualifications are Bachelor of Science of the University of New England.

(2) I received the following articles from Det Const Nicol of the Crime Scene Unit on the 20th day of Feb 1986

(i) Hair
(ii) Head hair
(iii) 2 jars of Fingernails
(iv) Panties.

(3) No examination was made of these items. Sallie-Anne Huckstepp was considered to be in the high risk category for AIDS and Hepatitis B and it was not possible for a screen of her blood to be made.

Given under my hand at Sydney the twelfth day of March 1986

G.M. Clancy
Forensic Biologist

On Monday, 24 February, Detective Nicol returned to the Division of Forensic Medicine at Glebe and collected the five items. These were then stored in the Sydney Crime Scene Unit Exhibition Room on Level 5 at the Sydney Police Centre where they remained for the next twelve months. In 1987, a further request was made by New South Wales Police for the fingernails to be examined. Vivien Gay Beilby, a forensic biologist at the Lidcombe Analysis Laboratories, examined the fingernails belonging to the right and left hands of Sallie-Anne Huckstepp. 'Human blood was detected on two of the fingernails of the right hand,' Ms Beilby concluded. 'But there is insufficient blood present for grouping purposes.'

No mention was made of the fact that the fingernails had been stored on a Crime Scene exhibition shelf for the past twelve months. As a New South Wales detective explained, 'If that blood had been examined after the first autopsy they would've wrapped up the Huckstepp case then and there.'

Arthur Gee, a forensic radiographist with the Division of Forensic Medicine took four X-rays of the skull and mandible of the deceased. The first radiograph was a lateral view; the second was an anterior posterior view; the third radiograph was a lateral projection of the lower skull showing the upper end of the cervical spine; the fourth radiograph consisted of four routine views of the excised larynx which still had the soft tissue surrounding the bones.

For some reason the X-rays were taken after the post-mortem. That seemed an odd procedure and I needed to ask why.

•

I met Dr Godfrey Oettle over a bruschetta at the Forest Lodge Hotel in Arundel Street, a few doors up from where he had worked as Director of the Division of Forensic Medicine. A tall, intelligent man with a white Abe Lincoln beard and long delicate fingers, Godfrey Oettle revealed how he had been called into the Huckstepp case by Assistant Commissioner Nixon after senior police had come under considerable political pressure. The initial pathologist was unable to give a cause of death so Godfrey Oettle spoke to the Homicide Squad and they examined the body, along with Dr Brighton and Dr Staraj, in 'the old murder room'.

Straightaway Godfrey Oettle knew it was a manual strangulation.

'If you look at the photos you can see the suffusion,' he said. He explained carefully about bruising on dead people, how the marks show up in the skin after the blood has drained. At that stage, Dr Staraj didn't know the cause of death because of the combination of three factors, drowning, asphyxiation and morphine.

'With respect,' Dr Oettle said, 'that's nonsense. It's quite simple, the findings have to follow a logical sequence of events. The cause of death was drowning as a consequence of manual strangulation and narcotic intake.

'Following the bruising to her neck she was still alive. My opinion was that a ligature was applied from behind.'

Dr Oettle said that the injury to the lip would have been made from the forefinger of the right hand and that the abrasions of the right-hand-side of her chin were consistent with manual strangulation.

'If sufficient force is applied, the carotid arteries are shut down. As a result of increased venous pressure and a lack of oxygen you get a weakening of the walls of the capillaries in the skin that then burst. You then get a small amount of blood similar to a flea bite. Characteristic of obstruction to the air passages and the venous return.'

Sallie was then dragged into the pond where somebody stood on her back.

'A person,' Dr Oettle continued in a soft voice, 'loses consciousness very quickly in freshwater drowning.'

I bought the doctor a glass of white wine. When I returned Dr Oettle mentioned that the coroner, Greg Glass, had requested that Dr Staraj not perform any further autopsies, that the Department of Health had decided to review his work in response to a request by the coroner. Dr Oettle had been given the invidious task of going through all Dr Staraj's back cases.

'Could you explain the incision he made?'

'It was our practice,' Dr Oettle said, 'that before you examine a body, you opened the skull, removed the brain and let the blood from the neck drain out. We usually put a headrest under the shoulders and drain the neck. The end result is that all the vessels empty of blood and the pathologist is unable to contribute to any additional bruising. So you don't confuse yourself, in other words. In the first autopsy this wasn't done.

'Also the incision made from the chin to the sternum was quite pointless because you couldn't see the sides of the neck. It would have been far better to have made two incisions from the ear down here.' He demonstrated with his fingers. 'And peel back the skin.

You would thus have had an unimpeded view of the neck muscles. I don't think the method used was adequate to show injuries to the soft tissue of the neck.'

I watched Dr Oettle segment his bruschetta into four equal pieces. 'What about the X-rays?' I asked. 'Was there any point in taking X-rays after a post-mortem?'

'Only if you're not sure what you're looking for.' He peered at me over the top of his glasses.

'The fingernails, the blood under her fingernails, would that have evaporated after twelve months on a police shelf?'

'You have to remember we didn't have DNA testing in '86. With hindsight what should have been done is that the blood should have been stored at −70°C until DNA testing was made available. Of course we were always short of staff then. The Analytical Laboratories at Lidcombe might tell you precisely when DNA testing was introduced in New South Wales.'

I thanked Dr Oettle for his time. We walked down Arundel Street and he told me of a case he'd been called out to by police a few years prior to the murder event. The body of a young man was lying on the floor in a house in Penkivil Street, Bondi.

'He was very dead,' Godfrey Oettle said. 'An overdose. The syringes had been chucked down the chute. In the next room I saw a beautiful young woman lying on a bed, full of heroin. It was Sallie-Anne Huckstepp.'

•

That afternoon I rang Lidcombe and spoke to the head forensic biologist. 'We weren't the first State to introduce DNA testing,' the man said, 'but we weren't the last.' The initial technology, borrowed from the FBI and first used in New South Wales in 1990, required large samples of blood or tissue and was extremely slow. Results could take weeks. I asked him what were the chances of recovering DNA from blood and skin under a person's fingernail clippings that had been stored in a glass jar. He said that although ultraviolet light and storage conditions can reduce the efficacy of DNA testing, the PCR (Polymerase Chain Reaction) technology available today is so sophisticated that DNA can be recovered from items that have been stored for many years.

He paused. 'Who did you say you were again?'

I told him I was investigating a murder case and put down the phone. Were Sallie-Anne's nail clippings still sitting on a shelf? Or had they been disposed of?

•

I waited outside the autopsy room in the Office of the Institute of Forensic Medicine. There is a great difference between the living human body and the dead human body, Professor Hilton, Director of the Institute told me. 'A dead body decays very quickly. Are you sure you're up to this?'

A young person lay on a stainless-steel autopsy table, thin-legged, hands rigid at the sides, toes pointing at the ceiling. 'When someone of this age is found dead in Darlinghurst,' the pathologist stated, 'we naturally suspect an overdose.' He placed a steel block under the shoulders and made an incision starting from the left ear guiding the scalpel cleanly through neck tissue at a 45-degree angle towards the throat, then extending the incision in a straight line down through the abdomen to the pubis.

His assistant, wearing a white apron, blue gown and yellow gumboots, stood on a red crate and snapped cheerfully through ribs and cartilage with a pair of surgical shears. She removed the breastplate and poked inside the viscera with a gloved hand, pulled out a bundle of intestines strung together like thick sausages. She placed all the guts in a plastic bag. The pathologist lifted out a connecting block of organs—tongue, trachea, oesophagus, stomach, lungs, liver, heart, spleen, pancreas—and placed it on a stainless-steel bench beside the sink.

The young person's limbs were streaked with dark blood, his ears plum-coloured. I watched the assistant slice through the top of the skull and peel the bloodied scalp down over the chin. Up until now it had seemed no worse than a butcher's shop. Once the face was removed and the scalp hung inside-out like a red bathing cap, the body looked surreal. With a vibrating saw she cut through bone and removed a large wedge-shaped section of the skull, sat it on the edge of the autopsy table, and then pulled out the brain.

I held onto the edge of my chair while the organs were separated one by one and dissected with a snipping of thin-nosed scissors.

Photographs of Sallie's autopsy show her lying on an identical stainless-steel tray with her scalp shaved and crudely stitched, her chest and abdomen sutured. There is a long scar on the inside of her right arm, track marks on her ankles. Close-ups show the petechiae in her eyes, deep bruising around her throat and lip. There are finger marks on her chin and what appear to be drag marks along her back. She is naked, of course, and seven males—four detectives and three forensic assistants—crowd around the autopsy table, staring down at her corpse. Her toenails are bright pink and shiny as if she has just finished painting them.

I watched the pathologist check for bruising on the young person's arms, paring away skin with his scalpel. The assistant scooped out litres of fluid from the body with a ladle and stuffed wads of fluffy white wool into the chest cavity and into the emptied skull. She replaced the wedge-shaped section of bone on the skull and stitched the scalp back together with surgical twine. The suturing was hard, physical work. The twine gleamed red through the needle. Slowly the face took on the appearance of a normal nineteen-year-old.

Outside the autopsy room a security guard winked and said, 'How did it go?'

I shook my head.

'Always bad the first time,' he said. 'Know what I do? I don't think of them as bodies, I think of them as plastic.'

I walked up Arundel Street, blinking into the sunlight. Why did I want to find out who'd killed Sallie Huckstepp? My friends said it was because she was attractive, that I was obsessed with the case. Yet it wasn't that simple. I'd already been accused once of trying to profit from the circumstances of her murder. And maybe there was some truth to that, but coming from a Kings Cross media solicitor it was a bit rich. 'So why are you interested in *this* woman?' he had asked in his third-floor chambers. I told him I wanted to satisfy a legitimate curiosity that her violent death had been fully and properly investigated. I said that through Sallie I might discover something important about this city. To be honest, the reasons were more complex and to do with my own life, but I didn't want to tell him that. Anyway, I didn't think Sallie-Anne would mind. She had always attracted attention. Even at her funeral, photographers were lurking in the bushes.

•

At 3 p.m. on Tuesday, 25 February 1986, the body of Sallie-Anne Huckstepp, sealed in heavy clear plastic wrap, was taken by Chevra Kadisha Funeral Directors, placed in a plain pine coffin and conveyed to the Jewish section of Rookwood Cemetery. 'The synagogue was full,' her sister, Debra, said. 'School friends came from Moriah College and Dover Heights, from all over the Eastern Suburbs. Sallie was well-liked.'

The rabbi referred to her as 'Sarah bat Jacov' and described the sadness of the death of 'a young person who hasn't even started to live yet.'

'Huckstepp, who had a keen sense of humour,' Wendy Bacon wrote in the *National Times*, 'would probably have laughed at that.'

Quiet Farewell to Sallie-Anne

Victim is buried as murderer stays free

Only a handful of mourners farewelled former prostitute Sallie-Anne Huckstepp at the Rookwood Jewish Cemetery yesterday. Twelve relatives and close friends stood at the graveside as a rabbi delivered the eulogy in Hebrew. The mourners included the dead woman's daughter, her sister and her parents. Police report no new leads in their search for the killer.

I drove out to Rookwood on a hot afternoon in January. Workmen, their blue singlets draped over headstones, were cleaning up between the overgrown graves in the Muslim cemetery. Grasscutters whined in the air. I parked outside the Jewish cemetery and walked between the rows of tidy headstones for ten minutes before I discovered the graves were arranged in chronological order. Apart from a woman swathed in black from head to toe watering lillies on a well-kept grave, the Jewish cemetery was empty. I rinsed my face under a tap and walked up and down checking dates on headstones. An elderly attendant limped over and asked who I was searching for. When I told him, the attendant stared at me. His face was crisscrossed with tiny scars as if he'd survived a serious motor accident. 'You a relative?'

'No.'

'Shouldn't be telling you this, but two detectives was out here yesterday. One of them had a folder with Warren Lanfranchi's name on it.'

'Lanfranchi. Why?'

'Wanted to know where her gravesite was.' The attendant pointed east. 'Number 684.'

I walked over to a plain black headstone with two stars of David on either side of a Hebrew inscription. Underneath, it said in English,

SALLIE-ANNE
KRIVOSHOW (HUCKSTEPP)
'We are but a fleeting shadow
on the face of time but live forever
in the light and love of our Lord'

I laid a sprig of mint on the grave and stood there for a moment, thinking about the Jewish custom of Tahara where the body is washed thoroughly from head to foot and wrapped in white cotton. The religious men and women who perform this task receive no payment. I walked back to my car, gazing around for the attendant, but he was gone. I wanted to ask him if he was certain about his facts, or was this just another rumour. Why, after all these years, were New South Wales detectives interested in Sallie-Anne's grave-site? Had new evidence come to light?

I got in my car and drove off slowly through Rookwood Cemetery, past the sweating workmen digging between the graves. Clouds of fine dust drifted past my windscreen. I needed to find out what this had to do with Lanfranchi. I needed to find out what was going on.

6

Lanfranchi

'I met Warren through a drugs contact and it was like a lightning bolt,' Sallie told a reporter from the *Sun*. 'He had the most beautiful blue eyes . . . electric. He used to send me dozens of red roses all the time, he was really generous. He was always buying me beautiful clothes and little gifts. He used to take my daughter Sascha shopping and buy her four pairs of shoes at once. When we first met, we lived in hotels together, including the Boulevard . . . I loved Warren, I loved Warren more than . . . I felt more for Warren than I've ever felt for any human being in my life. I would've accepted anything for Warren.'

•

In January 1981, shortly after her twenty-sixth birthday, Sallie arranged to buy five weights of heroin. The dealer drove her to a laneway in Randwick to test the quality and while she was preparing a vein she glanced over at his muscled arm resting on the steering wheel. At 22 years of age, Warren Charles Lanfranchi had all the qualities that Sallie admired in a man. He was young, handsome, exceptionally fit and bursting with energy. Released from Long Bay Gaol only four weeks earlier, Warren Lanfranchi had served four years and eight months of a five-year sentence for stealing colour TV sets—two-and-a-half of those years spent in solitary confinement. His father, Keith, a gunsmith, thought it was a harsh sentence for any seventeen-year-old, especially for a first offence.

'Warren started in crime,' Sallie said, 'doing kids' stuff, joy-riding in stolen cars, pinching little things.'

His brother Darrell added, 'Warren shouldn't have gone to gaol in the first place; he came from a broken home. He was a tough kid.'

In Long Bay, Warren fell under the influence of the gaol heavies, men like Arthur Stanley (Ned) Smith who Warren looked up to. 'Warren idolised Neddy,' Sallie told her barrister. 'He worshipped the ground he walked on.' Smith had made a name for himself in the heroin trade and boasted of the cops he paid off and the millions he'd earned. In gaol Warren learned as much as he could about the business. Many of his friends were addicts, but Warren despised drugs.

'He couldn't drink at all,' Sallie said. 'When he did he couldn't handle it. He liked a clear mind, he didn't like anything that blocked him.' Physical fitness became an obsession for Warren. A naturally gifted boxer, he had sparred with a leading professional in a Newtown gym when he was thirteen years old. In Long Bay, he held a champion middleweight to a draw in a fiercely contested exhibition bout and started to earn a name for himself as a young man with a bit of go. He came third in the prison's Iron Man contest only weeks before his release. No sooner was he on the streets than he looked up his mentor, Arthur Stanley (Ned) Smith, and started working for him. 'Frenchie was a good kid,' Smith wrote in his autobiography, 'but he was born in the wrong time. He was more suited to the roaring twenties.'

It only took Warren a few weeks in his new career to start pulling serious money. The heroin he supplied was 42 per cent pure compared to the usual 15 per cent found on the streets. It cost $150 for a gram and Lanfranchi usually carried a swag of 70 grams, in seven bags of ten. 'Warren was making $10 000 a week as an upper-level heroin dealer,' Sallie said. 'He was directly under the big dealers who brought in the heroin from overseas.

'About two weeks after I met him, two-and-a-half weeks, something like that, I started living with Warren. We didn't like to stay in any one place too long, there were so many motels we lived in . . . um, the University Motor Inn, the Marco Polo . . . and we were sort of looking for a place while we were moving around. He wouldn't settle down for a while. He didn't trust me at first. Most crims regard prostitutes as scum.

'Personally I was very attracted to Warren,' Sallie told the journalist Michael Willesee. 'He was almost schizophrenic. He had one persona that dealt with business matters which came from his gaol experience and he had another personality that was softer. I was an ex-prostitute. I was a heroin addict and I had to go through a trial by fire. Warren found junkies very weak. I was a very heavy user for many years, on and off. When I began working the streets in Darlinghurst I was a desperate addict. The year before I met Warren I started using a cocktail of heroin and cocaine. I was shooting up barbiturates and it was costing me $1800 a day.

'One of the problems with being a heroin addict is that you . . . you . . . shoot heroin to escape. There's something missing. Warren wanted me to get off it and I found it very easy to get off it, because I felt fulfilled. Warren gave me what I was looking for and it was very easy to come off it. He was wonderful.'

On the black market Sallie and Warren bought two bottles of methadone for $800 and Warren helped to wean her off heroin. 'He gave me two shots a day, one in the morning and one at night. He really tried to make me quit,' Sallie said. 'Gradually it worked. Warren got me off the drug for the first time since I was sixteen.'

To replace the needle Sallie started accompanying Warren to the gym where he worked out for two hours every day, running, doing sets of 250 pushups, hitting the heavy bag, swimming. In the late afternoon they often visited the Cranbrook School gym where Sallie's sister's boyfriend, Bruce, worked as a physical instructor. One of the many side effects for women of habitual heroin use is that it can interfere with ovulation. A woman may not have a period for several months or even years if her habit continues. Within three months of living with Warren, Sallie fell pregnant for the first time in eight years.

'Warren was a wonderful lover. He was a very horny guy and he desperately wanted to have our baby. He was an intelligent man too. He was so eager to learn,' Sallie said. 'He'd just never been shown things.'

According to one of his former cellmates Warren carried a baseball bat and had a reputation as a violent enforcer. Stories circulated of Warren bashing a man named McGroder to death in Wollongong over a non-payment of a drug debt, but Sallie denied this rumour. 'I don't doubt Warren was at the man's house, but just afterwards when I was in the cells at Central on a heroin charge he came in and bailed me out using his own name. It's ridiculous to suggest that if he'd just murdered someone he'd walk into a police station and say who he was.

'Warren had a gaol code of morality. Probably Warren only hit anybody with a baseball bat once or twice. Certainly he used the baseball bat as a threat, but Warren was pretty good with his fists, I mean, the threat was usually enough. He gave people a lot of chances, probably that a lot of other dealers wouldn't have. I wouldn't have been so tolerant. It's the only thing that these people understand.'

On 19 February, shortly after Sallie moved in with Warren, she was arrested at Long Bay Gaol. 'I went out to visit a friend in the late afternoon with Michael Maine,' Sallie told New South Wales Internal Affairs. 'We finished the visit and were waiting for the steel doors to open and let us out. Michael and I were the last to leave and I was halfway out of the gaol when I heard footsteps and two prison officers came running down the path behind me. I kept walking and one of the prison officers grabbed me from behind and said, "One of you has dropped some drugs in the gaol."

'I said, "Let go of my arm."

'He said, "I don't know which one it is but we're holding you both here and calling the cops." I got very angry and headed straight for the Superintendent's office, but he wasn't there. The screws followed us and kept us both prisoner in the room, there was some extremely harsh words between one particular officer and myself, his name was Probawski, I was rude to him and he was extremely rude to me, and then two Drug Squad detectives arrived and the prison officers spoke to them and much to my surprise we were handcuffed and taken to Maroubra Station.

'I was strip-searched by a policewoman who wasn't in uniform, she'd just won some sort of glamour contest, a couple of young detectives were watching and another detective dropped a silver foil containing white powder on the desk in front of me. "Look Sallie," he said, "this is a fair pinch, you either co-operate with me and wear that." He pointed at the foil. "Or you and Michael will be up for possession and supply." Then he showed me two plastic bags containing a much larger quantity of white powder. I had never seen either the foil or the two bags he placed in front of me before. He said, "I know I'm holding a gun to your head, Sal, but I have to make a pinch and the Superintendent's been complaining about the amount of drugs being smuggled into Long Bay." He told me that if he charged Michael and me with supply, Michael would not see daylight again as he had only just been released on parole on a drug charge.

'The deal was if I pleaded guilty to the lesser amount, Michael would not be charged. So I made out a handwritten statement basically saying that I had taken the drug to the gaol but that it was for my own use and that no inducement or threat was made to me to confess. The next morning I saw a solicitor [Greg Meakin] and when the matter came before the court I pleaded not guilty. I was remanded for hearing and then this same Detective C—sidled up to me and said he had statements from three prison officers swearing black and blue that they saw me drop the foil and he'd had a word to the magistrate and unless I changed my plea I'd cop three months for certain, so I changed my plea and when the matter was listed for sentencing I didn't turn up, because Warren had been put under surveillance and I knew that if I appeared in court I'd be followed and we had a real fear that his life was in danger.'

It was around early March that Warren came home from dealing one evening and told her of an Armed Hold-Up Squad detective he'd run into, a sergeant called Roger Rogerson.

'Mostly the things Warren said about this Rogerson were not good,' Sallie said, 'that he was, you know, that he'd killed a couple of guys before, that he was a madman. They had some discussions about Warren doing business for him, something like that. And Warren gave me a character rundown on Rogerson, telling me about the jewellery that he wore.

'We were sick of living in motels. Warren and I had been at the Marco Polo Motel in Ashfield for two nights while we were looking for a house, I'd actually got a house for us in Waterloo and we had to wait two days for the renovations to be finished on it. Sascha was staying with my husband for a week. I arrived at the motel at about 6 or 6.30 p.m. and also present was the wife of a friend of Warren's, Sue Walsh. I came into the room, saw Warren and said, "Hello darling, I'm sorry, I'm late, I'll jump into the shower right away, we're still going out for dinner aren't we?"

'And Warren said, "Why are you so late?" I said, "I got caught up having a drink with one of the girls." I emptied my bag out on the bed, I wanted to show Warren I hadn't spent all his money. I had a thousand dollars in cash and I got undressed.

'Warren and I were in the shower and then a whole lot of heads ran past the shower window. The next thing I know the bathroom door flew open and five detectives came running into the bathroom, someone grabbed me and pulled me out of the shower. Warren said, "What the fuck's going on?"

'"Drug Squad!" they were yelling at him. "Get out of the shower!"

'Warren refused, he wouldn't get out. I asked if I could get dressed and they threw me some clothes and Warren and the head detective, F— I think it was, they were talking very low and I heard him say to Warren, "Maybe something can be done."

'The other detectives searched the place and they found my thousand dollars and four-and-a-half bags of Warren's heroin in a blue coloured plastic pouch sitting on the bed. One of the detectives picked it up and whistled. "Guess what we got here." Then F—

came out of the bathroom and asked me about Warren and what we'd been doing in the shower. He wanted to know details about Warren's sexual prowess.'

Sue Walsh told Internal Affairs what she witnessed next, 'One of the police asked Warren for the key to his bike. The bike had a locked seat that you can put things in it. Warren gave him the key and the detective came back a couple of minutes later with a bundle of money in his hand and I think he said, "Look what we got here, fellas." There was $5000 in the bundle. Sallie indicated the dope was hers, but Warren didn't say anything. I could see that Sallie was trying to take the blame.'

All three were taken in separate cars back to Petersham Station and on the way Sallie asked if something could be done. 'The heroin's mine,' she said. 'Those other two don't know anything about it.'

'Where did you obtain this heroin from?' Detective Davies asked.

'I told you it's mine, that's all I can say.'

'How long have you known Warren Lanfranchi?'

'Look, he's just a fuck, he's got nothing to do with it.'

The police agreed to release Lanfranchi and Walsh if Sallie gave a statement and she was taken by the three Drug Squad members to Remington House. On the way they stopped and bought her a hamburger and Coke, trying to get friendly. At the station Sallie mentioned the name of a notorious New South Wales detective she knew and they said, 'Oh, yeah, Davo's a real bad bastard.'

Sallie asked them if she could do business. 'One of the detectives asked me to name a price, and seeing there was five of them, I thought $2000 a piece, and I said, "Would ten thousand do?"

'The head detective, F—, he wanted the $10 000 delivered to them that same night and then I would be released immediately. I said I couldn't do it, I said I wasn't the pizza girl.

'We can't take any chances with Internal Affairs, he told me, we'll have to do the deal through an intermediary, a solicitor or a barrister, they said they knew someone suitable and gave me a couple of names. Then they went off into a separate room and the youngest detective kept popping in and out, trying to be friendly.

Then all three came back fifteen minutes later and said I would have to be charged, but the money would have to be paid as well. They were concerned about Petersham detectives finding out no arrest had been made after the heroin had been found. I was then photographed and a fingerprint was taken and they drove me to Central and I was charged with possession of two bags of heroin. They kept the other two-and-a-half bags for themselves.'

Meanwhile Sue Walsh was waiting for Warren outside a telephone box in Petersham. 'Warren arrived one-and-a-half hours late and told me he thought he had been set up by Sallie,' she said. 'He said that they'd let him go on the pretext of him paying them a certain amount of money by the Monday. "Tough luck for them," Warren said, "because they aren't going to get it." He said the detectives had kept all the money they'd found in the motel room. I got on the back of his bike. He had this fear that police were following him so we drove around Camperdown, Glebe, Ultimo and Newtown. He dropped me off near my husband's mother's house and told me a second time he thought Sallie had set him up. He said that if they let her go he'd know it was definitely her.'

The next morning Warren turned up at Central and bailed Sallie out with $2000 in cash. She told him that she'd 'worn the blue' to save him from going to gaol for a very long time.

'Unfortunately,' Sallie told her barrister, 'I didn't know the police had taken the $5000 from Warren's bike, plus they'd lifted $910 from the $1000 I had on the bed and Warren was also making arrangements on his own to pay them an additional $5000. On top of that I was supposed to come up with another $10 000!

'Warren rang Davies up and said we were prepared to pay if all the charges were dropped against me, but Davies said, "That can't be done, she'll have to go to gaol."

'We were furious. The only way she can get out of it, Davies told Warren, was to give up your supplier's name. Nobody would know about it and he promised Warren he'd hand a special note to the judge. "Tell Sallie," he said. "I don't think Silverwater [gaol] will suit her."

'Warren was getting his gear from Ned Smith. The modus operandi was that Warren would buy heroin on credit and then on-sell it and having done so he could pay Ned Smith for the heroin and keep the profits. I knew that if I gave up Warren's supplier's name it was more than my life was worth.

'The detective said to Warren, listen, we can't drop the charges, but the analyst's report hasn't come back yet, if the fifteen thousand's paid we could have a satisfactory report come back.

'But Warren said, "No deal, we'll see you in court," and he hung up. When the matter was listed, I was chatting outside the courtroom to my ex-probation officer, and Warren went up to the detective and said in a loud voice, "I've got your ten thousand for you!" He reached into his back pocket. Everyone standing outside turned and watched and the detective went red in the face and stormed off. That was the end of our negotiations with the Drug Squad.'

It was around this time that Sallie and Warren first noticed that they were being followed. 'After we got busted at the Marco Polo,' Sallie said, 'they found the receipt for the house in Waterloo, so we thought we couldn't move in there, we moved to no. 3 Rosecrea Avenue in Randwick instead. We noticed . . . we started noticing there was a police car parked up the street and then a couple of detectives followed us from the court after my first remand. At first we just thought it was a bit of paranoia on our part and we were coming back from Cranbrook gym this night and I was driving, and a Kombi van followed us from Bellevue Hill to Pitt Street in Redfern. I changed lanes and Warren told me to put my foot down, which I did, and I went the wrong way down a one-way street and the Kombi van stopped on the corner and watched us. I pulled up and changed seats with Warren and we drove around the back streets for a while and then a panel van started following us and then the Kombi van came up right behind us and Warren just took off very fast, going the wrong way down all these one-way streets. We had a white Falcon with dark windows, tinted windows and it was fairly distinctive. The whole time we were at Randwick we were under surveillance. I mean, there were helicopters going over the unit all the time, over the car. It was quite obvious they were following us. But they never did anything, just followed us, sometimes they'd be there and sometimes they wouldn't, oh, it was ridiculous, like cops and robbers.'

To avoid the police Warren and Sallie moved to Warren's father's house in Salisbury Road, Camperdown. They stayed there a week and one night Warren told Sallie that he and a guy named Michael were going to rip off two drug dealers in North Sydney who'd previously ripped off Michael for $100 000. At midnight he came home and told her the deal had gone wrong.

•

'He was terrified,' Sallie told her QC in his Phillip Street chambers. 'And shocked.'

The barrister and his instructing solicitor studied her from across the desk and switched on a large black tape recorder. She had their undivided attention.

'As soon as Warren had showed them the money they produced seven bags of heroin. Warren hit one guy, knocked him straight out, grabbed the other guy, Ewen Cameron I think his name was, grabbed the dope, put one guy into the boot of Michael's car and put Cameron into the boot of his own car. Warren was representing himself as a police officer, trying to get them to spill where the rest of their heroin was. Warren said that he gave Ewen Cameron a real hiding and that Cameron yelled out, "Stop, stop, I'm working for the police."

'He pulled a card out of his pocket and Warren just slammed the boot on him. Left him there.

'A week later Warren got an urgent phone call. The wife of a prisoner who ran the heroin trade in the Bay told Warren that Roger Rogerson was going to shoot him on sight. She said the message was for Warren to lay low, be careful, that he was very tropical.

'That's when we knew Cameron was working for Rogerson.

'It was after this, we saw a report in the paper that Warren was wanted by the Armed Hold-Up Squad for the attempted shooting of a uniformed police officer. Warren went out that night and approached Neddy Smith to talk to Rogerson to see if they could do business. I went with him. I sat in the car outside the Broadway Hotel. Ned handles that kind of thing, he's got the "in" with the police. Warren was there about ten minutes, then he came back, he was worried, he said that Neddy wasn't sure anything could be done, that it would probably cost him a heap. Warren bought a pistol, I saw the name Smith and Wesson on it and Warren told me it was a 9-millimetre automatic. Warren bought it to protect us. He wanted to sleep with it next to the bed, he was afraid that Rogerson would find out where we were and run in and shoot us while we were sleeping.'

For the next three nights Warren and Sallie stayed in different motels under false names and then she found them a unit at 94 Kurraba Road, Neutral Bay. Sallie took the lease out under the name of Mr and Mrs Mark Lewis.

'There was so much happening, it was so hectic, we were moving, we were running around, you know, phone calls, ring, ring . . . going to see Keith [Warren's father], there was just so much going down and then on Thursday, 25 June, Warren got a message, he went out at nine o'clock and came back an hour later. "You won't believe it, Sal, Rogerson is going to do business."

'I said, "How much?" and he said, "Don't know. I have to see Ned again tomorrow." The next day, the Friday, Warren went out, I didn't go with him, but when he came back it was late. He told me that Rogerson wanted $30 000 to have the armed robbery and the shooting at the policeman dropped. Rogerson wanted $10 000 in cash immediately and Warren could pay him the other $20 000 at a later date. It was suggested that Rogerson could spear him into an armed robbery and Rogerson would then get his $20 000 plus a percentage.

'We went to bed, we were talking about what to do at great length. Warren was worried, he was talking about offering Rogerson an extra $20 000 to fix up the Marco Polo bust, but he didn't want to be involved in Rogerson's armed hold-up. He said too many guys had done armed hold-ups for Rogerson and found themselves in gaol, and it wasn't his thing anyway. He thought he could make the money through dope rather than put his neck on the line. Once this was over we could take off for Germany. We wouldn't have as much money, but we could go straightaway. He was concerned for my sake and for Sascha ... he didn't want police bursting into the flat, he said he was going to pay Rogerson the ten grand.

'We woke up about ten o'clock and Warren was running late, he didn't get into the shower until about 10.30. I looked out the front window and I saw a silver Celica waiting for Warren. It was one of the men Ned Smith had working for him. Warren went out wearing a big sheepskin coat and came home about twelve. He said that Rogerson wanted to meet him in a council car park in Redfern at two o'clock, but he'd vetoed the meeting place. It sounded a bit suspicious, he had been given instructions by Neddy Smith that he wasn't to wear the coat, in fact they didn't want him to wear a jumper. Warren told me that the deal was Smith would frisk both Warren and Rogerson to see that they weren't armed. Warren was pretty nervous about the whole thing.'

Sallie leaned back in her chair and pulled on her cigarette.

'The money,' her QC said, 'tell us about the money, Mrs Huck-stepp? Where did Warren produce it from?'

'From upstairs, he just came down the stairs with it.'

'How was he carrying it?'

'He had a manila envelope in one hand and loose notes bundled up against it, he brought it down like that. He just tipped it all out on the floor. I was sitting on the lounge in front of the television and Warren told me to make up two-hundred-dollar lots and then Warren got down on the carpet beside me and we started stacking these lots into one-thousand-dollar bundles, putting two crossed red rubber bands around each of them until we had a row of ten on the carpet. Warren picked up the rest of the money and shoved it into his back pocket.'

'What did he do then?'

'He was edgy, we were wandering in and out of the unit, into the courtyard, talking about it all, I'd been out shopping, brought him home some oysters and he ate his oysters, and we were just wandering around the unit. Pretty tense. He kept asking, "What do you think, Sal, you think it'll be alright?" We just didn't believe anything could go wrong, not in broad daylight, not in the middle of Sydney.

'He went outside and said it was too cold to go in just a shirt so he put on a jumper. I asked him for some money for myself and he pulled twelve hundred dollars out of his back pocket and said, "Here's two twenties, I've got to pay Ned the rest." Then he grabbed the money off the floor and packed it down the front of his pants.'

'What sort of pants was he wearing?'

'Beige wool pants.'

'How'd they do up?'

'With a fly and a button.'

'And he just shoved the money down the waistband?'

'No, he opened his fly and packed it down the front, he was grabbing it off the floor.'

'Did he put the money in his underpants?'

'Some of it. He put it down the front of his pants and then pulled the jumper down over the top of it.'

'And he put the money inside? Was it sticking up?'

'I don't remember . . . I wasn't watching, I went into the kitchen, I said something to him about bringing flowers home and he said, "Oh you never know, Sal, you could be sending me flowers." Then a car tooted outside.'

'You heard the toot?'

'Yes. I walked out the front door with him, it was like a little patio, a tiled area and I started to get anxious. I said what time will you be home because I'm going to be worried. He said, "Well, Sal if I'm not home by six o'clock you'll know they've killed me." And he kissed me on the mouth. I didn't want him to go. I had this feeling, an intuition.

'"Take the gun with you," I pleaded. "Leave it in the car, just in case something happens." And Warren said, "As long as I stick to my bargain, Ned'll make sure they're not armed. Ned's fixed it all up." I saw Warren open the car door and start to slide in and I turned away.'

'Did you see the car drive off?'

'No.'

'Did you get a good look at the driver?'

'No.'

'What time was it when Warren left?'

'Quarter to two.'

'What did you do then?'

'I stayed on in the flat,' Sallie said. 'I waited, I watched the clock, I paced up and down about the place. At six o'clock my heart sank, I was sick. I went down to the phone box and rang Warren's father who told me Warren had been murdered. He asked me if I was prepared to go public? And I said, "Yes." Keith said, "You realise that if you tell exactly what happened your life will be in danger?" '

'Then what did you do?'

'I went home. There was nothing anyone could say to me at the time that would have helped me get through it, because it all meant nothing. There is not a thing in the world that will compensate you for such a loss. I kept thinking we should have gone to Germany. But honest to God, it didn't seem possible. Now I would believe anything.'

'Tell us about the gun.'

'I went into the bedroom, I reached into the top right-hand drawer of our dressing table and took it out, it had a wooden handle and the metal was a sort of bronzey colour. A Smith and Wesson automatic pistol.'

'Was it loaded?'

'Yes, it looked new. There were nine bullets in it. I was worried that the police would arrive at any moment, I just grabbed a cab to Milson's Point, walked down through a tunnel to the pylon on the right-hand side. I stood at the fence and I threw it in.'

'Why did you throw it in the harbour?'

'I didn't want the police to plant it on his body. Warren used to say to me . . . that the deepest part of the harbour was under the bridge. Guns never get found there.'

• • •

The author, Richard Neville, was working for the 'Midday Show' when his phone rang late on Sunday night after the shooting. 'The papers were full of this hero cop Roger Rogerson in Dangar Place,' Richard Neville said. 'And this weeping voice came on the other end of the phone. "My name's Sallie-Anne Huckstepp," she said. "What they're saying in the papers is not true. I know too much, I'm scared. I need to talk to somebody."

'So I drove over and saw Sallie. She was staying in Blackheath at the home of a Push doctor. I was struck by her presence. I asked her why Rogerson had killed Warren. "It's all about smack," she said. "Rogerson supplies Parramatta gaol. He is the biggest heroin dealer in Sydney."

'I listened to her story and I guess I believed it. I felt straightaway this was too hot for the "Midday Show" so I rang Wendy Bacon at "60 Minutes".'

'Sallie-Anne surfaced very quickly,' the journalist Wendy Bacon explained. 'The first thing that struck me about Sallie was she was very different compared to other people in her situation—prostitution and drugs. She had a very strong physical presence. That's one of the reasons everyone was attracted to her. She was always well-groomed. She went to aerobics. Cops especially were attracted to her. I thought she was a very upper-middle-class product. She looked quite glamorous and was very charming.

'She told us her story and her main fear was the naming of Ned Smith. We decided at "60 Minutes" that we wouldn't use the name of Ned Smith even though we knew it was him. The other people working on the story were Ray Martin and Bruce Stannard and we went to the Hilton Hotel and checked Sallie in. I do remember that she booked herself in for a couple of massages that were quite expensive while she was there. So she lived it up a bit while she was on the station tab.

'That night she gave her story and clearly we believed her. She was definitely an actress, but there was such a ring of truth to her story. I mean it was interesting journalistically, because we believed Sallie-Anne. It was really a heady night. Ray Martin, Paddy Jones, Bruce, me and Sallie. We had a few drinks. But the next morning the lawyers looked at the tape very closely and found that there was material we couldn't use. The other thing that happened in the lead up to the story going to air was that Bruce Stannard and I had a meeting with Frank Walker, the Attorney General.

'When I came into his offices, Frank said, "Wendy, Wendy, they'll kill us for this!"

'He didn't want to know about it. In the end Frank Walker handed over all our statements to Internal Affairs. Then somehow it got to the Legal Aid Commission and then her stat decs were leaked back to Ned Smith via the police. Ned Smith let people know that he knew. Sallie had a real obsession about him. She had this real thing about Neddy Smith, that he'd raped her.

'Look,' Wendy Bacon said, 'I don't think you can underestimate the power Sallie had because she was attractive. She was in conventional terms very attractive and intelligent. Whatever that means it was definitely an element to Sallie-Anne. Like she could walk into "60 Minutes" and to the people there she was as compelling as Jana Wendt. She had that combination of intelligence and charisma. You can imagine, I mean if you go up round the Cross and see the state most heroin addicts are in and they're usually grotty, but Sallie-Anne wasn't like that. She kept herself together. She didn't lose it. Sallie always had a suntan and she wore sexy sort of clothes. The whole "damned whores, God's police" dichotomy was really relevant to Sallie-Anne. She was very conventional in the femininity thing. I knew a lot of prostitutes up at the Cross and they would be given expensive gold chains or bracelets. Many of them were very romantic types. As if they needed to be romantic types to keep on functioning.

'Sallie told me that Lanfranchi got her off heroin, he used to inject her to make her come down. She was definitely in love with Lanfranchi. I think she really wanted Ned Smith and Rogerson to get their desserts for what they did to him.'

EXTRACT: *SUNDAY TELEGRAPH*, 28 June 1981

Gunman Shot as he took aim

A **DANGEROUS** gunman was shot dead by police in a **High Noon shootout** yesterday. Just before 3 p.m. Detective-Sergeant Rogerson found himself walking slowly down Dangar Place, Chippendale. Walking towards him, in that grimy little back lane, was a gunman, a criminal suspected of three armed hold-ups and the attempted shooting of a police officer. Detective Rogerson took no chances. He knew how to handle a life-or-death situation. Suddenly the man pulled a gun and aimed it . . .

Rogerson pulled his pistol and fired. Quickly. Twice.

The gunman, Warren Lanfranchi, crumpled into the gutter.

For a member of the Armed Hold-Up Squad it was all in a day's work. And it wasn't the first time he had fired at an armed man, either. Rogerson, married with two young daughters, admitted that his family sometimes 'gets a bit worried' about his job.

EXTRACT: *DAILY MIRROR*, 6 July

Police Probe Missing $12,000

Girlfriend's claim on TV

The girlfriend of Warren Lanfranchi claimed on the TV show *60 Minutes* last night that the dead man was carrying $10,000 in his trousers and $1,160 in his wallet. But Lanfranchi's father, Keith, said, 'When I saw his body at the morgue he didn't have a penny on him, only his watch and neck chain.'

BANNER: *SYDNEY MORNING HERALD*, 3 November

Shot in Cold Blood: Father

EXTRACT: *SYDNEY MORNING HERALD*, 17 November

Lanfranchi did not take a gun, de facto wife tells

Miss Sallie-Anne Huckstepp told the Coroner's Court yesterday that her de-facto husband, Mr Warren Charles Lanfranchi, had been scared that Sergeant Rogerson was going to shoot him. 'We were both very nervous and not very trusting of the arrangement,' she said. 'Warren did not take a gun with him.'

EXTRACT: *DAILY MIRROR*, 17 November

Lawyer Throws $10,000 at Girl

A BARRISTER threw two wads of $10,000 in front of Mrs Sallie-Anne Huckstepp, a former prostitute, at Glebe Coroner's Court in a dramatic challenge to her evidence at the Lanfranchi inquest.

EXTRACT: *SUN*, 24 November

Mystery of the Faulty Revolver

Both police ballistics experts and the family of Warren Lanfranchi confirm that the weapon allegedly drawn by the deceased was defective. Experts confirmed that the silver Harrison and Richardson .38 did not 'index' properly. This meant that the chamber did not spin around to a true position adjacent to the firing pin after being fired. 'Why,' asks Sallie-Anne, 'should Warren take a defective pistol with him to meet an armed hold-up detective?'

EXTRACT: *SUN*, 25 November

The Man I Loved

A girl who has worked the streets and been a call-girl for eight years hasn't got a high opinion of men. So when Warren Lanfranchi courted Sallie-Anne Huckstepp in the old-fashioned way it took her by surprise. 'Warren was a gentleman. He wouldn't swear in front of women, he lit their cigarettes, he opened their car doors.'

An old-fashioned man who sent red roses.

'Warren was a wonderful man. I've explained it all to Sascha. She knows I've been a prostitute. I was always brought up to believe a woman should rely on her looks. Now I tell my daughter to use her brains and not her body to get things out of life.'

BANNER: *SUN*, 26 November

Lanfranchi was Murdered

BANNER: *DAILY TELEGRAPH*, 27 November

'Police Drugs' Link to Lanfranchi

•

'I've been paying the police for ten years as a prostitute,' Sallie told a national TV audience on 5 July 1981. 'My ex-husband was a criminal, I paid the police many times for him. I would have been quite happy to go on paying the police, because it's a way of life and it's the way you survive, but when the police become judge, jury and executioner, then somebody has to speak out, somebody has to come forward, somebody has to stop it.

'This is real, this is not something I've made up in revenge, this is cold fact. A lot of criminals are going to be very upset with me. I've upset the balance. A lot of detectives are going to be scared. It's going to be a lot harder for criminals to get away with a lot of things, but it had to be done.'

Within hours of appearing on '60 Minutes', Sallie went into hiding. She rang her friend Helen and asked her if she would take care of her eight-year-old daughter.

'I ended up keeping Sascha for a few months,' Helen said. 'I was shit-scared. Everyone knew that Sallie had a daughter. I went through all of Sascha's stuff, her bus passes and clothes and took the address and phone number off everything and I escorted her to school every day and made sure she got home alright until Sallie-Anne came to get her.'

The journalist, Jeune Pritchard, interviewed Sallie-Anne for ABC Radio. 'Sallie had no money and just the clothes she stood up in, but she was irrepressible,' she said. 'We held fears for her safety so we took her out of town to the Blue Mountains. It was the middle of winter and she desperately needed warm clothes. We bought her, among other things, a pair of ugh boots and a fleecy-lined nightie. Sallie was appalled at our lack of style and taste, lamenting the loss of the Double Bay dresses she'd worn on the Darlinghurst beat.'

A contract was taken out on Sallie's life by a top criminal. In revealing what went on in the Sydney underworld, Sallie-Anne had broken the criminal code. 'I wouldn't have said a word about paying police if they hadn't killed Warren,' Sallie told a reporter. 'If I go to gaol, I won't come out alive. I'll be found OD'd or stabbed. It doesn't take much to imagine a knife between my ribs. It's very possible that some members of the criminal world will try to kill me.'

Criminals weren't the only ones searching for her. A warrant was sworn out for her arrest for failing to appear on the Long Bay charge. A squad of heavily-armed police raided the house of Debra Krivoshow, mistaking her for her sister. 'I was pulling out documentation saying I'm Debra, I'm Debra!' her younger sister said. 'No, you're coming with us, they were saying. It was like these cops really believed I was Sallie-Anne and they wanted me. They had their guns drawn. They never showed any identification. It was very strange, very scary.'

After this Debra told Sallie she was getting herself a T-shirt printed—DON'T SHOOT, I'M DEBRA.

Two days later Sallie-Anne gave herself up. Her barrister made an urgent application to have the bail conditions altered so Sallie could remain in hiding.

EXTRACT: *NATIONAL TIMES*, 19 July 1981

Court Told of Death Threat

'A very large sum of money has been offered in the underworld to kill Sallie-Anne Huckstepp,' her barrister told the Supreme Court today. Justice Yeldham commented that the allegations were 'very dramatic'. At this point her barrister said that Ms Huckstepp was also 'terrified of the police'.

Justice Yeldham replied that the application was now 'getting into the realms of fantasy'.

Later outside the court, Huckstepp made it clear that she would not answer any questions from police concerning Lanfranchi's criminal associates.

Dissatisfied with the coronial inquest, two prominent barristers wrote to the Attorney General, Frank Walker, requesting a judicial inquiry into the shooting of Lanfranchi. Witnesses had been barred from giving evidence, the coroner repeatedly rejected evidence from Sallie-Anne, and the night before the hearing, Detective Sergeant Rogerson had called in to the home of important police witness, Neddy Smith, referred to as 'Mr G', and given him a copy of statements that he had previously made and coached him in detail about the case.

After a four-hour retirement, the jury found that Lanfranchi died from a gunshot wound to his chest, inflicted by Detective Sergeant Rogerson. The jury struck out the phrases 'in the execution of his duty' and 'in self-defence'.

The post-mortem was carried out by Dr Sergio Staraj. 'The body was that of a young Caucasian adult male,' he wrote, 'who weighed 74 kilos and bore a number of tattoo marks.' Three recent wounds were noted: an entry wound caused by a '.38 special' below the left ear; a second entry wound at the left side of the chest; and a large exit wound on the side of the right chest. 'The direct cause of death,' wrote Dr Staraj, 'was the gunshot wound to the chest, the projectile passing through the heart and right lung.'

Warren Lanfranchi left his flat with $11 160 in cash and no gun.

He was found dead 'without a zac on him' according to his brother, Darrell, and a revolver in poor condition with a non-functioning trigger return spring.

In a taped interview with Ian Barker QC, Sallie-Anne was asked if she had ever seen or heard of the antique silver Harrison and Richardson .38 revolver.

'Never,' she said. 'Not until after Warren was murdered.'

'Is it likely that Warren would have been given the weapon by Ned Smith. Before he met Rogerson?'

'Oh no ... Neddy and Rogerson were insistent that Warren come unarmed and dressed so that Rogerson could see he was not carrying a weapon.'

'Well, tell me this, do you think Ned Smith set Warren up, so he could be disposed of by Rogerson?'

'It's very possible,' Sallie said.

'Was there any trouble between Warren and Ned Smith to your knowledge?'

'Nothing serious ... Warren had got drunk the week before and had an altercation with another fellow there and he'd had words with Ned, but it was nothing—'

'You remember you told me that Smith raped you early in 1981. Was he interested in you as a woman after that?'

'I didn't give him the opportunity,' Sallie said, 'I kept my distance.'

'Was he jealous of Warren?'

'I don't know.'

'When was the first time you spoke to any police officer about this matter?'

'To be quite honest with you, for four weeks after Warren died I was off the planet, I mean, I couldn't tell you one day from the next.'

'Were you taking heroin?'

'No.'

'Were you taking any drugs?'

'No,' Sallie said. 'I was in shock, I was in hiding, up in Blackheath, up near Katoomba, I broke my foot ... I was quite a mess ... and the police found out I was there and Internal Affairs came up to see me, they left a message ... I was 10–12 weeks pregnant with Warren's baby and then I miscarried ... '

•

'Lanfranchi got her off dope,' her sister, Debra, said, 'but when he got shot she just went to pieces. Sallie-Anne fell in love very easily. She always needed someone to love her. Sallie always wanted that fairytale of a happy ending. Her and Sascha and Warren, but not living out in the suburbs somewhere. She wanted to end up in Vaucluse. Sallie should've been born in the 1920s. She would've made a great gangster's moll. There's a story going around that she was pregnant to Warren at the time—'

'Yes,' I said, 'she had a miscarriage.'

'Well, she didn't,' Debra told me. 'Sallie wasn't pregnant at all. She used to want things so badly she'd start to believe them. My father's wife and I were there at the Hilton. And Sallie *wanted* to be pregnant to Warren. We called a doctor because she said she was having a miscarriage and the doctor dealt with her and he came back out and we had a talk to him and he said, "No, no, she's just bleeding heavily because of the stress, there's no pregnancy there."

'Sallie told us that the doctor had given her a blood transfusion. So I pulled him aside and said, "Did you give my sister a blood transfusion in there?" He said, "I don't carry blood around with me." Sallie was fantasising. She desperately wanted to be pregnant to Warren. Especially once he was murdered. She was very romantic. She loved to be given flowers and she loved to give herself. She was always looking for love. She used to say to me, "You get so far down you don't know which way is up." '

•

Two weeks after the shooting, Sallie-Anne Huckstepp was interviewed by New South Wales Internal Affairs Police at Police Headquarters. Over the following two days she gave a detailed account of every payment she had made over the preceding ten years to Sydney's Vice Squad and Drug Squad detectives, culminating in the shooting of her de-facto husband in Dangar Place.

'Is there anything further that you can tell us before I conclude this record of interview?' Detective Inspector Ralph asked.

'Only that I believe that Warren was murdered in cold blood by Detective Sergeant Roger Rogerson and was not carrying a gun.'

'Are you prepared to sign this record of interview?'

'Yes,' Sallie said.

INTERVIEW REMOVED FROM TYPEWRITER AND HANDED TO MRS HUCKSTEPP. TIME CONCLUDED 8.30 P.M., 15 JULY 1981.

•

Rogerson was never interviewed by Internal Affairs Police over Sallie-Anne's allegations and, on 25 October, the New South Wales Internal Affairs investigation into the matter was suspended. The President of the Police Association and a future New South Wales Police Commissioner, Tony Lauer, said that Detective Sergeant Rogerson had been 'the subject of a continuing attack, well-financed with clear indications that it is supported by radical and even anarchistic beliefs'. Attorney General, Frank Walker, said that on the evidence available a judicial inquiry into the Lanfranchi shooting 'was not appropriate'. He said that the question of whether a Royal Commission should be held was one for the Premier, Neville Wran, who declined the invitation. Detective Rogerson agreed with the Attorney General, 'I don't think Miss Huckstepp'd be satisfied short of me getting twenty years.'

Posters sprang up on the walls of inner-city buildings.

WANTED

Det-Sgt Roger Caleb Rogerson
of the NSW Armed Hold-up Squad

for: MURDER of Warren Lanfranchi
RECEIVING BRIBES and protection money
HEROIN TRAFFICKING in association with
major Criminal Syndicates in Sydney

•

'I miss Warren,' Sallie told a reporter from the *Sun*. 'I miss so many things about him. But every night I miss his warmth beside me.'

7

Investigation

'Let me put you in the picture,' Geoff Prentice said. We were sitting in his caravan park on the far north coast of New South Wales. Three years retired from the Homicide Squad, Geoff Prentice was a big bear of a man with a red face and hands that gripped like pliers. He was wearing thongs, shorts and a white T-shirt that said ALL I NEED TO KNOW ABOUT LIFE I LEARNT FROM MY PETS.

'What used to happen in those days and it still hasn't been resolved since I was in the cops,' Prentice said, 'was that all matters arising from divisional work were always investigated by local detectives. With most homicides that were going to be difficult or involving notorious people or that were obviously going to be protracted inquiries, the Homicide Squad would get notified and we'd go over there and take charge of it. At the time there was not a laid-down format, so usually we'd go over and say, we'll give you a hand and mostly we'd run the show because we had the experience.

'Most times the changeover was pretty quick. With the Huckstepp inquiry, everyone wanted to get in on it, because it was going to be something with a bit of meat in it, a good brief as we used to say—a notorious person like her and all the ramifications.

'Everyone was excited about it because it was controversial, but from the department's point of view, they didn't give a stuff, so long as it went off the front page of the papers. Let's face it, there's a hundred people every week get knocked, druggies and that, and none of them would've got the treatment she got. The interest in her went on for years and years. All because of Sallie Huckstepp. All because of the notoriety of Rogerson. The bosses at the time couldn't give a stuff about Sallie Huckstepp. Never did. They only wanted to distance themselves from Rogerson.

'Real early in the piece, a couple of blokes from Maroubra, like Jimmy Waddell and a local detective named Bowles, were revelling in the publicity, and course we let 'em run, but then they started making all these blues. Bowles said to the family, words to the effect, that she was dead, and good riddance to her, thank Christ for that. Naturally the family were offended and he got the arse from the case. Then Waddell lined up Peter Smith to meet him at the Neutral Bay pub and we didn't have any input into it. Peter Smith was very suspicious and I wanted to get him on side and say to him, I've got some good information from the forensic that his girl could have some communicable disease and you better get it checked out. I was gonna give him that as a free one. Talk to him as a copper to copper. Unbeknownst to me Smith had this phobia the New South Wales Police were going to set him up. So we go over to Neutral Bay to meet and I'm sitting in the pub and Waddell's sitting there and this woman from Channel 10 walks up and she's got a clipboard and she says, "Sergeant Waddell? We've got the news crews out the front." And just as she says this Peter Smith walks in and she says, "Hello, I'm from Channel 10." Smith yells, "Get fucked!" Jumps right over our table and runs out the door. I said to Waddell, "What are *they* doing here?"

'Waddell says, "Oh, they wanted to interview him."

'I said, "You idiot, Jimmy."

'So I ring Smith up and say forget all that. I'll meet you tomorrow at 12.30 at The Rocks Police Station. So Smith rings up Channel 10 and asks where this female reporter will be tomorrow and they say she's due down at The Rocks on some special assignment and he goes, they've done it again! They've set me up! So he never turned up. And it was just a coincidence that Channel 10 were filming down there, but the bloke's totally paranoid.

'After this I went to the bosses and said look, you gotta get these other blokes off the job and give it to us. There was a lot of flack coming from Wendy Bacon through the *National Times* and a lotta speculation what was going on. Then a few of these names on the investigation turned up in Huckstepp's diary and we thought well, this is no good, bloody cops involved, and a couple of stupid things were done, so the bosses just barred them all and the whole inquiry come back to the Homicide Squad, and we opened up our own little task force in the CIB to work on it.'

As a result, Geoff Prentice took charge of the investigation assisted by three other Homicide Squad detectives, two detectives from the Drug Law Enforcement Bureau, and a plainclothes police constable to assist with the running sheet inquiries. He prepared a letter to the chief of the CIB and asked for a complete embargo on press releases. Senior police felt that Wendy Bacon and Geraldine Brooks were in fact hindering investigations into Huckstepp's death. 'And that's what happened,' Geoff Prentice said, 'The Assistant Commissioner of Crime ordered that no further press releases be made. We put a media black-out on it. We shut it down.'

'What about Neville Scullion?' I asked.

'He's another bloke. A junior bloke at Kings Cross who jetsetted into knowing all these crooks and Sallie Huckstepp was an expert at manipulating police, being a woman and a good sort and everything else going for her. Scullion was only in the police a couple of years. He polluted the whole scene before anyone even got there.

'Two things stuffed it up,' Geoff Prentice confided. 'First was handing it out to the divisional detectives. Fact that most of them blokes were in that sort of Kings Cross clique. You had Scullion, Spencer, Waddell—those blokes all knew Roger and that sort of group. Maroubra detectives knew her. All the Drug Squad knew her. So you get that scenario and there was probably the philosophy—like who gives a stuff—she's only Sallie Huckstepp, and then you get idiots like Bowles telling the family he was glad she was dead, and then it turns to shit because of the publicity, Wendy Bacon running around with all the lesbians, and then we get involved, and by that time a couple of weeks have gone past, it's got mould on it. And then we don't get the right blokes to work on it and then soon as all the sparkle went out of it, the department just dumps it.

'I really put a lot of work into the Huckstepp case, put a lot of my own bloody time into it. I maintained the integrity of it for years and years. It just got out of hand. It was a pest of a brief. Gee, we done some miles on it.'

•

Geoff Prentice had a golf game booked at four o'clock so we arranged to meet the following day. I sat down in my brand-new $50-a-night unit, which backed onto National Park rainforest, and read through the extensive police file on the Huckstepp investigation. On 7 February, the day Sallie's body was discovered in Centennial Park, divisional detectives conducted three interviews at Maroubra Station.

•

From day one Warren Richards' name had come up in the investigation; yet strangely, he was never brought in for questioning.

Debra Krivoshow stated that although she hadn't seen her sister for five months, she'd heard on the street that Sallie-Anne was seeing a Federal detective called Peter and getting a bad name. 'Then this New South Wales detective, Bowles, turns around,' Debra said, 'and in front of my father, me, Sascha and my father's wife, he says, "I hated Sallie-Anne Huckstepp and I'm glad she's dead!" And then tells me *I'm* a suspect in the murder. I mean the investigation from the start was just a bloody mess.'

Sascha Huckstepp, the second person to be interviewed, said she hadn't seen her mother since 25 December. During her interview she heard police mention Warren Richards; she also saw a mug shot of Richards and a statement of some kind sitting on a desk.

The third person to be interviewed on the Friday was Gwen

Beecroft who told police that Sallie-Anne had received a phone call at 11 p.m. the previous night from a man named 'Warren'.

Two days later Scott McCrae was interviewed at Maroubra Station by Detectives Neville Scullion from Darlinghurst and Dave Payne from Maroubra.

> TIME COMMENCED: 1.30 p.m.
> Q: How did you first meet Sallie-Anne Huckstepp?
> A: I first met her at a party that her sister Dee invited me to.
> Q: Do you know if she was using heroin recently?
> A: I caught her, I mean I discovered her using it and that's when I found out she was also dealing.
> Q: How would you describe Sallie's knowledge of the drug heroin?
> A: She was pretty clicked on with it. I don't think there was anyone wiser.
> Q: Do you know where she obtained her heroin from?
> A: Warren is the only name that I know.
> Q: How do you know the name 'Warren' was connected with drugs?
> A: Sallie has said to me on a number of occasions that 'I have to call Warren so that I can pick up.'
> Q: Can you tell us anything more about this person 'Warren'?
> A: No I can't, but Ashfield and Surry Hills were two suburbs that Sallie mentioned more than once.
> RECORD OF INTERVIEW HANDED TO McCRAE

The following day Neville Scullion interviewed Sallie's friend, Glenn Stone, at Darlinghurst Police Station where Stone handed him Sallie's 'dope bag', a black leather wallet tied with a small belt. The wallet contained a 'syringe wrapped in tissue paper, a spoon, two small empty plastic bags with a white substance coated on the inside and two square earrings'.

'When I first met her,' Glenn Stone told Scullion, 'she was using pretty heavily, but she was trying to get off it. Sallie never had money to buy dope, but when she wanted it she would contact a fellow by the name of "Warren", and she would meet him at

Ashfield or Centennial Park. She normally tried to get about 600, 700 or 800 dollars' worth. Most times she didn't have any money when she went out to see him, but she did tell me she had given this "Warren" some of her jewellery as security. I think that Sallie probably owed him some money for drugs, but she never had any money. During the time I was with her I paid the rent, bought her food and cigarettes.'

'When they were interviewing me,' Scott McCrae told me, 'the New South Wales Police implied that Peter Smith was involved in her murder. I spoke to Smith nine times on the phone, told him what was going on. I quite liked Peter Smith, he was young, eager, he'd fallen for her completely. Sallie was a pretty exciting woman. I went from being upset to angry to being frightened very quickly.

'I told the police what I knew and the nerves set in and I locked up. When I got back down to talk to them a couple of days later and got my head together a bit, it seemed off. Their questions weren't on course if you like. They were more interested in pinning it on a certain Federal Police officer than they were with Sallie's contacts with a known drug dealer and underworld figure. Basically at the time we didn't know what was going on. We didn't know who to trust.'

Scott McCrae had a friend who ran the Windsor Hotel and his girlfriend was seeing Warren Richards. The story she told Scott was that Richards and two prominent New South Wales detectives had a meeting at the Aircrew bar of the Texas Tavern in Kings Cross prior to the murder.

'A lot of paranoia was floating around,' Scott McCrae said. 'Apparently Richards believed that Sallie set him up years earlier—there was a car chase and Richards pranged his Porsche, the girl with him was killed and Richards blamed Sallie. He always thought that she set him up.'

Debra Krivoshow confirmed the story. 'When Sallie was alive, she and I would meet Warren Richards at the Central Plaza near Central Railway Station. There was a cafe-type shop in the front where Sallie, myself and other users would meet Warren to buy heroin. Sallie used to call him "Wozza". I remember speaking to

Sallie in mid-1985 and she said that she owed "Wozza" money for drugs and that she had given him jewellery belonging to Dave Kelleher to hold for security. I had an argument with Sallie over $1000 I owed Dave Kelleher for drugs. Sallie paid the money and we didn't speak again. At the end of 1985, I was buying drugs off Warren at the Central Plaza Hotel, I don't remember the exact words he said but they were to the effect, "Sallie set me up with the police, I ended up killing one of the girls when the cops chased us. Sallie owes me a lot of money."

'He was angry when he told me this. I remember him also saying that Sallie-Anne was going out with a Federal policeman and she was seen at the gaol and at the Cosmopolitan at Double Bay.'

In the week after Sallie's murder, Debra received five phone calls from a male voice, saying, 'You're going to end up in the same pond.'

At the inquest Debra was asked if it was true that Richards stopped selling her sister dope in 1985.

'That's right,' Debra said. 'The girl he was living with told me that Sallie wasn't getting any more dope from Warren.'

'Did it surprise you when you learned later he was selling to her?'

'It did, because Wozza was only doing two or three weights a day which was unusual for him to do such small amounts, plus I knew that she still owed him money, plus he didn't like her.'

'What do you mean?'

'Well, he told me he hated her.'

'Was Sallie frightened of Richards?'

'Yes,' Debra said, 'she was.'

•

Gwen Beecroft stated that when Sallie first started receiving phone calls at the flat from Warren Richards she seemed happy to get the calls and related to him in a friendly way.

'On one occasion Sallie said to me that Warren Richards fancied her, but she wasn't interested in him. She didn't explain why. About two weeks before she died her attitude to Richards changed suddenly and she didn't seem to want to go to these meetings alone.'

One other person who knew that Sallie was buying drugs from Warren Richards was Detective Neville Scullion. Six months after her murder, 'Scully' wrote in his statement,

> I am currently a Plainclothes constable attached to Darlinghurst station. Over a period of 5 years on beat duty I had reason to speak to the deceased Huckstepp. This was during a point in time when a number of drug dealers would gather at the 'Alice's Restaurant', they then moved to the 'World of Fun' pinball parlour. It was during this period that the deceased supplied me with her pager number so that I may be able to contact her. On one occasion Huckstepp contacted me in relation to two stolen furs. On another occasion she informed me of a person by the name of 'Warren Richards' who was the manager three nights a week at the Cosmopolitan hotel in Double Bay. She alleged to me that Richards was selling heroin from these premises and that he had in his possession a quantity of jewellery that belonged to her, and that she was given the jewellery by her ex-lover David Kelleher.
>
> I formed the opinion that Huckstepp was purchasing heroin from the person Richards and that she was frightened that Kelleher would become aware that Richards was in possession of the jewellery. I have also seen the deceased in company with her daughter in various drug hangouts, and it would be my opinion that she placed heroin on the person of her daughter for sale to other persons.

After interviewing Scott McCrae on 9 February, Scullion assumed that the 'Warren' referred to by McCrae was Warren Richards, yet this significant piece of intelligence was never passed on to Homicide detectives.

Five weeks after her death, the officer in charge of the CIB, Chief Superintendent Bradbury, told the media, 'We are very anxious to track the person Huckstepp went out to see on the night of her murder. We don't know who that person is but it is vital we contact him.'

Geoff Prentice was not aware that the 'Warren' referred to was Warren Richards until five months later when he re-interviewed Beecroft. It was only then that Homicide investigators turned their attention to the former judo and karate champion who had represented Australia at the 1976 Olympics.

Warren Austin Richards' phone number and his Croydon Park address were found in Sallie's blue and pink address book. Vehicles registered in Richards' name included a red 1974 Porsche, a red Holden sedan, a green 1967 Pontiac coupe and two motorbikes, a 1984 Kawasaki solo motor bike and a 1983 Suzuki.

I flipped through the 300 pages of the police file, the bulk of which consisted of a series of interviews with Peter Smith, Terry Muir and Gwen Beecroft. There was no record of interview with Warren Austin Richards. Nor was there a record of interview with Roger Rogerson or Dave Kelleher, two of the three men that Peter Smith had told State Police Sallie-Anne feared might kill her. The third man, Neddy Smith, was not interviewed by police until 22 months after her murder.

> New South Wales Police Department—RUNNING SHEET
> INFORMATION: On 30th December 1987, interviewed Arthur Stanley SMITH @ (Neddy). Occupation: Invalid Pensioner. He informed Police that he never knew the deceased. He maintains that he has never even spoken to HUCKSTEPP. He only became aware of her existence during the Coronial inquiry into the death of Warren LANFRANCHI.
>
> SMITH informed Police that he has known Warren RICHARDS since 1975. Further stated that he had seen RICHARDS enter the Iron Duke Hotel, Botany Road, previously owned by Bill DUFF, on one occasion carrying a motor cycle crash helmet. Also said that he has met with RICHARDS at the Iron Duke and that he has seen RICHARDS driving a red Porsche.
>
> SMITH also informed Police that it is his wedding anniversary on the 7th February and that he was at home on the morning of

the anniversary. This was confirmed by his wife Debra Joy SMITH who confirmed that he is at home on all special occasions (i.e. children's birthdays, christmas etc)

Detective Robert George Scott
Task Force Alpha

Attached to the running sheet was a Criminal and General Information Form filled out by Detective Sergeant Arnie Tees five weeks after the murder:

CGI FORM—FOR REPORTING ALL SUSPICIOUS PERSONS/ACTIVITIES/VEHICLES
INFORMATION.

At 7.15 p.m. on Friday 14 March 1986 in the Saloon bar of the Covent Garden Hotel, Hay St, City, I saw Arthur Stanley Smith a.k.a. 'Neddy SMITH'. I had a short conversation with SMITH and he told me that he frequented this hotel on a regular basis. At the time SMITH was in the company of Warren Austin RICHARDS, born 4.7.50.

SMITH and RICHARDS entered the bar together and on seeing Police, RICHARDS continued to walk hurriedly through the bar to another entrance and was lost from view. RICHARDS was not spoken to.

COPIES to Det. Sgt. Prentice. (Huckstepp Inquiry)
Crime Intelligence Unit C.I.B.

I kept searching for any mention of Warren Richards. At seven o'clock on the morning of 6 February, the day Sallie-Anne died, a dozen police raided the house Bryan Huckstepp had been living in, supposedly looking for stolen furniture.

'They didn't produce a search warrant,' Bryan Huckstepp said, 'they produced guns and questioned the woman that was living there about Sallie. The woman said I'd moved out a week or so, the police asked which room and she pointed it out to them, they drew their pistols and kicked the door in and found an empty room.'

RECORD OF INTERVIEW—Bryan Roger HUCKSTEPP.

> Husband of the deceased, however he stated that the marriage was one of convenience for the sake of their daughter and that he has been separated from Sallie-Anne since 1974. In this interview he said that he had information of Sallie's association with various drug-orientated criminals such as DAVE KELLEHER and he has told police that WARREN RICHARDS was responsible for Sallie-Anne's death. He further stated that he had knowledge of RICHARDS' movements on the night of Sallie's death but refused to disclose his source of information. It was pointed out to him that this information would be of great assistance to the investigation into his wife's death. HUCKSTEPP said he was reluctant to give any information to Police as he believed too many of them were associated with WARREN RICHARDS and NEDDY SMITH. Other information that HUCKSTEPP had is unsubstantiated (street talk) that WARREN RICHARDS was responsible for Sallie-Anne's death.

It was growing dark outside. I switched on the kitchen light and read through the remaining pages of the Homicide report. The State Opposition had called for a reward of $100 000 to be posted for help in solving her murder, but Labor Police Minister, George Paciullo, rejected the offer, claiming that Huckstepp's only association with State Police officers occurred during the course of normal police investigations. 'To suggest that there has been only a half-hearted attempt to bring her case to justice is rubbish.'

A senior officer in the Australian Federal Police had mailed me a confidential copy of the Huckstepp file. In his short hand-written note he said he was taking this risk with his career because he believed the AFP bore an ethical responsibility for Sallie's death.

He signed the note W.B. and asked me to destroy it.

SUSPECTS:

(1) David John **KELLEHER** Parklea Gaol, DOB 15/4/53
CRIMINAL HISTORY—Consorting, Malicious Injury (Car), Rape, Robbery, Larceny, Possess unlicensed pistol, Assault Police. Currently on Remand to Import Drug into Australia.

It is apparent that Sallie-Anne HUCKSTEPP had a close association with KELLEHER and knowledge of his operation in the drug trade. There have been numerous sources of information that HUCKSTEPP feared for her life from KELLEHER. These fears emanate from a combination of reasons ie:

(1) Her knowledge of his dealing and the methods of his operations in the drug trade.
(2) Her alleged knowledge of amounts of money mentioned at being $12,000,000 which he had hidden, the whereabouts of which were allegedly known to HUCKSTEPP and her talking to at least one witness of ripping KELLEHER off and going to Greece with the money.
(3) Her involvement with the Federal Police as an informer during which time she had exposed herself in various places in Sydney with Federal Constables Smith and Muir. It was common knowledge on the street that HUCKSTEPP 'had turned dog', ie Police Informer.
(4) That she'd been commissioned by KELLEHER to obtain documents and tape recordings relative to evidence against him in a substantial drug charge. Her role was to influence Federal Police Officers by offering them substantial amounts of money. It was apparent that KELLEHER was not happy with the progress in the dealings.
(5) HUCKSTEPP had become emotionally involved with Constable Peter SMITH and had expressed to a number of persons that she was in love with SMITH and there is little doubt that KELLEHER, even though he was in gaol, knew of the relationship.

David John KELLEHER has informed investigating Police through his solicitor that he had no reason to wish HUCKSTEPP harm, that he was not in any manner involved in her death and he has no knowledge of any persons who may be involved. KELLEHER could not have been involved personally in the murder as at the time of her death he was in custody in Parklea Gaol.

(2) Warren Austin **RICHARDS**—Croydon Park. D.O.B. 4/7/50.

CRIMINAL HISTORY—Indicted for Supply Indian Hemp, Goods in Custody

RICHARDS still has a number of outstanding matters of which results are not known including Conspiracy to import prohibited imports. Over the years RICHARDS has had a very large number of matters dismissed or discharged.

It is apparent that Sallie-Anne HUCKSTEPP had an association with RICHARDS, had knowledge of his involvement in the drug trade and his distribution of heroin. On the night that she died she had left her flat saying that she was going to meet a person called 'Warren', that she would be only four minutes adding 'at least this time I don't have to go to Ashfield'. Investigations revealed that—

(1) HUCKSTEPP knew RICHARDS and had been obtaining heroin from him and RICHARDS drove a red Porsche.
(2) On previous occasions HUCKSTEPP had told friends that she met RICHARDS at Ashfield and Centennial Park where she obtained heroin from him.
(3) That during the time she was living with BEECROFT, HUCKSTEPP had received a number of telephone calls from a person known as 'Warren'.
(4) Warren RICHARDS was in the Cosmopolitan Coffee Lounge at Double Bay when HUCKSTEPP had gone there with two Federal Police Officers and on seeing the Police RICHARDS had run from the premises. Apparently RICHARDS was dealing at the time and he told another person that HUCKSTEPP was a dog and tried to set him up.
(5) Information is that HUCKSTEPP had given RICHARDS some jewellery as a bond in respect of her purchase of heroin and that RICHARDS had refused to return it as she owed him

> a substantial amount of money. It is also alleged that HUCKSTEPP had been selling heroin for RICHARDS in an effort to pay off her debt, however she had started to use heroin again herself instead of selling it for RICHARDS.
>
> In summary of the above information I am of the opinion that Warren RICHARDS did contact Sallie-Anne HUCKSTEPP to meet him that night in the vicinity of Centennial Park. On previous occasions RICHARDS always made a meeting with her on short notice, to prevent her from contacting Police. There is little doubt that the night she met her death she drove to Martins Road, Centennial Park in her own vehicle. I suggest that this indicates she had voluntarily gone into the park to meet a person or persons in a similar manner in which she had done before.
>
> It is the opinion of the investigating Police that Warren RICHARDS is the main suspect as the actual person who may have killed Sallie-Anne HUCKSTEPP although there is no real evidence to suggest any conspiracy between him and David KELLEHER there are a number of factors which would indicate that both persons would have reason to wish HUCKSTEPP dead. Her emotional attachment to Federal Police Officer Peter Smith no doubt had caused great concern in the drug scene especially with KELLEHER and RICHARDS and there is little doubt that RICHARDS thought she was informing to Police.
>
> Warren RICHARDS was interviewed on the 10/7/86 at Bass Hill Police station in the presence of his solicitor, Val Bellamy. He refused to answer any questions.

I underlined the date that Richards had been interviewed—five months after Sallie's murder—and snapped the file shut. Outside my unit it was quiet and the rainforest lurked dark and shapeless beyond the park's high mesh fence. I sat there thinking about Sallie-Anne and how easy it was to get away with murder in New South Wales, until the lights went off in the windows of all the caravans.

There was a WBC welterweight title fight showing on Sky when I met up with Geoff Prentice the next evening in a run-down hotel overlooking the river. We got talking about boxing to break the ice and then I looked across at the former Homicide detective sergeant and said, 'Tell me about Warren Richards.'

'Well,' Prentice said, 'my philosophy with Richards was I knew he was gonna say nothing, so let him hang there. I knew that was the case, I said we've got a pretty good brief here and we've only got to get something concrete come out of one of these inquiries and we tie him up and we've got him. The bosses said no, that silly woman from the *National Times* was putting pressure on us. I argued with the boss. I said I know everything about him, all Richards has to say was yeah I rang her up, she owed me some money, but when I got there she wasn't there so I drove home. That's all he had to say.'

'But he rang her for sure,' I said.

'He rang her, course he rang her. He set it up. He rang her up, he organised it, he took her there, she was murdered. But all he's got to say to refute that: yeah I rang her up but she didn't show, so off I went.'

'And there was nothing the police could do about him?'

'He was interviewed, but he refused to answer. He's refused all the time, but he's dead-set involved. He was on reporting conditions over some charge. He pulled up in that red Porsche of his outside the station and I pinged him. "I wanna talk to you," I said. "My name's Detective Sergeant Prentice from the Homicide Squad." And Richards went as white as paper. His ears were shaking. I've seen it happen three or four times, when blokes get really frightened, their ears will shake. His ears were twitching.

'He said, "I want to make a phone call to my solicitor." He was frozen stiff with fear. I thought okay. He won't talk without him. So he makes a call. Then the first bloke that rings me is Billy Duff, I used to work with Billy Duff. "Have you got my little mate there," Billy says. "Is he staying or going?"

'And I said, "That depends entirely on him."

'"Right mate," he says and hangs up. I used to know Billy really well, but then he went down the sewer. I used to love Billy Duff. But Billy Duff flipped out, he went over the fence, started running with the crooks. Lost all perspective of what he was there for. Lost his house, his wife, his kids. Billy Duff and Rogerson were thick as thieves, but poor old Billy Duff never got a cent out of it. Next thing the little fat jew solicitor rings up, comes out there and soon as I put the questions to Richards, he wouldn't answer. "Do you know Sallie-Anne Huckstepp?" "Nothing to say." "Where were you on February 6?" "Nothing to say."

'It was futile going on so I signed him off and then all the colour pops back into Richards' face. He was up and rolling. The cops had nothing on him and that was the end of that.'

'So Richards was connected with Duff and Rogerson?'

'Oh yeah, course he was. They'd been seen in restaurants together and everything.' Geoff Prentice wiped his mouth with his hand. Two more schooners had arrived at our table.

'Did you ever discuss the Huckstepp case with Rogerson?'

'Look,' Geoff Prentice said, 'I didn't trust Rogerson as far as I could've thrown him. He was running around with all the crooks.'

I asked him about a newspaper report in which Rogerson claimed to have met Prentice in the street and Prentice had said: 'Everyone knows Warren Richards did it. But we can't prove it. If we had a few strong bosses we'd be able to lock him up.'

But Geoff Prentice denied saying that. 'What were the bosses gonna do? *I* was the one telling them not to do anything about Richards. Don't *make* me do anything. Wait until we've got something concrete. It was absolutely right 'cause when I pinched him, I said to me mate, "Take a look at him, he's shitting himself." Dead set he thought he was going in.'

'So you're sure he was involved?' I said.

'There's just no way he wasn't involved. Richards was an active drug dealer. I used to go down to the Covent Garden and see Richards down there. That was always a crook's pub. There's plenty of information on them being seen together, Roger, Billy, Neddy and Warren. I'd say Richards wouldn't have rung her up without being there. She was dirty on Roger and she used to have a band of followers going around bagging Roger, she'd gone the knock on some money and she hadn't been paying and she was back on the gear, all those things plus the fact that she's running around with

Federal cops. Kelleher was in gaol looking at doing 25 and she'd lost a fair bit of protection. You can imagine them sitting around talking about Sallie, saying she's going bad, she's causing shit with the Feds. Mate, what's she know? She knows heaps. Okay, let's get rid of her.'

'She didn't know much really,' I said.

'Well, what she knows and what she didn't know you'd never know because she never told anyone everything. She had blokes rooting her in motels; you wouldn't know what the hell was going on.'

'It's significant that she never told Peter Smith about Richards.'

'She'd have her guard up against him. She was too smart for him from day one. Peter Smith went out there with a shiny badge, thinking he was gonna stop crime in its tracks and he was getting burnt up something fierce. He was miles out of his depth.' Geoff Prentice clutched a schooner in his large hand.

'Look,' he said. 'I'll give you the scenario on Richards. We can positively identify him talking to her on the phone. There is evidence from other people that he met her in Centennial Park regularly for drug deals. Every bloke I spoke to in the Drug Squad knew Warren Richards, but no-one ever locked him up.'

'So he was protected?'

Geoff Prentice didn't answer, he looked up at the title fight and rubbed a hand against the bristles on his solid jaw.

'What about Kelleher, you don't think he was involved?'

'Well, Kelleher was in gaol, and there was no evidence that ever come up that Kelleher was dirty on her. He probably still held some hope that she could get hold of the Federal brief, know what I mean?'

I said I'd heard that Kelleher cried when he got news Sallie-Anne had been killed.

'Any glimmer of hope and he'd be hanging onto it because he wasn't coming out for a long long time.'

'And Rogerson?'

'Well the night she got knocked,' Geoff Prentice said, 'Rogerson and all them were out at Merrylands RSL drinking grog. Thursday night's a police pay night. They used to go out to cash their pay cheques.'

'There's no proof that he was ever there that night,' I said.

'There's no proof, but there was no doubt he was there. Look at it from Rogerson's point of view—every Thursday night they go out to Merrylands RSL, a whole heap of them meet to get on the piss. Make sure she goes Thursday night.'

'But he didn't sign in.'

'Well they never signed in. Roger'd be cunning enough to know. He'd have ten blokes to say he was there. He'd have had it done nice and quietly—whoa, got him!'

I looked up at the old Mexican fighter lying on the canvas, legs jerking, trying to pull himself up by the ropes, the ref signalling it was all over. The ring filled with scores of corner-men and well-wishers. I thanked Geoff Prentice for the drink and walked back to my unit and re-read through the 300-odd pages of the State Police file, looking for any reference to former Detective Sergeant Roger Caleb Rogerson.

•

On 6 May 1987 Detective Sergeant John Ferguson from the Armed Hold-Up Squad stated that in early February 1986 he arrived at the Merrylands Bowling Club about 9.40 p.m. and saw Sergeant Mal Spence, Sergeant Roger Rogerson and Dave Pike. Around 11 p.m. they drove in Spence's vehicle to a Lebanese restaurant in the Fairfield area for a meal and then the party of police returned to the Merrylands Bowling Club where they stayed drinking until 1 a.m.

In his initial statement Ferguson could not remember the exact date but one year later his memory had improved sufficiently for him to be certain that the evening in question was 6 February, the night Sallie-Anne was murdered, though he still could not recall the name of the Lebanese restaurant in Fairfield.

Malcolm Spence remembered the night and the club 'because it was a quiet little place. Never any trouble. They didn't worry too much about policing the door. Roger might not have been signed in.' Spence had attempted to 'mentally recontruct the exact date' but so far was 'unsuccessful'. Detective Dave Pike stated that he was at the Merrylands Bowling Club with Roger Rogerson, Mal Spence and John Ferguson, though he added, 'I cannot specifically remember whether this was the night Sallie-Anne Huckstepp was murdered.'

None of the names of Rogerson, Spence, Ferguson or Pike was entered in the visitors' book at Merrylands Bowling Club on Thursday, 6 February.

Eleven days after the murder, Roger Rogerson was interviewed very informally at his home by Detective Inspector Prescott who, according to Rogerson, said, 'Look Roger, I feel a bit embarrassed about coming here but I have been sent to ask you where you were last Thursday week.'

Rogerson said, 'Well, Aussie, where were you last Thursday week?'

'I wouldn't have a clue.'

Rogerson said, 'Well how do you expect me to remember?'

'Well, Roger,' the inspector said, 'it's about the Huckstepp death.'

Rogerson told him that it was his wife Joy who reminded him he was having a beer with Malcolm Spence at the Merrylands Bowling Club. 'Joy jogged my memory and I haven't forgotten it since. I got home at one or one-thirty, maybe a little later.'

'Did you speak to your wife when you arrived home?'

'Yes, I did,' Rogerson said. 'In fact she did most of the talking.'

•

I picked up the phone in the unit and after a chain of seven phone calls I contacted Joy Rogerson. I said I was investigating the murder of Sallie-Anne Huckstepp and that I was not a police officer. I asked her if she could confirm her ex-husband's alibi for the night of 6 February 1986.

'I never gave him an alibi,' Joy said. 'That's where *he* told me he was. Roger's capable of anything. Anyone who gets on the wrong side of him should be very very careful.'

'How do you mean?'

'Let's just say that Roger knew before he went to the Lanfranchi stakeout someone was going to die. And it wasn't a police officer.'

'Did he ever mention Sallie-Anne Huckstepp to you, Mrs Rogerson?'

'I'm no longer Mrs Rogerson,' Joy said. 'I've changed my name. With Roger you're dealing with a complex man who has led a double life for over 30 years. Even with his own family he was very manipulative. Decent people were frightened to say no to him.'

I wanted to ask her more, but sensed the apprehension in her voice. We talked a little about her ex-husband's close relationship with Arthur Stanley Smith—'Roger admired Neddy'—and then Joy hung up.

'I knew what Huckstepp was up to,' Rogerson had told investigating police, 'about having her daughter Sascha with her, secreting heroin deals in her daughter's panties. I knew the sort of person she was which was quite contrary to the image she was trying to make out for herself.'

Rogerson had made no secret of his hatred of Sallie-Anne and Smith despised her. Then there was Billy Duff riding shotgun for Warren Richards.

•

At dawn next morning I drove back to Sydney. I had no idea of the whereabouts of Warren Austin Richards but on a hunch I rang Corrective Services and asked if Richards was in custody. 'Yes,' a woman with an Indian accent said. 'He's being held at Parramatta Remand.'

I rang Remand and found that Warren Richards was presently on trial for heroin dealing in the Downing Street courts. An hour later a boyish security guard was fanning the lower half of my body with a metal detector. A bewigged barrister was up on his feet in Court 1.4 of the old Mark Foy's department store in front of a jury and an elderly judge wearing a red sash. I sat down and stared at the accused.

Warren Austin Richards.

From side-on he had a rugged face. His hair was cropped to gaol length, his nose had been broken and his thick muscled arms were folded tightly. 'Be careful of Richards,' a sleepy-eyed solicitor had warned in the corridor. I listened to the barrister question a witness, while a number of exhibits were passed around the court showing sets of electronic scales and a photograph of a safe filled with white plastic bags. Not once did Richards look my way and I was the only person in the public gallery.

At four o'clock the judge dismissed the eleven-man jury exhorting them not to discuss the case with anyone. Richards' barrister pleaded for bail, accentuating his client's 'serious asthma condition'.

'This case is going swimmingly, Mr Summers. I don't want any interrruptions to it on Monday. Bail refused.'

Richards glowered at the judge and then an overweight security officer approached the dock. Not until 'Wozza' stood up did I realise how short he was. He was around 158 centimetres with built-up shoulders, a strong jawline, and a low centre of gravity that would have assisted him in his judo career. He glared at the blue notepad in my hand and hugged his pregnant blond wife, Michelle Hughes, formerly Neddy Smith's lover. It was a small world, but an even smaller underworld.

If anyone knew why Sallie-Anne was murdered, Richards did. There was an abundance of evidence to implicate him in her final hours. Richards would not say a word to Homicide police, so there was no hope of him talking to me. And I couldn't think of how to approach him. I left the courtroom and gripped the polished rail out in the corridor, staring at a bunch of Drug Squad detectives huddled together by the long window.

Sallie-Anne had gone out at 10.55 p.m. to meet her supplier. Even though she was afraid of him, she needed to score so badly she met Richards in an unlit park on her own. Had he killed her, or had he set her up? Was it because she was running around with

Federal Police? The Drug Squad appeared to be no barrier to Richards' business activities, so why would a pair of junior Feds worry him? Unless Sallie knew who he was getting his gear from. Unless it was Richards' suppliers who wanted rid of her.

Two days after she was murdered, Detective Sergeant Billy Duff withdrew his appeal against a decision of the Police Tribunal recommending he be dismissed for misconduct. Evidence given before the tribunal in 1985, by Detective McNamara from the Criminal Intelligence Unit, was that Duff and Rogerson were getting ready to 'fly some smack down from New Guinea shortly' and Neddy Smith had arranged to on-sell it. 'Roger and I have it all worked out,' Duff had told McNamara. 'If we don't do it some other cunt will . . . the Feds are sweet, we have a couple of senior blokes on side.'

Was it coincidence that Billy Duff was the first person Richards contacted when questioned by Homicide police? Who were the two prominent New South Wales detectives who met Warren Richards in the Aircrew bar prior to Sallie's death? Why was information linking Richards to Sallie-Anne not passed on five months earlier to senior investigators? I went down in the lift answering my own questions. I had to remind myself that this was real.

Outside waves of office workers were rushing for the trains. I stood on the slippery wet steps of the courthouse and watched the rain angle across the city. The night Sallie died it was raining hard. Her sister, Debra Krivoshow, was lying in bed. She remembered that night like it was yesterday.

'It was pissing down with rain,' Debra said. 'I woke up and looked at the clock. It was five past eleven. And for some reason I thought there's someone out there getting really wet. I felt sorry for them. I didn't know if it was a hobo or what made this thought come into my head. Or why I was worried about people being out in the rain. Normally I would have gone straight back to sleep, but this night I remember thinking, there's someone out there who's really wet, there's someone out there who needs covering.'

8

Fame

'Three months ago the man I loved and lived with was shot dead by a Sydney detective,' Sallie-Anne wrote. 'The slow squeeze of the trigger began the first day Warren walked into gaol. A violent man on the outside, yes. But a violence that had been nurtured by five years in NSW prisons, two-and-a-half of these in solitary confinement. For the sake of these people and their families, who it would seem are sentenced along with them, do something, do anything, write, hassle, lobby . . .'

The appearance of her first published article in *The Review* brought Sallie to the attention of a wider audience. Her prose was naïve, passionate and she wanted to come to grips with her writing.

'I remember Sallie very clearly,' the agent Jane Cameron said. 'She came to me shortly after Lanfranchi's death. She had a lovely charisma, absolutely attractive. She was a terrific girl, awfully vibrant, quite funny, awfully straightforward. She showed me something that she'd written and I remember thinking I'm not dealing with an incompetent here. She had talent. I liked her writing, but it was her personality that I liked most. She had a real warmth and we connected. So I rang Andy who was editor at *Penthouse* and he agreed to see her.'

'Sal came to my office and started chatting,' Andrew Cowell said.

'It was obvious she had a great sense of humour. She was fascinated by the seedy side of life. She'd always wanted to write. She saw it as a window out of that world. I think she also wanted to have a profile as a writer because she felt safer. To make it harder for people to harm her. She'd written something that I quite liked about Kalgoorlie. We published that and it got a good response. Sallie wasn't terribly good at sticking to deadlines though. We put her on the masthead as a writer. She used to come into the office and got on pretty well with the staff. At *Penthouse* they were a fairly hard-bitten group. She wasn't absolutely gorgeous, but she was charming. She was vivacious. She won them over. Everyone liked her and her copy was pretty good. She didn't need much editing. She was a natural writer, she really was.'

'In the beginning,' Sallie wrote, 'I went to bed with men whom I "loved". Later on I simply did it for fun, but there were a few rather unsatisfying one-night stands so I have given them away. Nonetheless I don't judge anyone else's sexual behaviour; I simply accept that their way is not right for me. This brings us directly to the point of male hypocrisy. I strongly suspect that men who use terms like "tart", "slut", and so on are actually trying to compensate for feelings of sexual inadequacy. Encountering a sexually experienced woman, they probably become worried that their own performance will be found lacking in comparison. For what other reason would a guy want to marry a virgin, a woman who would have to be taught all the laborious details of sexual technique?'

Double standards, prostitution and police corruption were subjects on which Sallie wrote with verve, humour and authority. For someone with no training in journalism she took to it easily. She also fed *Penthouse* information for some of their investigative stories.

'Every so often she would become depressed,' Andrew Cowell said, 'and you would see glimpses of her dark past. I remember her getting quite upset one afternoon and telling me that people were out to kill her. She knew who it was and she told me who it was, but I don't think I want to say. She told me about a New South Wales policeman who had given her heroin and she had gone to see a friend and she gave the heroin to this girl and the girl died. The heroin was cut with something.

'Denis Whitburn did an interview with Sallie, an extensive interview and I kept the tape at my house in Glebe but it was lost in a burglary. A great tragedy. Strangely all the burglar took were the tapes.'

'Sallie certainly fed us information,' Denis Whitburn added. 'We couldn't publish the interview at *Penthouse*, because she named a lot of police officers and politicians of the time. You get the impression from the Royal Commission that it is just police, but corruption in New South Wales goes very high. It always has. Sallie had her head screwed on. She knew she was a marked woman. She was also a naturally good writer. She used to drift in and out of heroin and when she was using the doom side of her came out. The tape that I did with her was pretty hot. Andrew was as nervous as hell about it. You couldn't publish it, she named people such as [*senior New South Wales politician*]. I guess we'll never really know what happened to her. You can never get to the truth. The thing I remember about Sallie was that she was very confident. She had a great sense of humour. I guess a lot of really good humour comes out of black situations. Sallie was at the crossroads of a lot of the corruption that went on in this State. She kicked in the door.'

•

'Considering the circumstances of the evidence presented and the coroner's directions,' Sallie told reporters at the conclusion of the Lanfranchi inquest. 'I'd say the jury came up with a very fair verdict. I'd like to thank the jury for their patience through this whole terrible ordeal.'

'Do you think this is the end of the matter, Mrs Huckstepp?'

'No, definitely not. This is only the first round.'

'What do you mean by that?' a reporter asked on the steps. 'What do you intend to do?'

'When my legal counsel has gone through the transcripts we will release a detailed statement. We will be calling for a judicial inquiry into Warren's death.'

During the Lanfranchi inquest, Sallie became a media celebrity. Each day of the hearing she was on radio and national television. Her picture appeared in every metropolitan newspaper. One of the first things she did was to engage a prominent solicitor.

'Sallie approached me in a state of nervous agitation,' said the solicitor, who did not wish under any circumstances to be identified. 'It was just after she'd accused Rogerson of murdering Lanfranchi on "60 Minutes". It was high drama. Front page of the *Telegraph* and the *Mirror*, and Sallie loved it. She loved the attention. She was genuinely affected by Lanfranchi's death, but she was also enjoying her role as an anti-corruption crusader.

'Sallie was attracted to the anti-corruption side of female politics and I think she had to reconcile that part of her personality with using and dealing in heroin. I mean Sallie was an actress. She was a bright girl. The level of adrenalin she was receiving then enabled her to keep away from heroin. People in the arts were dying to meet her. A lot of men were enchanted with her. She was intelligent, she had a certain panache, a confidence and she enjoyed being coquettish, qualities that appealed to male publishers and editors.'

'She was just a great girl with great one-liners, a terrific lunching companion,' Andrew Cowell said. 'I had lunch with her every couple of months. In my experience she was a really amazing mother, very protective. She still felt threatened so she was glad to have an outlet to protect her. I was paying her a regular retainer. We'd go through ideas, one of which was she went off and road-tested a number of male prostitutes.'

'If you are a regular reader of Australian *Penthouse*,' Sallie wrote, 'you will know of my own experiences as a street girl on Darlinghurst Road in Kings Cross. Male prostitution, despite the greater degree of sexual liberation, isn't for every woman. But the woman who is looking for a purely physical relationship without emotional strings can now pay a man, take her pleasure and walk away without any guilt.'

To find a man for hire Sallie sifted through the display ads for escort agencies and settled on a parlour that offered a great selection of males. Over the phone she chose the house recommendation: a 34-year-old male of Maltese extraction, five feet ten, dark, handsome, intelligent and a good conversationalist. All very well, Sallie asked, but was he good in bed? The cost was $200 and she booked 'Charlie' for the following evening. All the women in the office were hungry for details of her adventure. 'The general feeling was that it was all a lark,' Sallie wrote, 'and just as acceptable as finding a casual sex partner in any other manner. We were all surprised at the price scale, and decided that decent men just don't come cheap these days.'

She sat down to wait. An hour later and she was still waiting. Another half an hour and there was no sign of her escort. She was ready to ring and cancel when there was a rap at the door. Apprehensively, Sallie opened it. Instead of the handsome man she'd imagined, her escort was an unattractive, scrawny-looking character with a severely battered face. 'He was well-dressed—if you like John Travolta's style in *Saturday Night Fever*—but Charlie was a far cry from my fantasies.'

Sallie decided to press on and they drove to a restaurant which she'd booked. Over dinner her date started to relax. 'Charlie was a pretty amazing guy,' Sallie wrote in *Penthouse*. 'If only for the fact that his ego was so enormous. He had little interest in any conversation that didn't focus on himself apart from the odd bit of insincere flattery.'

At one stage he leaned over and whispered to her: 'You are so lovely. Next time we go out I won't charge you.'

'My only thought,' Sallie wrote, 'was if there was ever a next time he'd have to pay me. Over the veal he provided me with some very explicit descriptions of his prowess at oral sex. I realised I'd made a horrible mistake in booking Charlie.'

Back at the motel Sallie was in two minds whether to go to bed with him. Eventually she decided she really had nothing to lose, and she figured he must have been good in bed because he certainly didn't have anything else going for him. Charlie, naked, was no Adonis. His sexual skills were non-existent. His continual boasting of his prowess at oral sex was just that. He was totally inept and clumsy, handling her like an ice cream cone. 'When he entered me,' Sallie told her readers, 'after very little foreplay and despite my protests, his rhythm could only be compared with that of man hammering a nail into a piece of wood.' When she tried to stop him and make her own needs apparent, he disregarded her totally, caught up in his own efforts to climax. Again Sallie felt like the prostitute instead of the client, but when she tried to push him off, it was obvious Charlie wouldn't be happy with anything less than orgasm so, in order to end the whole terrible business, she faked it.

After complaining to her editor, Sallie rang the agency and explained that she had been promised a handsome, intelligent and sexually competent escort, and found herself with a man who struck out on all counts. The manager was stunned. 'Apparently I was the first customer to make a complaint,' Sallie wrote. 'About ten minutes later I received a call from an irate Charlie. He'd just been sacked. "You seemed like a nice person, but you're just a bitch!" he yelled. "Don't worry, you'll get your money back!" Charlie hung up in my ear. I never did get my money back.'

The next day she called a second agency and booked a 28-year-old blond called Craig. He was no male model but good-looking in a rugged Australian way. When Sallie had undressed he gave her a sensual massage that went on and on, all the time talking to her, whispering. He never hesitated to do anything she asked and his whole manner was flattering, respectful and seductive. 'Although it wasn't the greatest sexual encounter of my life,' Sallie wrote, 'it was at least satisfying.'

When Sallie had climaxed, she slipped the fee into Craig's hand; embarrassed, he thanked her for the evening.

'Consequence-free sex is basically what the male prostitute is offering to women and men have been able to get that for thousands of years,' Sallie wrote in *Penthouse*. 'I feel it's about time women had the same opportunities. The typical Australian male attitude to sex apparently prevails even when it's being sold. Where the female prostitute learns to become suppliant, able to satisfy most male needs, the male prostitute hasn't even attempted to learn about the nuances of the female body. The fact is that all women love satisfying sex.'

•

'My sister has been accused of a lot of things,' Debra said. 'But she was never a hypocrite. She despised them. She was upfront about her past, drugs, sex, prostitution. She was totally honest. She never hid anything from her daughter. Her philosophy was if you hide it from children, they'll think it must be really good and want to do it. And Sallie loved to write, she really loved books, she used to devour them. She always wanted to be a writer. She had a natural aptitude for language. She used to go to bed for days and read anything, novels, fiction, non-fiction. At school she was the top student in English. I thought she wrote beautifully, poetry, prose. She was very proud of her writing. She'd write stuff and show it to me and say what do you think of this? Her autobiography was brilliant, it was just so funny.'

For the first weeks after Lanfranchi's death Sallie stayed at the house of a doctor in Blackheath, a member of the 'Sydney Push'. One evening the authors, Richard Neville and Julie Clarke, drove over to see her.

'She was in a very bad state,' Julie Clarke said. 'Physically she looked terrible, dark shadows under her eyes. She was frightened. She kept on talking about how Warren was murdered. I wasn't taking it all in. She was just going on and on about the police doing armed hold-ups and trafficking in heroin. It seemed terribly unlikely. I kept thinking if this is true the whole system is corrupt.

'Sallie was a strange mixture, she was really likeable, very very bright and I couldn't make sense of why someone like her was living like this. She came up out of the underworld. I felt that she had this air of danger around her. I was always worried for her. We became friends. Richard was fantastic with her. I thought she could be saved through her art. I was trying to be a cheer-leader. I imagined her becoming a very successful writer. We wanted to help her, that's why we rang Martin. She wasn't a no-hoper. She was unusual, a delightful person, but very self-destructive. It was almost as if she had a death wish.'

'Sallie-Anne was a person who was brighter than the context in which she operated,' Richard Neville explained. 'She could've had padded shoulders and been running a corporation and here she was a prostitute and a crim's moll. She was intelligent, articulate, candid and she used her sexuality consciously. She was a sexual being in a way that was out of style even then. I guess I'm trying to say she had a strong sexual appeal. And she was street-wise.

'She told me that Lanfranchi had a premonition that he was going to die and I said why? And she said, "He used to make love to me seven times a day." Naturally my ears pricked up at this. And talking about it with her she said that she would sleep on top of his body with her head resting on his chest. If she moved away to turn on her side, he would pull her back in his sleep. He could not touch her without fucking her. She said Warren's sexuality was so relentless, he had to have sex so often that it was almost as if he knew he was going to die young.

'I was very fond of Sallie,' Richard Neville continued quietly. 'She was pushing at the behavioural frontiers, she had a doomed quality about her I guess, tangled up with a sort of relishing of her own notoriety, an exaggerated fascination for the criminal milieu, rather a French thing really; it goes back to the poet Villon, the French have this fascination with the underworld. I think Sallie was rather a spontaneous woman, quite gutsy. She could've just shut up about the police, but she didn't. She was loyal to the memory of her lover. She didn't take on just any cop, she took on Roger Rogerson, winner of a police medal, and she brought him down in the end. It was a brave thing to do. Her story deserved telling and it was a lucky circumstance that there were two old libertarians working in the mass media at that time.'

•

While Sallie was in hiding in Blackheath, Debra Krivoshow received a message that her sister had been taken to hospital. 'Well, I thought they'd got her!' Debra said, 'I thought the police or the crims had murdered her. Then I get a phone call from a man who identifies himself as a police officer. He wants to know which hospital Sallie-Anne is in. I thought well, why are you asking me? I said, "I'm not telling you anything." Then five minutes later someone else rings back. "I'm Superintendent So-and-So. I want you to tell me where your sister is." And I said, "I'm not telling you either. How the fuck do I know who you are?"

'Finally I found out that Sallie had climbed up onto the roof at this doctor's house to adjust the aerial with a bottle of bourbon in one hand and she'd fallen off and broken her leg. So they moved her down to Martin Sharp's place and she stayed there a few months. Martin encouraged her to write. Sallie loved all that bohemian scene.'

The artist, Martin Sharp, was unaware of Sallie's background when Richard Neville rang and asked if he could accommodate a young woman. Sallie-Anne arranged to meet Richard at a Darlinghurst restaurant. All the orange people were there dancing and hugging to a group called Orange Juice. Sallie arrived dressed in black. She was spaced out on Mandrax, slurring her words. She dropped lots of names. She said a senior New South Wales Labor politician and a Sydney media personality were investors in the heroin trade. She needed shelter immediately. Richard thought Martin would be good for Sallie and that Sallie might be good for Martin.

'It was quite a household here,' Martin Sharp said. 'She had a broken leg when she came, she was on crutches and Richard told me she'd had a miscarriage. It wasn't a blessing to have her, but there was enough room. She had a little daughter. Some guy used to come and visit her, quite a tough guy on a very expensive motorbike. He definitely came from the underworld. She started writing when she was here. She wrote very well, I think she could've become a great writer, because she had a real story to tell, she had too much of a story. It was quite a creative house.'

Martin Sharp was busy working on the Tiny Tim film and Luna Park, so he didn't do a lot of talking with Sallie, but he liked her.

He thought she was going to get it together. She was healthy and strong and recuperating.

'I thought Sallie was a terrific person,' Martin said. 'There was a beautiful photo that William Yang took of her. She certainly had a large personality. She was a star in her own way. A mythic figure. Very brave, she showed exemplary courage. Ultimately one of the great women.'

The photographer, William Yang, was also staying at 'Wirian', Martin Sharp's mansion in Bellevue Hill. 'She fitted in well,' William Yang said. 'She liked the lifestyle there. She was chilling out. She was very direct, forthright in her writing. She'd channelled her own sexual encounters as a prostitute into these articles, it was journalese, but I liked it; she wrote quite well, she didn't have any literary pretensions. She was a very honest, straightforward person. I remember delivering some photos to her after she'd moved to Edgecliff Road and her current boyfriend had ripped the front door to her apartment off its hinges. My impression was she lived in turbulent circumstances. I believe people create their own turbulence. There was always an undercurrent of drama around Sallie. She did like a bit of drama.'

While Sallie was staying at Bellevue Hill, Michael Willesee produced a documentary on her life, interviewing her father, her sister, her nine-year-old daughter, and even a clairvoyant and psychic healer called Madame Hildegard who, ten years earlier, had filmed the teenage Sallie hugging a tree when she was pregnant in the Cross.

'How far back do you have to go?' Willesee asked, 'to determine what turns nice little girls into nasty little girls?' With her thick panda eye-shadow, bleached blond hair and white gapped teeth, Sallie smiled and responded to every personal question, disarming the interviewer with her charm and candour.

'Is it possible you're bad?' Michael Willesee asked.

'I suppose it's very possible I'm bad,' Sallie said. 'But I'm good too, there's good in me too.'

Mixing with the flow of artists, musicians, actors and film-makers at 'Wirian' gave her renewed confidence. Sallie began to consider herself a writer. She was now earning $800 a month on a retainer from *Penthouse*, receiving between $600 and $1800 per article and working for the ABC as a research consultant. Journalists wanted to interview her; TV producers would ring her to verify their facts about the Sydney milieu.

'Sallie was very adept at making you feel you were the only person in the room,' the producer Ted Robinson said. 'She was an extraordinary mixture of the beguiling overlaid with this persona of danger. She'd tell you stories of parties she attended where the Attorney General was present along with major underworld figures and I'd say, "Stop, stop! Why are you telling me all this for? Why don't you just keep quiet?"

'And Sallie told me what Roger Rogerson had whispered to her at Lanfranchi's inquest—"The moment you're not in the headlines you're for the knock."'

•

In December 1981, Sallie signed a contract to write her autobiography. The publisher at Penguin Books, Brian Johns, paid her a $5000 advance, a substantial fee at the time for an unproven author.

'I saw a piece of hers that she'd written for *Penthouse* and I thought she was a natural writer, and you don't get too many of those,' Brian Johns explained. 'I mean it wasn't just an exposé, it wasn't just a piece about her notorious life. It had depth and imagination. My impression was that Sallie would produce a good manuscript if she had the discipline to do it because she had the talent. So I arranged to meet her before we signed. I remember picking her up in Edgecliff Road and taking her to Rose Bay, to the Pier Restaurant, for lunch. Now this is what stands in my mind:

'She was a woman of considerable intelligence. She had a rather show-off quality that took away from her frankness and directness and the realism of where she'd been and what she was doing. It was a bit disconcerting. She was very forthright about her sexuality and sexual experience. I remember her recounting in detail how one of her clients would pick her up in Rose Bay Park and she'd be dressed in a schoolgirl's uniform. I was veering her off that. I was more interested in her as a writer and what she was going to do with her life and how she was going to portray it and make it more than I-was-a-prostitute sort of thing. I don't know how it came up but she suddenly said to me, "Do I look like a tart?" I said no, but in fact she was, she was tarty. She was a lovely looking young woman, she had strong features, but she'd said it and she was right. Ironically there was a Federal politician at lunch, Barry Jones, and Barry, I reckon, looked over at us and thought, *Ah huh, I've got him!*

'So I took Sallie over wilfully and said, "Barry Jones, I'd like you to meet a future Penguin author." '

•

By now Sallie was writing every morning on a small electric type-writer, going out in the evenings, entertaining her new-found friends with stories of brothels, fetishes, right-wing politicians and drug-dealing businessmen.

'She came to a few parties we had,' the journalist Wendy Bacon said. 'Academics were dying to meet her.'

A Melbourne mathematics lecturer, John Ryan, read Sallie's first story in *The Review*. 'Of all the things that I've experienced,' John Ryan said, 'it moved me so much it changed my life. It was such a compassionate piece of writing. I rang some friends in Sydney and said I wanted to meet the author.'

Sallie was in hiding and Ryan got a message through to her. He sent her some flowers and a note. Sallie-Anne got a message back thanking him and she gave him her address and when Ryan went there, she said, 'Come in John,' and they just clicked. The more he talked to her the more he was impressed by Sallie, for all her faults. A religious man, Ryan had been involved in the anti-Vietnam war movement in Melbourne. It didn't worry him that she was a working-girl. He was impressed with her courage and her honesty and he found himself a close friend in no time at all.

'He gave her money, he used to fly up to Sydney at the drop of a hat and he was like an old sugar daddy,' one of Sallie's female friends recalled. 'I don't think it was sexual, though he really adored her.'

'It's pretty widely known that I paid the rent quite often,' John Ryan said, 'that I put food on the table. They were always out of food. You can't have heroin and food too. Time and again I would call on Sallie. We had a method of communication where I'd fax her up and I might say "Sent packet of 150 this afternoon, signed Zorba." I used to send her money to get her out of scrapes. A lot of journalists were naturally anxious to ask about my relationship with Sallie-Anne. I told them, "I loved her, but not carnally."'

Ryan's friends warned him that the sub-editors would delete the word 'not'.

A few months after Lanfranchi's shooting, Ryan was sitting with Sallie in the Cross and she was sewing. It just seemed so unlike her, Ryan felt, darning a sock. So he reached over and touched her on the cheek.

'No, John,' Sallie said, 'it's too soon after Warren.'

He tried to explain to her that he meant nothing sexual.

'There was never any sexual intercourse between us,' John Ryan said. 'I was happily married and it would have ended our friendship. She would've seen me as just like all the rest. Sallie liked powerful men and I was the odd one out. It was just that she could trust me.'

•

It was around this time that Sallie met up with Scott McCrae. He'd lived next door to her in Neutral Bay when she was living with Lanfranchi but had never spoken to her. 'It was just after Sallie had been on "60 Minutes",' Scott McCrae said, 'and she came to this party in Paddington. Everyone was saying, "Sallie Huckstepp's coming, Sallie Huckstepp's coming!" She was quite a big deal then.

'What she'd done was come out and reveal what everyone in Sydney knew but was too frightened to say. I wanted to meet her and when she walked in she was a knock-out. You could tell she revelled in the attention. I got talking to her and later that night we went for a drive. One of the New Zealand guys renting the apartment had a Ferrari, and he took us for a spin down through Vaucluse to Double Bay flying around those sharp bends. Five of us in this sleek black Ferrari. I don't know how fast we were going, but everyone was petrified except for Sallie. I just wanted to stop, I had my eyes shut, and Sallie was screaming faster, faster, faster. And then this wild manic laugh.'

Scott McCrae was so enthralled he began to see Sallie regularly. 'Sallie took me to the Pimp and Prostitute's ball at the end of '81,' Scott McCrae said. 'I had a friend with me who was straight, no drugs, no crime, and he thought he could do a Pretty Woman on her, he thought he could rescue her. The thing was, Sallie didn't want to be rescued. She had an insatiable appetite—for relationships, for drugs, for money. We went to dinner and she was referring to her addiction in the past. She talked of going to the UK and interviewing Terry Clark and other major criminals. I remember asking her if Roger Rogerson was really as heavy as people said and her voice dropped to a whisper: "Scott," she said, "there's not many men I'm afraid of, but he's the worst." She had a lot of drive and enthusiasm back then. She didn't need drugs for a while. She was living way out on the edge.'

'While there's publicity I'll be safe,' Sallie told her probation officer. 'Probably for the next twelve months, but each day after that I'll be less and less safe and Rogerson will get me in the end.'

•

'You have to give her credit for what she did,' a senior barrister who acted for Sallie in 1982 said. 'Back then New South Wales had arguably the most corrupt police force in the English-speaking world. Elite squads were organising armed robberies, running the drug trade, extracting huge pay-offs from prostitution, gambling and licensing, and murdering criminals who got in their way. Sallie stood up and spoke out against it. It wasn't the Labor Party, it wasn't the Catholic Church, or the Law Society. It was a 26-year-old single mother. It took a lot of guts to do what she did.'

'Corruption is a dirty word,' Sallie wrote in *Penthouse* in April 1982. 'But never more so than when applied to the police. Currently there is a massive outbreak of corrupt practices in Australia and in some States it has reached an all-time high, with police knowingly and happily involved in drug-trafficking and importation, bank robberies, armed hold-ups and, in extreme cases, murder and conspiracy.'

'After Lanfranchi died, Sallie knew she was putting her life on the line by speaking out,' her sister, Debra, said. 'She knew she was dealing with heavy boys and that she had upset a lot of people. She knew there was going to be reprisals. We were standing in Pinocchios up at the Cross one night. Waiting at the counter for a take-away meal and in walked Rogerson and some other detective. He had to walk past us to get served and he looked at Sallie and me, and if looks could kill we would've been dead on the spot. I went ohhhh. Just this evil look he gave. But Sallie stood there and stared him back, straight in the eye.

'Then after Warren's inquest she walked into the Iron Duke Hotel and in front of everyone she called Neddy Smith a dog. I don't know if anyone's ever told you but Sallie had a mouth on her.'

•

When she appeared in court over the Long Bay charge the *Daily Telegraph* ran a full-length photograph of her beside the headline:

Lanfranchi Girl took Heroin to Jail: Police

The police prosecutor was Sergeant Mal Spence (who five years later would attempt to give his colleague, Detective Sergeant Roger Rogerson, an alibi for the night Sallie was murdered).

'What is your occupation, Mrs Huckstepp?'

'I'm a writer.'

'Isn't it the situation that on the occasion you went to visit

Long Bay Gaol you didn't have a certain portion of your clothing on?'

'No,' Sallie said, 'that's not right.'

'Isn't it the situation, Mrs Huckstepp, that you were affected by drugs?'

'No, that's not right at all.'

'Isn't it true that you were under the influence of drugs and weren't wearing any panties?'

'I beg your pardon.'

OBJECTION—DISCUSSION ENSUES.

'Is she alright?' The Bench asked. 'Is the witness alright?'

'No your honour, she is not.'

'Is the police prosecutor asking me to continue with this case? I don't like to continue with a witness who obviously appears to be in some distress. Do you know what the problem is? She appears to be crying.'

The problem, her counsel tried to explain, was that in the past nine months, Ms Huckstepp's lover had been shot dead by police, she'd suffered a miscarriage and broken her leg. He neglected to add that Sallie was coming off heroin, drinking heavily, taking Serepax, living in a succession of temporary safe houses and frightened to go outside her door for fear that she would be killed.

'She really liked it at Martin's,' her sister said, 'it was a lovely place, but when she moved out of there, she started using dope again and pills, she started getting messy. Sallie was desperate to stay on the tracks, but she kept falling off.'

'I remember having lunch with her in August '82,' Andrew Cowell said, 'and she was pretty unhappy. She tried hard to leave her past but the people from the underworld kept dragging her back.'

Gripped by bouts of severe depression, Sallie contacted a psychiatrist at Prince of Wales Hospital who wrote on her file: 'Sallie is a long term drug user who is in mourning for the death of her boyfriend who was shot dead last year. She is currently working as a freelance journalist.'

Psychiatrist: Do you smoke?
Sallie: 40 cigarettes a day.
Psychiatrist: What is your drug of choice?
Sallie: Heroin or cocaine.
Psychiatrist: How much do you use a day?
Sallie: 1 weight/gram.
Psychiatrist: How much do you spend a month on drugs?
Sallie: $2,500.
Psychiatrist: How many times have you overdosed?
Sallie: Never.
Psychiatrist: How many times have you had detox?
Sallie: Five.
Psychiatrist: Do you exercise?
Sallie: Yes, go to the gym.
Psychiatrist: Have you ever been to hospital?
Sallie: Yes, two ovarian cysts.
Psychiatrist: Any recent abstinences from heroin?'
Sallie: Sixteen months. From March '81 to July '82.

At 9.32 a.m. on Saturday, 25 September 1982, ambulance officers responding to an emergency call attended Unit 6, 10 Ocean Street, Bondi. On their arrival they found a woman, Naomi Sutherland, d.o.b 22/8/48, collapsed on the lounge room floor and her de-facto husband, John O'Brien, d.o.b 21/10/37, and a blond woman giving her mouth-to-mouth resuscitation. Ambulance officers examined Sutherland and found the body to be deceased.

'It was really a very, very strange thing,' Sallie told the journalist Graham Gambie. 'I'd got messages from a prominent New South Wales detective that I was a walking dead woman and he was going to kill me. I thought the only way he can ever get me is by giving me a "hot shot"—the most common way is to mix the gear with battery acid or strychnine.

'I really didn't touch dope for a long time—really I was so careful. And then after the anniversary of Warren's death I was going through very bad times and I got back into dope. And I went to my doctor and I went to a psychiatrist and no big help. And it just got worse and worse and it just happens like that and you're back into it before you know what's happened. And I became a bit blasé about it and I started not to really care for my own safety.

'Naomi and a male friend arrived at my flat at 6 a.m. with some heroin. I'd been sick all night and I'd had about 10 to 15 Serepax to get me through the night . . . with all that Serepax in me and the heroin I just fell asleep. When I woke up she was dead on the bed next to me. It's almost impossible to die like that from an overdose. It is bizarre. I really think there is something going on. I couldn't understand how she died. I don't want to think about it too much, you know. It's really scared the pants off me.'

When police interviewed Sallie at Bondi Police Station they asked her to outline the circumstances of the deceased woman visiting her flat.

'When Naomi and John arrived,' Sallie said, 'I was still groggy from the sleeping tablets. They came into my bedroom and I dozed off. Later I went into the kitchen to make coffee and I had one of those Sunbeam coffee makers, it takes some time to drip. When the coffee was ready I took it into the lounge room, I yelled out, "Coffee's ready." John came into the lounge room with me, we started drinking coffee and talking I don't know how long for, I think we realised Naomi had been in there quite a while, and we went to check on her. She was on the bed. I couldn't find a pulse beat and her lips were blue. I started to give her mouth-to-mouth, and John tried to give her mouth-to-mouth, and that didn't work. I tried to give her heart massage, I kept saying to John, "She's dead, call an ambulance." We moved into the lounge room, and I still kept trying to give her heart massage when the paramedics came.'

'Where was your daughter Sascha at this time?'

'Running around the house.'

'Who was in your bedroom when you awoke?'

'John and Naomi.'

'Can you tell me why this syringe was located on the floor behind your cat basket?'

'I don't know.'

'Can you tell me what this red liquid substance is?'

'Blood.'

'How did this blood come to be in the syringe?'

'I don't want to incriminate myself.'

'These two syringes were located in the bottom right-hand side of your dresser. What can you tell me about them?'

'They belong to me,' Sallie said.

'Ambulance officers have also located a blue plastic bag in your garbage closet containing 42 syringes with needles, 5 needle caps, one spoon, Codral 4 and Serepax foils, one empty brown bottle marked poison, pink tissues with blood on them and two pieces of paper with white powder on it. Did you place that bag in your closet?'

'I've already hung myself for a lamb,' Sallie told police. 'I might as well hang myself for a sheep.'

Debra Krivoshow remembered that Saturday morning. 'I got there in the afternoon,' Debra said. 'I was working nights. This couple had come around and they'd brought Sallie a free taste. Now let me tell you it is pretty unusual in the junkie scene to come around at 6 a.m. and say here's breakfast. Especially when they know that she sells dope. Also what they did was turn up with the two syringes already mixed. The other girl had more in hers than Sallie did, so when she's not looking, Sallie-Anne swaps them over to get the bigger taste. They both crashed out and when Sallie wakes up the girl is dead on the bed beside her.'

•

'Seven or eight months after the "60 Minutes" thing,' Scott McCrae said, 'was when it all hit her. She'd lost a bit of support she had with people. I actually think she was seen there for a little while as a white knight. I know she got a number of compliments from some senior underworld figures. It was Lenny McPherson who called her across to his table and said, "You must have a lot of balls to have done that, girl." That's the way she presented the story later on. But that was Sallie—she used to tell you things and hope that you'd swallow them. She used to mix fantasy in with the truth.

'After the hip people started to drop off and she wasn't out having nice lunches on Saturday afternoons with writers and editors, I used to see her at two or three in the morning waltzing back to the Cross looking wrecked and on her way home. I saw her at five o'clock in the morning on New Year's Day, '83. That was probably the clearest picture of what was happening. She waltzed around the corner and she really didn't look good at all. Not the way she could. She just sort of wrote her number down quickly for me and said, "I've got to get home for a taste."

'And she just sort of disappeared off. She was in a hurry. She spoke openly about the fact that something could happen to her, but generally for a good year afterwards she gave the impression that no-one would be game and if anything she was the aggressor. That goes back to the Lanfranchi inquest, I think Roger Rogerson said that "He feared for his life from this person", and pointed the finger at her.

'Sallie enjoyed that. She played on that for a while until no-one listened anymore and then she faced facts, that she really didn't have a great deal of clout and she didn't have a great deal of money.'

'If she'd been able to stay focused she probably would still be alive today,' her sister Debra said. 'She was pushed into that "60 Minutes" thing with Lanfranchi. They bamboozled her. She was still in shock, she was taking Mandrax and Tuinal and Valium and Serepax, and drinking bottles of bourbon. She was under enormous pressure. People wanted to meet her and know her. Everyone saw her intelligence and the magnetism that she had. Then Dave Kelleher came back into the picture and Sallie stopped writing, and started using more and more, and once someone starts giving you dope on credit you know you're gone. Sallie always wanted to be somebody. She always wanted to be a star. If she couldn't make it in a straight sense she was going to make it in the underworld.'

•

Sallie's solicitor from those days is a ruddish, well-fed man with a delicate voice and a pair of heavy black-rimmed glasses balanced halfway down his nose. I met him in an alfresco coffee shop three doors up from where the Royal Commission into the New South Wales Police Service was holding its final hearings. All around us lawyers in sharp dark suits were lunching in the autumn sun.

'I remember her father, Jack, was in Police Headquarters with Sallie and I,' Sallie's solicitor said softly, 'and he wore gold jewellery. The whole family liked gold jewellery. I think Sallie had an identity crisis. Part of her enjoyed the persona of being a corruption fighter; but she was also drawn to the drugs, the criminal lifestyle. I mean she had terrible taste in men and she was very incautious about talking. She was a mix of the fool and the hardy. She told me that Lanfranchi gave one of his clients battery acid. I mean this was Sallie talking about her lover. She was attracted to men like Lanfranchi and Kelleher, criminals with a certain rugged charm.'

Sallie's solicitor nodded at two barristers settling into the neighbouring table. 'Sallie was full of contradictions. On the one hand she was a grossly ineffective mother, but she was around a lot. She was unreliable but consistent in her love for Sascha. Seeing them together I used to think that Sascha was the responsible one. I used to think that she would switch the stove off, that kind of thing. I remember when Sascha was about eight or nine, Sallie came into my office, and was talking about Dave Kelleher who'd just come back into her life. Sallie prattled on like a schoolgirl and Sascha gave me this wise, grown-up look. Sallie related to men and women sexually—the way she walked, the way she talked. Sallie didn't know how to relate in any other way. I mean she was a ratbag, but she had style.

'She told me once, "I can't live on $300 or $400 a week." She was used to living on $1500 a week. Once you get a taste of the easy money, drugs, the high life, it's very difficult to leave that and to go back to the nine-to-five routine. When Lanfranchi died Sallie had her chance to cross over, she was getting her fifteen minutes of fame, but she didn't take it.'

The solicitor stirred his coffee, spoon gripped between thumb and a ringed forefinger. 'I remember going out to see her at Mulawa in late '82 on a possession charge,' he said. 'Sallie had stopped writing and she'd drifted back into drugs and the criminal milieu. I felt pissed off with her. She had made the choice to go back to a dangerous lifestyle.

'Sallie was a middle-class junkie, a girl of high drama. She was pretty saleable as far as the media were concerned. Here was this glamorous ex-prostitute telling the world she would be killed. And then she was.'

9

Inquest

The Coronial Inquest into the death of Sallie-Anne Huckstepp began at Glebe Coroner's Court on 20 January 1987, in a blaze of publicity:

EXTRACT: *DAILY TELEGRAPH*

Police in Murdered Girl's Diary

MURDERED heroin addict and prostitute Sallie-Anne Huckstepp had recorded the names and phone numbers of five NSW detectives in a diary shortly before her body was found in a Sydney lake. It has been alleged Huckstepp was having an affair with a Federal Police constable and also had an affair with a detective at Darlinghurst Police Station. Solicitor Andrew Haesler who will appear on behalf of Huckstepp's relatives described the police investigation as '*somewhat relaxed*'.

The coroner, Greg Glass, who was officially in charge of the investigation, took offence at this public criticism.

'Any co-operation that had been shown by Counsel assisting up to this point stopped,' Andrew Haesler confided in his chambers, 'and we never regained it. Now this was not an on-the-record conversation I had with the journalist, I probably did use those words in an off-the-record briefing, but that sort of reporting does not help the level of trust in a case. That is why I am so hesitant to talk to you.'

I had driven down to Wollongong to interview the Public Defender for a second time. Like all lawyers, Haesler had to be cautious of what he said. A short man with dark hair and a fawn beard flecked with white, he was working over a ham and salad on brown rye amidst a pile of law books, a cup of coffee steaming on his desk. Every few minutes his phone would ring and twice a court official pushed open the door and fired off a volley of questions about the forthcoming drugs case he was defending.

I switched my tape recorder off and on.

'To be brutally honest,' Andrew Haesler leaned back in his high chair, 'I regret having agreed to talk to you in the first place. I don't like petty criticisms of counsel, police or the coroner. My criticism is of the whole coronial system, that the coroner is expected to have two functions: one to investigate suspicious deaths; the other to sit as a judicial officer and act judicially. And those two things can't always be reconciled. Coroner Glass reconciled them on the grounds that he would be a solid and staid magistrate rather than taking an active and participatory role in directing the inquiry. He left it up to Counsel assisting. We did not get on. I didn't like the way Counsel assisting was running it and she didn't like me criticising the way she was running it. I presume that she did not trust me not to communicate confidential material to my clients, Bryan and Sascha Huckstepp. I've done other inquiries where police and Counsel assisting were very forthcoming in providing information. Certainly nothing like that occurred in this case. Everything was kept very close indeed.'

'Did you know Sallie Huckstepp?'

'I didn't know her personally,' Haesler said, 'I'd seen her back in the Lanfranchi days. If one makes a moral bourgeois assessment of Sallie Huckstepp, she took drugs, she lied, she cheated, she broke laws regularly, but yes there was an element of judgmentalism in the case.'

•

SECRECY SURROUNDS PROSTITUTE'S DEATH

From day one of the inquest the mood at Glebe Coroner's Court simmered with mistrust. New South Wales Police let journalists know they were critical of the way their Federal colleagues had 'mishandled Sallie Huckstepp', citing her visit to Long Bay Gaol with Peter Smith and Terry Muir shortly before her death. 'Every prisoner would have known she was an informant,' a police source told the *Daily Telegraph*. 'Among crims that's enough motive for murder.' Detective Sergeant Geoff Prentice, in charge of the homicide investigation, questioned the Australian Federal Police's training methods and the lack of supervision of Smith and Muir.

Although Federal and State authorities publicly maintained there was 'absolute co-operation' between them, State Police privately referred to regional Federal Police Headquarters in Redfern as 'Fawlty Towers'.

In an urgent Minute Paper to his Assistant Commissioner, Chief Superintendent P.J. Lamb spelled out Federal Police priorities. 'It is understood the coronial inquest will be used as a forum for allegations emanating from Huckstepp's family of Police complicity in, or negligence resulting in Huckstepp's death,' Lamb wrote. 'It is a strong possibility the AFP will be the target of negative publicity. Urgent consideration should be given to protect the interests of the AFP.'

The Federal Police employed a top barrister who took silk during the inquest and is now a Judge of Appeal. The AFP briefed extremely well. They acted on their barrister's advice and put a lot of effort into it. They were successful in keeping to a minimum any damage the fur coats could have done. It didn't leave members of the Huckstepp family with the feeling that the inquiry was full, open or frank. If there was absolute co-operation between Federal and State authorities, they asked, why were they so reluctant to share material? Andrew Haesler submitted that the Federal Police were negligent in their management of Sallie-Anne Huckstepp as an informant.

OFFICER LOST FAITH IN INVESTIGATION

On the second day of the hearing, Peter Smith revealed to a packed courtroom that he had received information about two persons involved in the death of Sallie-Anne Huckstepp.

'Was one of those persons Warren Richards?' Counsel assisting the coroner asked.

'Yes,' Smith said.

'And the other one was a State Police officer. Is that correct?'

'Yes,' Smith said.

'And you also knew that the Homicide Squad of the New South Wales Police were investigating her death, didn't you?'

'Yes.'

'And yet you didn't make any contact with Detective Prentice or any other New South Wales Police officer and give them that information?'

'No.'

'Why was that?'

'Because,' Smith said, 'at the last meeting the New South Wales Police arranged to set me up with the media.'

'And you thought that was sufficient justification to withhold information as to the murderer of Sallie-Anne Huckstepp?'

'I didn't trust them,' Smith said. 'I had serious doubts about the way New South Wales Police handled their investigation. I had grave fears for myself and for the safety of my informant.'

HUCKSTEPP SECRETLY TAPED POLICE

Terry Muir told the court that he had listened to a tape recording Sallie had made of a State policeman.

'Correct me if I'm wrong,' Andrew Haesler asked, 'Was the constable asking or pleading with Sallie-Anne to be kept on the payroll?'

'Yes,' Muir said, 'words to that effect.'

'Do you recall anything else from the tape?'

'Only this State policeman apologising for locking up one of

Sallie's runners. He said, "That came from higher up. I had to do it." '

DRUG SQUAD DETECTIVE'S MEMORY LAPSE

On 23 April 1987, Gary Adam Spencer, a detective constable attached to the Drug Law Enforcement Bureau of the New South Wales Police gave evidence that Sallie-Anne had phoned him at 4 p.m. on 6 February 1986—seven hours before she was murdered—and asked to see him.

'I told her I was busy,' Spencer said. He admitted that Sallie had secretly taped him in the Golden Sheaf Hotel in Double Bay in December 1985.

'Have you been shown a transcript of that tape-recording?' Counsel assisting asked.

'Yes,' Spencer said.

'Would you turn to page 3, halfway down the page, the question attributed to yourself, "*How did you know about that, who told you?*" And a response by Huckstepp, "*Every copper I come across, oh, Trent?*" Does the nickname Trent refer to you?'

'Yes.'

'What does that exchange mean?'

'I can't recall.'

'Then Huckstepp says, "*It's been a bad week, I lost a twenty thousand dollar ring.*" Do you know what sort of ring it was?'

'No.'

'You don't remember anything about the ring?'

'That's correct.'

'The comment by Huckstepp, "*Don't forget where your meal ticket is*", do you know what that refers to?'

'No, I can't recall,' Spencer said.

'Would you turn to page 9, to the words attributed to you, "*I'm in the shithouse now.*" Can you tell the court what that refers to?'

'I'm sorry, I just can't recall.'

'I take it Constable that you have read through the whole of this document prior to seeing it in the Witness Box?'

'Yes.'

'So you are not being faced with these passages for the first time?'

'No.'

'Well on page 14, again attributed to yourself. "*What do you want me to do about it?*" Can you tell the Court what that is related to?'

'Yes, well, I was just putting to her, to Sallie-Anne you know, she's been charged, you know, what do you want me to do, that's like . . . end of story.'

'So it wasn't an offer by you to do anything to assist her?'

'No.'

'Turn to page 15 please and the words, "*Well give us a job where we can make it up to you.*"'

'I was trying to get Sallie-Anne to give me a job, because she'd been done, done badly by in the past and I was trying to get her to do a job for me and I'd give her assistance through the official channels.'

'Did you log that conversation with Huckstepp in your duty book?' Andrew Haesler asked.

'No.'

'Constable Peter Smith of the Australian Federal Police has given evidence in this inquiry that Huckstepp told him that you were a police officer involved in corrupt practices. Is there any truth in that allegation?'

'None whatsoever,' Spencer said.

'You don't recall mentioning being on the payroll of Sallie-Anne?'

'No.'

'You weren't upset that Sallie-Anne hadn't paid you.'

'No, that's totally false.'

When asked by Haesler if he knew Gwen Beecroft, Spencer replied that he'd arrested her 'a couple of months ago'. But he had no idea that Gwen Beecroft was Sallie-Anne Huckstepp's flatmate.

'So you weren't aware at any stage that she was to give evidence in this inquiry prior to being arrested?'

'That's correct,' Spencer said.

WITNESS HARASSED AND TAKEN OUT TO DINNER

In an interview with Homicide detectives in New Zealand, Gwen Beecroft was asked if she knew Gary Spencer.

'Oh yes, he is a detective who came to my house after Sallie died and searched it and I was charged with a cocaine offence. While I was at CIB in the Remington building Detective Spencer went into a room nearby and came out and he was sniffing and he said that I could make some money. I told him I wanted nothing to do with it.'

By the time Gwen Beecroft gave evidence at the inquest, she was totally rattled by her treatment from New South Wales Police. 'Here was a person with no prior history who suddenly got arrested twice,' Andrew Haesler said. 'She was terrified. Now if that's not pressure on Gwen Beecroft because she nominated Warren Richards, then I don't know what is. There are a lot of police in New South Wales so why was it that the two involved in this inquiry—Scullion and Spencer—just happened to be the ones who arrested her?'

On 24 April, Neville John Scullion gave evidence that he had offered his assistance to the investigating police within hours of Sallie's body being found. He and other police arrived at Huckstepp's flat in the early evening, confiscating Sallie's diary and all her personal belongings.

Haesler: And you interviewed Gwen Beecroft?
Scullion: Yes I did.
Haesler: And you weren't convinced she was telling you everything she knew.
Scullion: No, I was not.

Haesler: You then said, 'We're going to arrest you because you haven't told me enough?'
Scullion: No, that's incorrect.
Haesler: But you did arrest her?
Scullion: She was arrested, yes.
Haesler: And she mentioned the name of Warren Richards?
Scullion: Not to me, she didn't.
Haesler: Did you ever have dinner with Gwendoline Beecroft?
Scullion: Not with her, I did not.
Haesler: So when Gwen Beecroft says that she had dinner with you and a female journalist, you say she's lying?
Scullion: No she's not lying.
Coroner: Well she's made a mistake.
Scullion: No she's not made a mistake.
Haesler: So you did have dinner with her and a female journalist?
Scullion: Yes.

'Scullion took me down to the Cross,' Gwen Beecroft said. 'Took me to this sleazy bar where everyone knew him. He was a very flirtatious man. "Detective Scully" they called him. He was part of the investigation. All he wanted to know, was what I knew about him.'

DEEP SUSPICION OF POLICE

Andrew Haesler's questioning at the inquest was based on a deep suspicion of the management of Sallie-Anne by Scullion and Spencer.

'Even little things, like Spencer had a telephone call with her on the night of her death,' Haesler told me. 'That took months before that information came out. And then he couldn't recall the exact words of the conversation. One would think that if you had a conversation with someone and then they had been found dead the next day then what you'd said to them would be pretty clear. Police are trained to recall conversations. A lot of people—friends of Bryan

Huckstepp's—saw what happened to Gwen Beecroft and were scared off.'

'Primarily our suspicions involving State Police involve the names in Huckstepp's address book,' Andrew Haesler submitted to the coroner. 'Now some officers have come forward and volunteered an explanation which is both plausible and acceptable. Others—and I refer specifically to Detective Scullion—are far less plausible. His arrest of Gwen Beecroft on the day the body was discovered and his conduct with her on a subsequent occasion—taking her out to dinner—we submit have substantially hindered this investigation. We don't know what to make of Detective Spencer's evidence. His memory is not precise and he has in fact contributed substantially to the muddying of already muddy waters. Detective Conrad Moores had dealings with Warren Richards, he had dealings with Sallie-Anne Huckstepp, but he kept no notes, he kept nothing in his head about meeting them. Why, when this is such a public inquiry, did State Police who knew of her death and knew of Warren Richards' dealings with her not come forward earlier and been as frank as we would have anticipated?'

COCK-UP OR CONSPIRACY?

Andrew Haesler lowered himself into his highback chair and gazed out his window at the steel city.

'Was there a lack of interest in the investigation because she was Sallie Huckstepp?' I asked.

'Well there seemed to be a lot of fervour from Maroubra Police early on to get to her flat,' Andrew Haesler said. 'And then it died quickly. Now maybe that was because she was Sallie-Anne Huckstepp. If Scullion, Spencer and Moores all had information about Sallie's involvement with Warren Richards, why was there a hiatus? By the time Geoff Prentice got to Richards five months later it was stale and that was never explained. There's a theory that says that if you have a choice between a conspiracy and a cock-up, the cock-up wins every time. It may well be just a cock-up. It was either gross incompetence on behalf of somebody or there was a conspiracy in the New South Wales Police Service between certain police officers to sit on information. Scott McCrae's evidence about two detectives meeting at the Aircrew bar with Richards suggests a conspiracy.'

'So nothing could be done about Warren Richards?'

'They could not force Richards to say anything,' Andrew Haesler said, 'but the police could have investigated him. They could have brought him in straightaway. They could have put a tail on him. They could have taken a proper and detailed statement from Gwen Beecroft. They could have subpoenaed Telecom records for Richards to see whether he had been making calls to her flat. They could have canvassed friends of Sallie-Anne's at the time as to her contacts with Warren Richards. If Richards had been regarded as the murder suspect from day one—which he should have been—there should have been a much more detailed investigation. Just because someone won't co-operate doesn't mean you can't investigate where they were. You can ask other people. They didn't do that. Once Richard's solicitor said he wasn't going to talk, the police just walked away. It was absurd.

'Look,' he went on, 'just because a suspect refuses to co-operate doesn't mean the investigation stops dead. The laws under the new Evidence Act allow for hearsay evidence that is contemporaneous to be used. It allows for statements such as "I'm going to meet Warren" to be given in evidence. That law was not available back then. This investigation called for a bit of flair, imagination and a degree of intuitive thinking. It may well be that Geoff Prentice and his offsider were just snowed by some of his colleagues in the State Police, some of whom have now been found to be corrupt.

'What you had was a clear picture that Richards had been supplying Sallie,' Haesler said. 'Then they had a falling out. Richards would not have anything to do with her because he thought that she'd set him up. Suddenly—just weeks before her death—Richards is the only person who supplies her. No-one else will supply her because she's been seen with the Feds, but good old "Wozza" has her on a string. Now that is very odd.'

KEY MURDER SUSPECT REFUSES TO ANSWER

When Warren Richards was called to give evidence at the inquest he was asked by Andrew Haesler, 'Do you know Roger Rogerson?'

'I refuse to answer on the grounds that it might incriminate me.'

'Do you know Neddy Smith?'

'I refuse to answer on the grounds that it might incriminate me.'

'Did you kill Sallie-Anne Huckstepp?'

'I refuse to answer on the grounds—'

'Your Worship, I would press that the witness be directed to answer the question.'

Counsel for Richards objected. Folding his thick arms tightly, Warren Richards refused to answer further questions and was dismissed.

'The coroner cannot compel anyone to answer a question that may incriminate them,' Andrew Haesler explained. 'The Coroner's Act goes further, it says that they cannot draw any inference one way or the other. Now that flies in the face of commonsense, but it's an essential protection for anyone, that you can't be required to incriminate yourself. The exception is a Royal Commission.'

NEW TWIST ON HUCKSTEPP'S LAST HOURS

On 23 April 1987, a friend of Sallie's, Wayne Leslie Cook, came forward and told the court that he had rung her at six o'clock on the morning of 6 February 'to get a hit'. Cook didn't know where Sallie was living but thought it might be Bondi.

'She was living all around the place you know,' Cook said. 'I never went to her place. I remember on this particular occasion Sallie said, "Usual place. Eight o'clock. Be early if possible." It was at the back of Candies Hotel in Oxford Street, you go down this lane in a back door which was always open and make the deal.'

'What did you purchase from Sallie?'

'Half a weight.'

'How much did you pay her?'

'$150. She took the money and pushed it down her strides. She told me she had to meet someone else. She was very uneasy, very worried. And I said to her, "What's the matter, Sal?" She said, "Doesn't matter, I can handle it." I said, "Come on mate, I've known you for years, do you need a hand?" and she said, "Don't worry about it, Cookie, I can handle it myself."

'I said, "Do you owe money?"

'Sallie didn't answer, but I formed my own opinion that she did owe money and I said to her, "Has this got anything to do with the fur coats, everyone knows you've been working for the Feds."

'Sal said, "It's got nothing to do with it Wayne, I've got a lot of worries, I've got to meet Rogerson and Wozza. I've got to go." She was crying. I offered her a lift and she said, "No, I'm right." And I got into my car which was parked in Oxford Street, outside the pub, and I drove to a back street nearby and I had a hit.'

'Why didn't you come forward with this information until now?' Counsel assisting asked.

'It's been chewing up my guts for twelve months,' Cook said. 'I've known the family for years that's why I come forward. I don't think it's fair that someone should get away with murdering her, you know.'

Cook asked for his name to be suppressed because of death threats he was receiving. His tyres had been slashed and a male person was ringing him at nights terrifying his family, 'You're going to die, you're going to die.'

The coroner asked him, 'Do you say Mrs Huckstepp had an appointment to meet Rogerson that day she was killed?'

To which Cook replied, 'That's correct, that's right.'

'You're very clear about it?'

'Very clear and another person by the name of "Wozza". It was common knowledge around the Cross that Warren Richards was dealing in drugs and selling to Sallie.'

'Is there anything else you can tell the court?'

'Only that Rogerson was giving her a hard time.'

'In what manner was he giving her a hard time?'

'He was threatening her. Threatening to get her busted if she didn't lay off. Apparently Sallie was out to get him over Lanfranchi's death.'

FAMILY KEPT IN THE DARK

I waited for Andrew Haesler to brew himself another coffee. 'So what about Rogerson?'

'When we were preparing our case,' Andrew Haesler settled into his chair. 'We went through each of the people with a motive to kill her. We had this list of names. There was Neddy Smith, there was Dave Kelleher, there was Warren Richards, there was Roger Rogerson. We called them the nasties.

'Then there was Scullion, Spencer and Moores—three New South Wales detectives involved in some way with her, who she may have had information on or who may have had a motive. There were the two Federal Police—Smith and Muir—who may have had a motive. Now some of these suspects could be eliminated reasonably satisfactorily, for instance, the Federal Police. Others could not. It was a question of saying, have they been eliminated? Yes. Is there any evidence to implicate them? In most cases, no. Or are there unanswered questions calling for further investigation—yes.

'Now in the final category Kelleher and Richards appeared. In the middle category were Rogerson, Neddy Smith and the State Police.'

The phone started up on Andrew Haesler's desk. He let it ring. 'Rogerson's evidence wasn't truthful,' he said. 'It was an attempt to use the coronial process. Rogerson came across using the same techniques he'd used for twenty years to convince juries he was the kindly Uncle Roger. Very good, but because he had no control over the brief and didn't know what the other evidence was his answers were exposed as being untruthful and malicious.'

•

On 4 May 1987, Roger Caleb Rogerson gave evidence. Described as the most notorious, disgraced policeman in New South Wales history, the 46-year-old Rogerson refused to give his address: 'There are people in this court who I would not like to have my address.' He admitted he was angry when Sallie-Anne allegedly defamed him on '60 Minutes'. 'She rubbished me and caused a lot of harm,' Rogerson said. 'I knew the sort of person she was.' Apart from seeing her sometimes at Kings Cross, Rogerson said he had no association with her in 'any way, shape or form. I have never made arrangements to meet her anywhere.' The Drug Squad kept him informed on Huckstepp whom he was interested in 'purely from a human point of view'. Rogerson said it was 'correct' that he would rather not have had her around, but that he would not resort to having her killed.

Rogerson told the coroner that a man had telephoned his home three times last month saying that the journalist Wendy Bacon was the instigator of Huckstepp's murder because she'd had 'a lesbian relationship with Huckstepp' and that Bacon had been 'put in a compromising position' and arranged to have her killed.

The allegation caused an uproar in the public gallery. 'It was pretty funny stuff,' Geoff Prentice said. 'I couldn't help laughing, all them lesbians up the back moaning and crying foul play.'

But the coroner was not amused. 'Rogerson's accusation is not only dishonest,' Greg Glass wrote, 'but he has brought discredit upon himself and in doing so was guilty of disrespect to this Court.'

Wendy Bacon denied the allegation. 'Poor old Sallie would be horrified by this vindictiveness,' she said.

Andrew Haesler submitted in court that Rogerson had come to the inquest 'to drop a bucket on Wendy Bacon' because his own alibi 'was not one hundred per cent.'

•

'There was no actual corroboration for where Rogerson was on the night of 6 February,' Haesler explained. 'All Malcolm Spence has said is that they went out for a drink on a pay night in February.

Now that's not an alibi. The Homicide investigation wasn't thorough. It wasn't as thorough as one would have expected and part of the blame is that there wasn't a Homicide investigation for some weeks or months afterwards. If Assistant Commissioner Nixon hadn't got involved, if he hadn't approached Dr Oettle and said do a second autopsy I don't know what would've happened. There is no explanation other than gross incompetence or conspiracy. Take your pick.'

'And Neddy Smith?' I asked.

'Smith was not called.' Andrew Haesler got up from his desk. He had a deep booming voice and the red light on my Sony tape recorder flickered.

'The police had a dossier on Smith which they made available to Coroner Glass. It was not—in his discretion—made available to us. Nothing was made available to us on Neddy Smith. We had no evidence against him. There were certain tapes which the Commonwealth and State had but they were never made available. We were given bland assurances that these tapes could not assist the inquiry. We weren't prepared to believe those assurances. We weren't happy with those assurances. We were given assurances by Coroner Glass and Counsel assisting that all investigations of Neddy Smith were dead ends and that it was not worth pursuing. We were told that all relevant material was produced.'

'Extensive police inquiries indicate that there is *no evidence* to reveal any involvement by Neddy Smith in the death of Sallie-Anne Huckstepp,' Coroner Glass wrote. 'No submissions were made by any interested party that he should be called as a witness.'

Despite the coroner's firm assurances, no record exists of Neddy Smith being interviewed by New South Wales Police over Sallie's death until *22 months* after her murder. Smith then casually informed police that on the morning of 7 February 1986, he was in Newcastle, with his wife, Debra Joy Smith, celebrating his wedding anniversary.

I told Andrew Haesler about the Criminal Intelligence form linking Warren Richards with Neddy Smith. 'They were seen together at the Covent Garden Hotel by Homicide detectives five weeks after Sallie's death.'

'We were never given that information,' Andrew Haesler said. 'This is why we were so frustrated because the Federal and State Police did not trust us to open the books and say have a look at what was done. We couldn't get anything unless it was to be tendered at the inquest. Whatever information the Federal Police or the National Crime Authority or the Joint Drug Task Force had on Sallie and her dealings with Kelleher was never made available to us. Whatever investigations that were made by the Homicide Squad that did not result in a statement and someone being called to give evidence were not made available to us. In retrospect I should have subpoenaed more than I did. Whether I would've been given access to Homicide running sheets and briefing notes I doubt very much. Because they related to a continuing murder investigation. Now the rules with regard to production of documents of privilege change once someone has been charged. The police aren't going to tell you two-thirds of the way through a murder investigation where they're going.

'Let us presume, as they did, that Debra, Bryan and Sascha Huckstepp could not be trusted to keep the information to themselves, the police are not going to tell Bryan Huckstepp or his scumbag legal aid lawyer where they are going or what their investigation has uncovered. Certainly nothing linking a meeting between Neddy Smith and Warren Richards was ever relayed to us. This is the problem that where the degree of secrecy may well be justified in one view it also stops people with information from coming forward that can fill in other pieces of the jigsaw or even place those pieces on the board. That's how I saw the Huckstepp inquiry—as a jigsaw puzzle with the State and Federal Police hiding half the pieces from me.'

I watched Andrew Haesler pace the floor of his chambers, hands gesturing as he spoke.

'There were some very odd things. There was a lot of secrecy. We were staggered that simple inquiries hadn't been made. I don't want to be too critical of Coroner Glass. He was a well-meaning and reasonable magistrate, but sometimes it requires imagination, an inventive frame of mind and initiative to put all the pieces together. That was the problem with the Huckstepp case from day one. Inquiries weren't made. Material wasn't passed on. We were kept in the dark. Then they brought in Task Force Alpha and nobody ever told us what Task Force Alpha actually did.'

BROTHEL MAN TELLS: 'FETISH FOR BODIES IN WATER'

On 9 December 1987, Task Force Alpha was formed under the command of Detective Chief Inspector Stephens after the Internal Security Unit of the New South Wales Police received two tape recordings of an alleged conversation in a Kings Cross brothel between Detective Gary Spencer, Warren Richards and former Detective Sergeant Roger Rogerson. According to the tape recordings the three had decided that Huckstepp 'has to go for certain' because 'she knows too much about an Asian–Australian drug operation involving NSW detectives.'

The Special Weapons Operations Squad secured Redfern Local Courtroom when boxer, Lee Henderson, handcuffed, gave evidence that he was told by former Kings Cross doorman and close friend, John Dale, that on the night of 6 February, Rogerson, Richards and Spencer met at Kiely's brothel on Darlinghurst Road.

According to Lee Henderson, Richards rang Miss Huckstepp from the 'bondage room' in the Kingsdore Motel.

'It's called the black room and they've got a rack in it, you know,' Henderson told police. 'It's a domineering type of room that people use to have their fuckin' kicks. And any rate they were in there drinking and carrying on and everything and they spoke about the killing of Sallie-Anne Huckstepp. She was going to come to Richards' house but he told her not to. He told her to meet him in Centennial Park. It was Gary Spencer and Warren Richards who popped her and Rogerson took back the tapes she had on her.'

In a statement read out to the inquest, former brothel owner, Michael Kiely, said that Richards was paying Spencer money for protection.

'There was a general conversation taking place about their drug operation and the drama Huckstepp could cause,' Kiely said. 'Apparently it was a joke amongst the cops that Spencer had a fetish for bodies in water.' Kiely admitted there was a drug-based relationship between himself, Spencer and Richards. He told police he knew which one of the three killed her: 'When the police tell me what they can do for me and my family I'll give them the name they want.'

Four days later Michael Kiely suddenly retracted all allegations against Spencer, Richards and Rogerson. He told the court that he had no information whatsoever on Huckstepp's death. 'I never once met the girl.' Kiely said he was now telling the truth 'on the advice of his conscience'.

Lee Henderson was interviewed by Task Force Alpha detectives and admitted in a ten-page record of interview that he had manufactured the tapes in the Sewing Room of the Protection Wing of Parklea Prison. Henderson told police that he had used his own tape recorder for the conversation and another tape recorder to play background music. He used jugs of water, glasses and dice to give the impression of making drinks with ice. He had other prisoners play the part of Spencer and Richards while he impersonated Rogerson. To give the impression that Gary Spencer was using cocaine, snorting noises were made.

'From the Task Force's point of view Constable Spencer has been cleared of any wrongdoing,' the coroner wrote. 'There is ultimately no reason why Constable Spencer should not be believed that he had no part in the death of Sallie-Anne Huckstepp. Mr Haesler suggested a close relationship between Spencer and the deceased. There was no evidence to support this other than an assertion by Sascha Huckstepp that she had telephoned Spencer once at her mother's request to say "Sallie will be late". Spencer denied receiving such a call. Considerable resources have been made available to Detective Chief Inspector Stephens' Task Force, including a liaison with the National Crime Authority. The Alpha Task Force was responsible for a complete overhaul of the investigation into Huckstepp's death. Every claim, every piece of evidence was checked and re-checked.'

But Detective Sergeant Geoff Prentice was not so laudatory of Task Force Alpha's efforts. 'I couldn't get any help on the Huckstepp case for years and then they brought in another Task Force who done absolutely nothing, tripped all over the place and dumped it back onto my lap,' Prentice said. 'I spent weeks at a time following leads that went nowhere. People crawling out of the woodwork lying their heads off. Greg Glass was notorious for not making a decision in my opinion. What I would've done was use my authority to stand over a bit more. Not trying to chase every rabbit down every burrow.'

HUCKSTEPP DEATH: FINAL CLUES TO BE CHECKED

'The investigation of Alpha Task Force was never made available to us,' Andrew Haesler said, moving about his chambers. 'By this stage a level of exhaustion had crept into the family's camp and we didn't want any more red herrings. We didn't have any funds to hire private investigators. One could think up a wonderful conspiracy of Neddy Smith, Warren Richards and Roger Rogerson getting their heads together to get their combined revenge on Sallie-Anne. But that's more in the line of detective novel stuff.'

'That's what I do,' I said.

Andrew Haesler stopped pacing.

'Write detective novels.' There was a long silence. 'So you don't think Smith and Rogerson were involved in her murder?'

'My hypothesis was that Richards was beating Sallie up and he went too far,' Haesler said. 'What we do know is that Richards set up a meeting in Centennial Park and that Sallie-Anne never survived that meeting. Rogerson hasn't got a hundred per cent alibi. We know that Smith and Richards had a connection. And we know that Rogerson and Smith had a connection.

'This is the problem with lawyers.' Andrew Haesler watched me carefully. 'We're bound by ethical rules. You can't make allegations without a basis in your instructions or a basis in proof. You can't submit Roger Rogerson murdered Sallie-Anne Huckstepp unless there is evidence before the inquiry that can support that. Kelleher was the person with the strongest motive. I wouldn't discount Kelleher. He's a dangerously evil man whose influence stretches far beyond his cells in Goulburn Gaol. He put on a few performances at various times.

'Once there is a prima facie case against someone the inquest has to stop. If you look at the inquest there was not enough evidence to charge anyone. There were lines of inquiry that were shown or should have been followed, but weren't. The whole exercise from my point of view was one of incredible frustration. To be able to suggest things and be ignored but not being able to follow it up. There could've been far more done on Richards and his connection with Smith or Rogerson. The problem with me making that criticism now is it is open for the police, Coroner Glass and Counsel assisting to say all that was done. It may have been. We just weren't told.

'And if we go back to the analogy of the detective novel, I suppose if I'd spent six months of my life just devoting it to this case going around as a private dick at the Cross trying to dig up the truth, I don't know if I would've achieved that much more.' Andrew Haesler opened his filing cabinet and fished out a sheaf of papers. 'At the conclusion of the evidence,' he said, 'each of the parties made a submission to the coroner. This is mine.'

I took the file and thanked Andrew Haesler for his time. He was due in court on a supply heroin case in three minutes. I was halfway out the door when he called to me, 'Have you ever been out to Long Bay?'

I shook my head.

He picked up a pen and began sketching lines rapidly on the back of a Law Society Circular. 'This is the maximum security prison. It's got a different name now. When the two Federal Police constables went to interview Steven Murray they took Sallie-Anne through the gates where there were many prison officers and sweepers, through a second gate, across the yard here and then around to the Special Purpose prison. They ran into prisoners who knew they were Federal Police officers. They marched her through a yard where prisoners had access to. That march would have signalled to anyone at Long Bay that she was dealing with Federal cops.

'What they did was negligent, grossly negligent. The notion of taking a well-known woman like Sallie Huckstepp into Long Bay is an odd thing. For her to agree to it showed she was not a hundred per cent with it. To even be suspected of being an informer in serious drug matters is a death warrant.'

THE WOMAN WHO LIVED DANGEROUSLY

I walked out into the corridor and down the wide stairs underneath Wollongong Courthouse. On a wooden bench that faced a glassed-in native garden I sat and read through Andrew Haesler's submission to the coroner.

'It's clear that throughout her life,' Haesler wrote, 'Sallie-Anne Huckstepp placed herself in a position of danger. She also placed herself in a position where she was used by many people. She was used by Kelleher. She was used by her dealers. She was used by Federal and State Police officers. She mixed with a dangerous milieu and that made her a valuable informant to the police. Perhaps as she got older the risks became greater. It's clear that she was a drug user; that she'd worked as a prostitute. She associated with heavy criminals. She associated with police, but all those associations don't lead to any conclusion that she deserved to die.

'This is an important point because at various stages witnesses have said that because of the sort of person Sallie Huckstepp was she was in some way to blame for what happened to her. We say she was murdered. My clients would like to know who killed Sallie-Anne and why. We hope that someone will come forward with information which will lead to these two questions being answered.'

NEW WITNESS TELLS OF MEETING IN PARK

On 30 November 1990, when the coroner was about to announce his finding under the Act, a new witness stepped forward. Timothy Paul Hiron gave evidence that Warren Richards, whom he had known since 1982, 'asked me if I wanted to earn some drugs, which I did.' Hiron drove Richards to Centennial Park in Richards' silvery blue Holden.

'Warren told me he would be back in a little while,' Hiron told the court. 'He got out of the car and walked into the park through the big stone gate posts. I remember sitting in the car for about fifteen minutes or so and then I got out and walked a short distance where I was able to see Warren speaking with a girl who was sitting on the edge of a pond in Centennial Park. Warren was standing in front of her, pointing his finger a lot in an abusive way. Warren then handed the girl something and she started looking around to see if they were alone. I ducked behind a tree. She then leaned to the side and appeared to be injecting something into her arm.'

Hiron saw Richards shove the girl backwards towards the water. He then ran back to the car and waited, but Richards did not return for another 25 to 30 minutes. When Richards finally got in he barked at Hiron to drive them to Granville. Richards was 'mentally preoccupied' and would not be engaged in any conversation, despite Hiron's frequent attempts.

'About six or eight months later,' Hiron said. 'I saw a photograph of Sallie-Anne Huckstepp in the newspaper and I realised this was the girl I'd seen.'

'What colour hair did she have?' Counsel asked.

'Sandy light colour,' Hiron said.

'How much light was there in the park?'

'There was adequate light to see what I've told you I've seen.'

'Who do you fear?'

'I fear Warren Richards,' Hiron said, looking around the packed court. 'I fear his associates and I fear for my life because of what I know.'

•

When Detective Sergeant Geoff Prentice gave evidence he was asked by the coroner if he had attended the murder scene when Sallie's body was recovered from Busby's Pond.

'Yes I did,' Prentice said.

'Now in relation to that day when you first went to the scene of the crime and what you saw the day the previous witness Timothy Hiron led you into Centennial Park, what can you say about the two occasions?'

'Well Hiron led me to the exact same spot where I first saw the deceased on the ground near the water.'

'So he led you to the same pond where the body was located?'

'Right to the area, sir, there's a large concrete slab adjacent to where the deceased was placed on the ground and he took us exactly to that area.'

But when pressed to give a date to the night he saw Sallie Huckstepp in Centennial Park, Hiron could not be specific: 'It was late in the year.'

'End of November, December?'

'Somewhere around there, yeah. I remember it was light, just getting on dark when we were driving towards the city.'

'Despite the witness Hiron being unable to give a definite time and date,' the coroner informed the court, 'his evidence is fairly convincing and certainly links Richards with the deceased, but falls short, in my opinion, of being cogent evidence that would justify the court terminating the inquest under section 19 of the Coroner's Act and forwarding the papers to the Director of Public Prosecutions. While the evidence heard at this inquest casts suspicion on Warren Richards as being implicated in the death of Sallie-Anne Huckstepp, it takes it no further.'

Warren Richards sat listening in the public seats at the back of the court.

HUCKSTEPP KILLER STILL NOT KNOWN

After four years, and nineteen sitting days, Coroner Greg Glass handed down his finding on 22 February 1991, that Sallie-Anne Huckstepp drowned, following asphyxia due to strangulation inflicted upon her, by a person or persons unknown.

'There can be no doubt that Sallie-Anne Huckstepp was murdered,' Coroner Glass wrote. 'The question that remains is by whom? In my opinion a compelling case could be made out that Huckstepp was killed because she was a Federal Police informant. For her own reasons—those of helping Kelleher—she formed an association with officers Smith and Muir. She had inhabited the shadowy world of heroin addiction for a long time. She had numerous criminal convictions. She had sought and obtained media publicity. She was well-known in the circles in which she moved. It is probably accurate to say she had a much better appreciation of the risks involved of being seen to associate with police officers than they had. At 31 years of age, Huckstepp was a far more sophisticated person than these two young Federal Constables. This is not to suggest that she was "a bad person". It is merely intended to dispel the notion that she was a hapless, unsuspecting innocent woman who was duped. No-one is saying that Huckstepp's death was Huckstepp's fault, but *she* cannot have been unaware of the enormous risks she was taking.'

I dumped the coroner's report on the wooden bench and stood up. I kept thinking of what Andrew Haesler had said, that this was either a cock-up or a conspiracy. A former detective sergeant in the New South Wales Homicide Squad, an ex-colleague of Geoff Prentice's and friend of Rogerson's, had told me off the record, 'Look, it's the easiest thing in the world to hoodwink a coroner. The coroner only knows what the police tell him.'

SALLIE-ANNE—THE MYSTERY REMAINS

After five years of exhaustive inquiries, Homicide police had come up with insufficient evidence to charge anyone with her murder. Aside from divisional detectives from Darlinghurst and Maroubra Stations and the nine detectives assigned to Task Force Alpha, the assistance of the State Drug Crime Commission, the Drug Law Enforcement Agency, the Federal Police and the National Crime Authority had also been sought in relation to Sallie's death. Due to 'the sensitivity of certain issues', her murder was discussed 'at the highest level' including the Commissioner of Police, the Minister of Police and the New South Wales Opposition Spokesperson on Police Matters. Investigations were pursued interstate and overseas. A reward of $50 000 was offered by Liberal Police Minister, Ted Pickering, for information on Sallie-Anne's murder. At the completion of the coronial inquiry, police investigations were described as 'on-going' but, in terms of man-power, her file was closed.

I climbed the stairs of Wollongong Courthouse. There was a musty smell in the air, a mix of shoe-leather, old law books and dried sweat. The idea of giving up on the case and driving home up the coast pulled at me like a magnet. Did it really matter what had happened to Sallie-Anne? People were getting murdered every day. I pressed my fingers against the plate-glass door. I had finally come to a dead end.

'If you can get anything on a meeting between New South Wales detectives and Warren Richards at the Aircrew bar before or after her murder,' Andrew Haesler had said, 'then you would be on a goldmine.' But the chances of that happening were next to zero. If the coroner and the Homicide Squad could not dig up anything solid with all their resources then what hope did anyone else have?

It was getting dark outside and I stood between the courthouse and Wollongong Police Station watching the shapes of people darting past. I had my suspicions of who had murdered Sallie-Anne and why, but I needed to hear it from somebody else's lips.

10

Kelleher

Long Bay Correctional Complex clings to the eastern edge of Anzac Parade in the small coastal suburb of Malabar, three kilometres north of Botany Bay. Proclaimed in 1914, Long Bay replaced the overcrowded Darlinghurst Gaol as the prime place of detention for Sydney's growing army of criminals. The words *gaol* and *prison* are no longer used in Corrective Services terminology so that buildings within the complex, such as the *Reception and Induction Centre*, have a welcoming ring to their names, but there is no mistaking where you are as you pull into the car park and walk through the sliding steel gates of the city's oldest, continuous, State penitentiary.

David John Kelleher was not expecting me. He had not answered my letters and had declined to respond to my phone messages. His reputation in the underworld was of a violent man who commanded respect. According to one former associate, Kelleher had a 'fearful reputation both inside and outside the prison system'. Neddy Smith described him as having 'the biggest ego of any man I knew'.

Nicknamed 'The Boss', Kelleher was arrested on 13 September 1985 by the Joint Drug Task Force on a charge of conspiracy to import a commercial quantity of heroin. Conveyed to Long Bay Gaol, Kelleher ended up, in the words of the journalist Bob Bottom, 'in the biggest and best cell, reserved for the gaol's head sweeper who, after 22 years on gun and theft charges, gave up his bed for Kelleher.' At his trial, Kelleher denied that he was one of the gaol heavies, but agreed that he was 'no shrinking violet'.

'I am not a good person in any respect,' he told the jury, 'I have been a criminal nearly all my adult life. My ethics are in the gutter.'

When the Homicide Squad tried to question him about the murder of Sallie-Anne, Kelleher sent a message through his solicitor that he would not have any conversation with any member of the New South Wales Police, Federal Police or Corrective Services concerning this matter. He told Geoff Prentice, to 'write out the questions that you want answered and I might answer them for you.' Geoff Prentice never did. At the inquest, Andrew Haesler asked Kelleher, 'You've been questioned about your relationship with Warren Richards?'

'Yes.'

'And you said that it's your code that you wouldn't inform on anyone?'

'That's correct.'

'No-one from the gaol has told you anything about who killed Sallie-Anne Huckstepp?'

'People have told me things but I'm not about to repeat them to you.'

'And I take it nothing his Worship or anyone says would beat that out of you?'

'That's correct.'

'And you'll carry that information with you to your death bed?'

'Yes.'

'No further questions.'

•

Sallie-Anne had first met Dave Kelleher in 1979 at the Star disco in Bondi Junction. Situated above a coffee shop near the Grace Bros department store, the Star was a familiar haunt of the new wave of Eastern Suburbs criminals intent on taking over Sydney's thriving drug scene.

'Sallie met Dave up there and they ended up having a drink,' Sallie's sister Debra said. 'I had a lot to do with Sallie-Anne and Dave over the years. She loved him and was respectful. You *were* with Dave—very respectful. Dave wasn't a talker. He was a big man, a violent man. He taught Sallie years before that you always have some sort of protection. Especially when you're dealing with drug dealers. Sallie always had a baseball bat. Plus her mouth was a lot of protection. If she was angry you knew. It was not unusual to have some sort of protection. She wasn't this wicked swearing Kings Cross junkie. She believed in manners and doing the right thing; she wasn't the type that went around with her tits hanging out. She kept it together. She could mix in any company, but she could be strong if she had to. In our lifestyle you never knew if someone was going to come around and rip you off.

'One time we were living together and this Yugoslav guy from the Cross—they called him the Chief—he and these other guys walked into our flat around 10 p.m., picked up the television and picked up her jewellery and they walked out, and there was nothing Sallie and I could do about it. We had to say *take what you want, just don't rape or kill us*. Another time Sallie came home and there were guys in the living room with shotguns. Dave and some friends of his had raided one of the police crops. They were shooting out of the back of their car with the police after them. See Dave ended up going to gaol for life. He started off working for other dealers and then went out on his own. He ended up taking more control of the drug business than the police. He was getting bigger than the cops. And they couldn't handle that.'

'Now Huckstepp,' Kelleher told the jury at his Supreme Court trial. 'Huckstepp and I knew each other back in about 1979 I think. We had a relationship which was very covert if you like. I had been married for fifteen years and back in 1979 she was virtually a mistress, for want of a better term. Round about 1980 I discontinued that association with her. I did so because she was getting involved with heroin, she was using heroin. She then took up with a person whom I am sure you are all aware of, a person known as Warren Lanfranchi. I am sure you have heard of him. He was shot in a lane in Dangar Place. Shortly after, Huckstepp and myself resumed a relationship. Then I was arrested and while I was in custody on that charge Huckstepp reverted back to using heroin again. I found out about that and I discontinued my association again.'

'If Sallie didn't use dope Dave would've given her the world,' Debra said. 'She was a very sexual woman. She told me Dave liked it Greek style. He'd come around to our flat to mix up the stuff, to cut it with Glucomed. He used to tie a teatowel around his face so he wouldn't inhale the heroin. Dave was terrified of getting addicted. He hated drugs, he hated Sallie using so she had to hide her habit. I can remember he was dropping off some dope in O'Sullivan Road and we'd been waiting, hanging out from the night before and we'd run out. Dave knew that I used and he didn't care about me so I was allowed to test it. He finally turned up this afternoon and Sallie and I'd taken all these Codral 4 and we had stomach aches and we were sweating and we were that sick we'd start laughing. We were lying on the floor as sick as dogs and you get hysterical, you know it's coming and one hour seems like ten. Dave finally got there. Sallie-Anne jumps in the shower because she's been sweating and has to make herself look really really straight and I'm sitting there and he's got this bag and I'm right into it and Sallie had to go and have sex with him.

'Now the last thing you want to do when you're hanging out is to have sex, the last thing you want to do is have someone touching you, your skin's crawling, you feel sick, you're hot and cold, your senses are so heightened when you're withdrawing that you can orgasm when someone touches you, and Sallie was sitting there almost frothing at the mouth dying to get into this dope and she had to entertain Dave first and he bought her back a ski-jacket and it was winter and Sallie nodded off and she burnt a hole in it and she was terrified that Dave would find out that she was using, because burn-holes are a sign of nodding off. He was a generous man. We'd go to the Hilton and have a steam bath and a massage. He bought her clothes, jewellery, a beautiful gold chain. He treated Sallie well, he treated her very well. As good as that style of man would. I never saw Sallie with a black eye but apparently he gave her a few slaps. When I lived with Sallie I heard him going off at her once or twice, but I never saw him beat her. In that scene he was such a violent man anyway. Sallie used to call him her Blond God.'

•

At the far end of the Long Bay complex a narrow path winds between a row of palm trees to the Industrial Training Centre. I didn't hold great hopes of Kelleher speaking to me. When he was on the outside Kelleher carried a copy of a letter from his solicitor warning police that if approached he would not talk to them 'under any circumstances'. At Sallie's inquest Kelleher said that he would not talk to members of the Joint Task Force 'if his life depended on it'. A New South Wales detective had revealed that of all the places he and his partner had visited during the Huckstepp investigation it was here at Long Bay that he had heard the most convincing explanation of why Sallie-Anne was murdered.

'If anyone knows what happened to my sister,' Debra Krivoshow had told me, 'Dave would know.'

Coils of barbed wire were strung along the roof of the Industrial Training Centre and a Corrective Services shuttle bus was parked outside the gate. Inside an airless booth I filled in a green Visitors Form with my correct name and address and handed it to one of the guards. 'Identification?' he said. I produced a driver's licence and the guard wrote down my details, then checked the inmate's name in a large black book. David John Kelleher. No. 129397. The guard passed me a zip-up bag and instructed me to place inside it keys, cash, comb, licence. The guard closely watched me empty my pockets. 'Are you a relative?' I shook my head. 'Friend?' he said. 'No, an acquaintance.' The guard turned to his partner. 'How do you spell acquaintance?' The second guard picked up the phone and said into the mouthpiece, 'Visitor for Kelleher.'

I stood outside a huge metal gate, then a hatch in one corner opened and ducking my head, I stepped through into the yard. A third officer ran a metal detector over my ribs and the pockets of my trousers. More guards stood around in the middle of a windy, open-air yard. Inmates in green track suits were embracing girlfriends, wives, mothers and children at plastic chairs and tables bolted into the concrete floor. I found a chair that was dry and with my back to the main gate, waited for David John Kelleher.

•

Twelve months after the shooting of Lanfranchi, Kelleher reappeared in Sallie's life. She had moved into a flat in O'Sullivan Road in Rose Bay with Sascha, and Debra, and had started dealing at the Astra in Bondi to cover her habit. Kelleher would drop the two sisters off a ten weight bag and they would use half that and sell the rest to pay him back.

'We used to keep money in Sascha's panties,' Debra said, 'when we were working up at the Astra. We never got Sash to hold the dope, but she held money. She had her underpants full of hundreds of dollars. She was so aware of how to handle the police. This little girl at the door and she'd ask them for a search warrant and say, who are you?'

It was while they were living in O'Sullivan Road that Sallie told Debra that Neddy Smith had raped her. 'They were out at some pub where the crims used to hang,' Debra said, 'and Smith tried to get onto her and she wasn't interested. Sallie told me that he got her when she was leaving the pub, bashed her around and raped her. She was a good-looking girl, the sort of woman that men wanted to attain. When she knocked him back,' Debra said, 'Smith was determined he'd have her anyway.'

On 22 October 1982, Sallie-Anne was sentenced to three months hard labour on a charge of possessing heroin. She appealed against her conviction and while she was awaiting the outcome of that appeal she was committed for trial on a charge of 'Supply Heroin' relating to the Marco Polo bust.

In a taped interview with journalist Graham Gambie, Sallie revealed that the Drug Squad were out to get her. 'They want to nail me,' she said. Two weeks later, Drug Squad police raided a house in William Street, Kings Cross, and found Sallie-Anne lying on the floor. 'On a table nearby was a shoulder bag containing a plastic bag with $240 cash and 124 pieces of glossy wrapped paper containing white powder believed to be heroin,' a police source said. 'We also found a syringe, two spoons, a spatula and a set of scales.'

She pleaded not guilty to the charges and was remanded in custody. Most of her time now was spent fighting court cases. Her appeal against her conviction of 22 October was dismissed and the Department of Corrective Services ordered her to attend a Pre-Sentence Report.

> SALLIE-ANNE HUCKSTEPP—D.O.B.: 12/12/1954.
> Mrs Huckstepp was previously known to this service, when in 1975 she was placed on a three year recognizance. Mrs Huckstepp is a 28 year-old married woman who separated from her husband nine years ago.
> RECENT HISTORY: Mrs Huckstepp would appear to have above average intellect, but apart from some recent journalistic work, she has not utilized her abilities. In January 1982, the offender signed a contract with a large publishing firm in Melbourne, to write a book. This company still looks forward to publishing Mrs Huckstepp's work. The offender is currently being supported financially by her boyfriend, Mr D. J. Kelleher, and he indicated this situation would continue.
> CURRENT RELATIONSHIPS: The offender has been involved in the current relationship and has known the person for five years. This man professes not to use drugs, and his fit physical condition would tend to confirm that fact. However, he is currently in custody, bail withdrawn, awaiting hearing on various charges. His current marital situation precludes him from residing with Mrs Huckstepp.
> CURRENT DRUG SITUATION: The offender attended Mosman Clinic last October, for detoxification and therapy, over a nine day period. Reports from the clinic indicate that she assumed the role of therapist, rather than that of patient, during the group therapy sessions.

> ASSESSMENT: Mrs Huckstepp professes to desire a stable relationship for herself, her boyfriend and her daughter. However, while she continues to rely on a male friend to supply this stability for her, she remains emotionally vulnerable. Whether she has the strength of character to evolve out of her need to be dependent, to mobilize her own resources and to be self-sufficient emotionally, remains to be seen.
>
> Bondi Junction District Officer

On 1 March 1983, Sallie was sentenced to three months hard labour for possession of heroin. The day after her release Sallie reappeared in court relating to the Kings Cross charge. Despite her protests to the magistrate that she had been 'loaded up', she was sentenced to 100 hours community service. Val Bellamy—who was to represent Roger Rogerson, Warren Richards, Neddy Smith and Dave Kelleher at various times in his career—acted for her.

'I'm like an old hooker myself,' Val Bellamy admitted in his city office. 'Anyone who wishes to flag me down can get my services. Over the years I acted for Sallie in a lot of shitbox charges. I got her some sort of community service order at Waverley court. She was supposed to read books onto tapes for the blind. They reckoned she got the tape recorder off the Blind Society and then sold it and stuck it in her arm. I don't know if that was true, but everyone was very shitty about it.

'There were times when she was utterly infuriating, even contemptible, but most of the time she was a pretty nice girl who'd had a rough time. I was always fond of Sallie. I thought she was harmless, but obviously somebody didn't. She was entitled to kill herself with an overdose rather than have some prick strangle her. She had this thing about running around with gangsters. She was infatuated with Kelleher.'

•

Out of gaol Sallie-Anne spent time looking for a flat, staying with her sister, and working at the Nevada brothel in Bayswater Road. It boasted the biggest bed in Australia. The women would stand on the balcony and call down to passing men in the street, 'Come up, come up, and do your body a favour!'

'Sallie hated it,' Debra said, 'It just wasn't Sallie-Anne. Sallie used to say, "I hate it, I hate it." First night she didn't make a cent. I had to drag her up there. She'd only work until we got out of trouble and then she'd quit.'

While Sallie was struggling with her habit and trying to write a book, her boyfriend was having troubles of his own. Kelleher was arrested outside the Star disco in Bondi Junction for possession of half a kilo of heroin and attempted bribery. He spent the next seventeen months in gaol. On Friday, 11 November 1983, Kelleher noted in his diary: 'Sallie turned up at court today. I told her to piss off. Bellamy gave me a letter from her. It was full of a lot of excuses and bullshit.'

When the matter went to trial Kelleher convinced a jury that a team of police and Armed Hold-Up detectives had planted the half kilo of heroin in his red Mazda. According to a transcript read in court, Kelleher had asked a notorious NSW detective why he had 'been loaded up', was it over 'the police crop'?

'Mate, you had to go,' the detective replied. 'It's as simple as that.'

The release of Kelleher in September 1984 added to his formidable reputation. He had taken on detectives from the toughest squad in the State and won. Sallie-Anne boasted of their relationship.

'Her constant references to Dave were how smart he was, how tough he was,' Scott McCrae said. 'That never dissipated. She constantly referred to how much she loved him. Sallie was always looking for a hero, to be with someone who was notable, but she was also frightened of Dave. He gave Sallie-Anne some kind of repectability in the underworld. People in the drug world were scared of him. Dave was a big time heavy. He was on a mission to rule.'

On 15 October 1984, Scott McCrae ran into Sallie-Anne at the

Woollahra Hotel. 'She looked great, fantastic, really healthy,' Scott said. 'She was sitting there, wearing new clothes, looking stunning. I sat down opposite and all of a sudden her eyes averted and she said nervously, "Someone's sitting there, Scott." It was odd, because she was usually so friendly. I stood up and behind me was this well-developed guy, blond, solid build. It was Dave Kelleher. He sat down without a word to me and I could see that Sallie didn't want to talk, so I darted off.'

'It was surprising that Sallie-Anne got on with Kelleher,' the journalist Wendy Bacon said. 'Kelleher was very smooth, middle-class background, Trinity Grammar, but a particularly nasty type who had been convicted of pack rape.'

'Dave hit me once,' Debra Krivoshow said. 'For cocaine money I'd blown. I was sitting on Sallie's couch eating a cheese and tomato sandwich and he asked me where the thousand dollars was that I owed him. I said, "Don't worry, I'll get it." Next thing a hand came across and the plate and toast and tomato went flying and I burst into tears. After that whenever he'd come around to the flat to see Sallie I'd hide in Edgecliff Park. But Sallie-Anne had a temper on her too. I had an argument with her once and she was standing at the door giving me a mouthful so I just shut the door in her face and next thing Sallie's fist came right through the bevelled glass.'

On 13 September 1984, Sallie had moved into a luxurious apartment overlooking the harbour. Telecom records show that the phone was connected to 28/22 New Beach Road, Darling Point under the name of Sallie Stepp. The monthly rent was part-paid by Kelleher who moved Sallie 'into the joint to keep an eye on her' and to use it as a base for his couriers. Sallie was moving up the food chain, dining in Sydney's best harbourside restaurants, accompanying Kelleher to the snowfields.

'Sallie wasn't just a girlfriend,' her sister Debra said. 'She was one of the players. Sallie was living with Dave in Darling Point when Dave was trafficking big, big time. He was making millions, getting into gold, organising runs to Hong Kong. And Sallie was doing well. Designer clothes, beautiful jewellery, all this lovely furniture. Dave was giving her ten weight bags so she could make her own money. Dave told Sallie he was going to leave his wife for her.

In December 1984, Kelleher wrote in his diary: 'Gail accuses me of writing to Sallie and some bullshit about me supposedly going to go away with her somewhere.'

When John Ryan visited Sallie in her sixth floor apartment, with its white shag-pile carpet, she told her old friend that she was physically afraid of Kelleher.

'Dave belted me, picked up $1200 and walked out,' Sallie wrote in her diary. On another occasion, when Kelleher took Sallie to Jeff Fenech's IBF bantamweight title fight at the Hordern Pavilion, Sallie got drunk and Kelleher ended up striking her in public. Sallie told Scott McCrae: 'I shot my mouth off and copped a backhander from Dave. I probably deserved it.'

'In 1984 I was seeing Huckstepp,' Kelleher told the jury at his trial. 'We were not having a sexual relationship but I was seeing her. I stopped that abruptly because I became aware she may have been using heroin. Huckstepp and I were reunited for one single night. While I was in Manila, Huckstepp went into a rehabilitation centre. She admitted to a friend that I was trying to get her off it.'

In a telephone conversation taped by the Joint Drug Task Force, Sallie-Anne told Sharon Smith, 'Do you think I should tell Dave, you know what he's like. He'll kill me if I even think about it.'

'I suppose,' Kelleher said at his trial, 'she only meant that in a metaphorical sense.'

•

While Sallie was copping backhanders from her Blond God, the Crown Prosecutor wrote confidentially to the Attorney General over the Marco Polo bust:

> If this matter proceeds to trial no doubt the accused, Huckstepp, will try and use it as a platform to air her grievances over the death of Lanfranchi. And while that man's death has nothing to do with this

> case his involvement with police and their alleged corruption does, to a certain extent, have a bearing on the matter. For example, one of the allegations is that the $10,000 bribe which the accused was supposed to pay police coincided with a $10,000 bribe Lanfranchi had to pay. In the circumstances it does not seem to be in the public interest to distract a consideration of the merits of the evidence against Huckstepp by attempts to litigate the rights and wrongs of Lanfranchi vs The Police. For those reasons, I recommend that a bill not be found in the case of Regina vs Huckstepp.

The Drug Squad was furious and lodged an official disapproval that the matter was not to proceed to trial. New South Wales Police had not forgiven Sallie-Anne Huckstepp nor had they forgotten Dave Kelleher who continued to flaunt his considerable drug wealth around the Eastern Suburbs of Sydney, living with his wife, Gail, and two young children in a luxury home in Watson's Bay, driving a Mercedes or one of his two brand new Jaguars over to visit Sallie at her new $1400 a month penthouse in Eastbourne Road, Darling Point, accompanied by his three English sheepdogs. For a smart man he seemed to be asking for trouble.

In early 1985, the Joint Drug Task Force targeted Kelleher. Listening devices were installed in his plush new office suite on Level 9 of the Aetna building, corner of Bathurst and Castlereagh Streets. The officer involved in electronic surveillance on Operation Postscript—using a Marantz super scope professional recorder—was Trevor David Haken who, ten years later, would roll over to the Royal Commission into the New South Wales Police Service. Kelleher was put under around-the-clock surveillance. His phones were tapped. Sallie's telexes were intercepted; her movements monitored. She was captured on videotape. Although Kelleher would later claim that Sallie-Anne only played a minor role in 'this escapade' she seemed to be a trusted member of his inner organisation. Kelleher carried a police scanner in his car and Sallie started to do the same. Her apartment was used to make international phone calls and as a safe house for Kelleher's couriers, one of whom described how, after arriving back from Hong Kong, he was introduced 'to a blond girl called Sallie-Anne' at 17/2 Eastbourne Road and 'spent time at her crib resting and sleeping'. At Kelleher's request, Sallie wrote a note to the man before he left on his next run saying, 'No coins, no jewellery.' Another time, the courier went to a private hotel in Watson's Bay and met 'the blond lady who came out of the bathroom with Dave'. Sallie carried a pager and used the codenames 'Harry' and 'Boris'. 'Boris spoke to Mr Honda today,' was a reference to Sallie-Anne speaking to Ping Kwong Fan, Kelleher's main supplier. Kelleher referred to himself as 'Jesus Christ' and 'Lionel Murphy'.

On the police tapes she says, 'Dave is making my life a misery. I love him, but he won't talk to me.'

Desperate to keep her Blond God, Sallie-Anne checked into Langton Clinic on 10 July to detox. Dr John Stanhope remembered her clearly:

'Sallie was so distinctive,' Dr Stanhope said. 'She gave the impression of being considerably older and more mature than the average user. Heroin really started to become popular in the late 1960s in Sydney and Sallie belonged to that baby-boom generation. She used to ring up frequently and say she might come in for treatment. She told us her boyfriend Dave was very keen for her to be drug free. She wanted some kind of help.'

The day after Sallie was admitted, she told her support group that nobody had suffered like she had. On day two she rejected Narcotics Anonymous and the Twelve-Step program. She was verbally aggressive and disruptive. She told the nurses that her boyfriend Dave was straight, that her husband Warren was killed by police and she felt 'that certain powerful people in Sydney wanted revenge on her'. At seven o'clock the next morning she was found in a drowsy state and although denying she had smuggled in drugs, and despite her threats to expose the clinic publicly, she was discharged. She had lasted three days.

On 13 July she rang Kelleher's lieutenant and told him that she was still using heroin. 'What do you think I should do with Dave? Should I tell him or not, he will probably kill me.'

At 5.45 a.m. on 13 September 1985, a squad of heavily armed

police gathered at Canton Beach caravan park near Toukley. Kelleher appeared at the front door of his caravan naked. Detective Sergeant Paynter said, 'David John Kelleher, you are under arrest for conspiring to import eleven kilos of heroin into Australia.' Detective Paynter asked Kelleher if he would like him to read out the search warrant.

Kelleher said, 'I've got fucking eyes, you cunt.'

When Sallie-Anne got news that Kelleher had been arrested, she contacted lawyer, Val Bellamy, urgently and asked if there was anything Dave needed. She could not understand why she also hadn't been pinched. When she met with Peter Smith on 7 December she badgered him for information about the Joint Drug Task Force: 'How long was there surveillance on Dave? Did they have surveillance on me? Why wasn't I picked up when Dave was?'

Smith couldn't come up with the answers because he had no idea about the Task Force and he knew if he said anything it would only show his ignorance.

With Kelleher in custody and unable to pay the rent, Sallie-Anne was forced to move out of Darling Point and into Room 22 of the Alice Motel in Bondi. She continued to receive weekly telephone calls from Kelleher and regularly caught taxis out to the Bay.

'David was always ringing Mum to do certain things for him,' Sascha Huckstepp said. 'On 6 December, I recall that David rang for Mum at our room in the hotel. It was about 9 p.m. He was ringing from the gaol and I recognised his voice. Mum was out this time so David told me to tell her to come out and see him tomorrow. I forgot to give Mum the message.'

Sallie was furious. They argued and Sallie sent Sascha to live with her former husband in Kissing Point Road, Dundas. At some point during the next week Sallie wrote to Bryan. The letter was undated, but in the top right-hand corner of the page Sallie noted the time—*Ten p.m.*

Dear Bryan,

Please ring me when Sascha arrives home—it seems to be an awfully long trip, or perhaps I'm just 'unusually' sensitive to time at the moment, as I'm sure there's not a lot of it left for me!

Oh well, I suppose we all take our chances and get the breaks we deserve—something I should have thought about earlier. Have been receiving rather cryptic messages I can't understand on the voicecall. Either I'm off the air 'something to dwell on' or I'm just not remembering the codes. Either way it seems not good—things I'd rather not think about. Look after Sascha for me if things somehow go wrong—I don't want to seem depressive, but I think I may not be able to make any choices for myself in the near future—

Give her all my love, always,

Sallie-Anne XXXXX

On Christmas Day, Sallie-Anne visited Bryan at Dundas and told him that Dave had instructed her to 'dig up the money'. She mentioned going to Greece with it instead. 'Dad just kept saying that Mum should leave,' Sascha Huckstepp told the coroner, 'and that what Mum was thinking of doing was dangerous. Dad also told Mum they might "get me". I recall the amount of money Mum mentioned was $10 000. I know too that in the past Mum used to sell drugs for Kelleher.' Sascha said that Dave Kelleher gave her mother presents and that she'd seen her mother give a lot of money to Kelleher. 'Bundles,' Sascha said, 'I mean I used to count it.'

When the Joint Task Force were informed by Smith and Muir of a large amount of money and heroin that Kelleher had buried in Narrabeen, the State Commander of the Joint Drug Task Force personally attended Regional Headquarters and listened to a tape that Peter Smith and Terry Muir had made of Sallie. It was suggested to Smith that he try to set up a partnership with Sallie to cut Kelleher out of the picture.

'This idea was not met with a great deal of enthusiasm by Sallie,' Peter Smith reported back, 'basically because she said that if she even took one dollar from that money, Kelleher would have her killed.'

•

From across the windswept yard of the Industrial Training Centre a well-built man with a shaved head was striding towards me. His eyes never left my face. Casually I looked around for the guards, but there were none in the vicinity. I stood up expecting trouble, but the man brushed straight past me for the main gate. Two small girls and a willowy woman appeared and the man scooped up both children in his arms and squeezed them so tightly you could hear their squeals above the sound of the wind cutting through the yard. I watched the woman stroke the man's back, running her bitten fingernails across his shoulder blades. All around the yard women and children were huddled beside men wearing green track suits. I waited another five minutes alone and then walked back to the main gate and told them that Kelleher hadn't come out.

'He's a strange case,' the guard said. He rang through to the cells. 'Visitor for Kelleher.' He gave my name. Minutes passed and then the phone rang. The guard picked it up and listened, observing me closely. 'Kelleher won't see you.'

Even though I'd expected it, I was disappointed. Long Bay was my last hope. There was no doubt that Kelleher knew what had happened to Sallie-Anne and why. At her inquest he put on a performance, knocking over the microphone, toying with Counsel. When asked about his relationship with Sallie he replied, 'it didn't amount to a hill of beans'.

'She's been a friend of yours for a period of time?' Counsel asked.

'Yes, yes.'

'And there were times when you helped her out financially?'

'She was forever snipping me here or there.'

'Do you recall going to Thredbo with Huckstepp?'

'Yes.'

'What can you recall about it?'

'The snow was good.'

'Do you regard this as amusing?'

'No I regard it as an abhorrence. I shouldn't have to put up with months and months of torment, thinking well who's going to jump in next and start telling lies about me for something that I had absolutely nothing to fuckin well do with.'

'Mr Kelleher,' the coroner interrupted, 'I'm not interested in speeches.'

'Well, I'm not interested in you either,' Kelleher said. 'You can stick it—'

•

I walked back along the narrow path, skirting the canteen and the Long Bay art gallery. Going over in my head what had happened to Sallie-Anne in those frantic early weeks of December.

Steven Edward Murray, an addict Sallie had known since the late 1960s, came down from Brisbane to buy some drugs. Sallie believed that Murray had been planted on her 'to get information about Dave'. She contemplated giving him an overdose with her rock of heroin but never did.

Her solicitor Val Bellamy said, 'Steven Edward Murray was a guy who was giving up various people. He took refuge with Sallie and he was giving evidence against a client of mine. My barrister and I tracked Sallie down because we heard this guy was with her and she agreed to tape him and indeed did tape him using our tape recorder and while she had the machine she did a bit of freelance taping of her own to help Kelleher. We had a conference with her in Elizabeth Street and the following morning the coppers grabbed her and put the frighteners on her.'

By 17 December 1985, something had changed. Sallie had grown tired of running out to the gaol for Kelleher. She told Smith and Muir that she was not interested in the brief anymore.

'Dave's given me such a hard time over it,' she said, 'I'm fed up. I love Dave, but I'm sick of wearing his backhanders.'

There was no doubt she was scared of her Blond God. She told Glenn Stone that if Dave knew she was sleeping with other men 'he would knock her'. She told Gwen Beecroft, Scott McCrae, Bryan Huckstepp, Peter Smith, Terry Muir and Neville Scullion of her fear of Kelleher. She told them that, 'Dave might kill me.' But even with her arm in plaster she staggered out to see him in Long Bay.

For two years after her murder Kelleher said nothing. Then he stood up in the dock towards the end of his Supreme Court trial and addressed the jury: 'Sallie-Anne Huckstepp's name has been dragged before you,' he said. 'I want to tell you who killed her and why they killed her. I refrained from telling the whole story at the Coroner's Court. I didn't lie to them, I just told part of what I am going to tell you today.

'Sallie-Anne Huckstepp rang Long Bay Gaol. She practically begged to come out and see me and I said, "No." I said, "I don't want to see you. Full stop." I didn't want to see her. She said, "It's very important Dave, it's something to do with your case, your trial." And after a couple of phone calls, I think it was, and I think I got a letter off her, I'm not sure anyhow what happened, she actually came out and I accepted the visit.

'"Dave," she said, "some police came and saw me a short time ago and they told me they were looking for some furs." She told me that the police had these furs hidden in a safe house. I have already touched on what a safe house is. A safe house is where nobody knows where it exists and they can keep informers or protected people or what have you in places like this. They had a person called Steven Murray in this safe house who stole some furs. The furs belonged to some high-ranking policeman and the police didn't like the idea of Steven Murray stealing the furs from their safe house. So they wanted to get them back. I said, "Look, what are you telling me all this for?"

'She said, "The crux of the matter is I have struck up a deal with them, if I help them get the furs back nobody will get arrested, and they will help me get a brief of this trial for you." Now a brief of a trial is virtually what the Crown or the police are going to do. That might be a big thick folder, it might contain all the letters and telegrams. The brief might be this big or it might be bigger. I don't know. She told me this. And I said, "Frankly, I'm not interested in the brief. I don't want it. It's as simple as that." Then I thought, Hang on, don't throw the baby out with the bath water. Let's see what we can do here.

'I said, "Alright, I'll tell you what to do. What did they actually put to you?" She said, "They want $15 000 for the brief." Plus she had to help them get the furs back. Now this is not out of my mouth alone. There is evidence of this from the detective who did the deal. He tried to skate around the issue, tried to say, "Yes, we did it, but we were only conning her. We were conning her to con Kelleher." Not so.

'I said, "Get a tape recorder, a little mini one and tape these people trying to bribe you." She said, "Alright," and went away. When she came back she said, "We have got them, Dave." She said, "Cold as mackerel." I said, "Fair dinkum?" She said, "It's all on the tapes." I said, "Okay, that's great. Now look, take the tapes, make copies straightaway, bury some of them in the back yard where you are living." I asked her where she was living and she said she was living in Botany with three or four other people. I said, "Get the originals to my solicitor, Val Bellamy." And she said, "How will I do that?" and I said, "I will get my mum to meet you."

'What transpired then was stupidly my mother—a lady of about 65 at the time and quite ill—talked about it with Sallie on the telephone. Somebody's phone was bugged. They met outside the Hordern Pavilion and no sooner than Sallie pulls up the police pull up behind her. They jumped out, they grabbed her, they took her bag, searched her, pulled the tapes out. My mother witnessed all this. They took Sallie away and my mother was left there. Further down the track the police said, "Yeah, sure all that happened, but we were only conning Kelleher." Now if it had only been a con why didn't they search my mother's car. Why didn't they at least expect that my mother would have the $15 000 in her handbag. They didn't search my mother's car. Now Sallie was taken from there to some police station and bashed. The tapes were taken off her. She rang me up and told me she had a broken rib and pains in the side.

'The police were not happy because you see if a person has a tape of anyone you can't ever be sure that there are no other copies. And that was the predicament these police found themselves in.

They could not be positive there were no other copies. I am sure you have all heard how Sallie was found in a pond, floating face down. She had been strangled. They claim she was a police informer. As far as I am concerned she was not. They tried to label Sallie because they were having dealings with her. I can't prove it, but I can tell you that the police killed her.'

•

I got into my car outside Long Bay Gaol and drove off through the back streets, up Malabar Road hugging the coastline, through the beach suburbs of Coogee and Bondi, heading north through Dover Heights along Old South Head Road to Watson's Bay, and past Kelleher's security-screened property in Dunbar Street. I didn't know whether Kelleher really believed the tale he had spun at his trial or whether he was simply making a last ditch stand to deflect attention from the weaknesses of his own defence. Either way the Supreme Court jury didn't buy his story. Convicted of conspiracy to import a commercial quantity of heroin, David John Kelleher was sentenced to life imprisonment.

On 22 May 1989, he was recalled to the Coroner's Court to give additional evidence at Sallie's inquest. During his testimony Kelleher denied that he was jealous if Sallie slept with other men and added, 'I was never in love with Sallie-Anne Huckstepp. I have only been in love with my wife.' He described his friendship with her as 'definitely off' in 1985. But the coroner wrote, 'There is no doubt that Kelleher is a jealous man. The weight of the evidence including the contents of Huckstepp's diaries suggests strongly that Kelleher was Sallie-Anne Huckstepp's lover throughout the months of 1985 up until he was returned to custody.'

Sallie's sister, Debra, said, 'Dave always taught Sallie-Anne to stand up for yourself. If you get caught with dope you never give anyone up. Sallie lived by that code. I remember Sascha and I went along to the courts and Dave sent a note out via his solicitor that he hadn't killed her. He did love her, I mean I think that's why he was so hurt that he thought Sascha and I thought he murdered her.

'We suspected him at first, but Dave would never have killed Sallie-Anne, he was very upset, because she really did do the right thing by him. Because she was such a staunch person. She started hanging with the Feds to do a deal for Dave to get him out of gaol. Then Dave was in there and this Federal copper was out here and you have to understand, Sallie always needed someone to love her.'

•

I swung down through Vaucluse, along New South Head Road to Double Bay and into Darling Point where Sallie had entertained her big Blond God. I drove through Elizabeth Bay, Edgecliff and back through Bellevue Hill. Sallie always wanted to end up here with Dave living in a big white house with sandstone walls, but Kelleher was never going to leave his wife and kids for her. In the end she must have realised that. I kept coming back to the letter that Sallie had written to Bryan Huckstepp, saying there was not a lot of time left for her. Why at this point did she feel unable to make any choices for the future? What were the cryptic messages she was receiving that she didn't understand? Were the codes to do with Kelleher's drug business? *Look after Sascha for me if things go wrong*. She had written those words on or around 14 December 1985, two days after her thirty-first birthday, two days after she had told Peter Smith and Terry Muir in a Japanese restaurant in Chinatown about the $13 million Kelleher had wrapped in plastic and buried in bushland north of the city. Although Kelleher would later dismiss 'her buried treasure story' as fantasy, there was no doubt that she believed he had money hidden.

'Dave always knew he was going to get caught so he buried a lot of money and heroin,' Sallie said. 'I helped him wrap it.'

At the inquest Kelleher said he knew Warren Richards personally and that he didn't believe he was responsible for Sallie's murder. So who was responsible? Did Richards come back into Sallie's life and start dealing with her just so he could set her up? Is that why he kept her on a tight schedule? According to Andrew Haesler, Dave Kelleher was the person with the strongest motive. But why was

Sallie murdered in February? Kelleher knew that she was seeing Peter Smith by late December. He knew of their relationship. He must have seen through her ruse to deceive his mother with the police tapes. Yet Richards met Sallie regularly throughout January. If his role in this was purely to lure her to Centennial Park, why didn't he do it earlier?

Darkness was spreading over the harbour. I kept driving in circles, gazing at shadows in doorways, staring up at the silhouettes in the high apartment windows. Trying to figure out the truth.

11

Task Force Snowy

'The day Sallie was found,' Mrs Krivoshow revealed on the telephone, 'Jack rang me at lunchtime and said Sallie's dead, she's been murdered. I had an excellent psychic. Her name was Joan Moyland. I'd seen her twice before and once she was just brilliant. So I thought I'll go to her. I said to Debbie we'll need something that Sallie wore. Debbie went to the police and asked for her sister's jewellery and they gave it to her. So I took Sallie's gold watch and a gold bracelet up to the psychic and I said this person's been murdered, we want to know if you can pick up anything that might help. I didn't mention names, I didn't mention anything about her.

'So this woman described Sallie. She said, "She's small, she's attractive, she's got strong language." She said, "It happened about five to midnight." When Sallie went through some trees a guy was there and he threw a packet of white powder on the ground. As Sallie bent to grab it he grabbed her by the neck. She reached up and scratched his face. There was another man waiting up the top. They'd come in a dirty police car or wagon. The guy wore jeans and Italian loafers. He'd killed before. He took jewellery from her neck and, after the murder, they took a police scanner from her car which was parked nearby.'

I asked Mrs Krivoshow if I could drive over to talk to her. She gave me an address in Vaucluse and a time to call and I put down the phone. There was a knock at the door. I stepped into the hall and unlatched the chain. Two men were standing outside. One was tall, slouched, with a grey speckled beard and weathered skin. He studied me for a long moment. 'I'm Detective Con Moores from Task Force Snowy,' he said. 'Can we come in?'

Stepping outside, I clicked the apartment door shut behind me. His partner stood on my right side and brought out a notepad and pen. Typed across the top of the manila folder he was holding were the words: LANFRANCHI–HUCKSTEPP.

Detective Moores leaned forward. 'I want to talk to you about inquiries you've been making into the Huckstepp murder. Have you had any criminal convictions?'

'No.'

'Have you spoken with Debra Krivoshow?' he said. 'I don't want you talking to witnesses. I can't prevent you, but it might upset delicate investigations in progress.' His partner watched me in silence, writing down my name and date of birth. 'We'll be speaking to you again,' Moores said. The two police walked down the corridor.

I went inside and chained the door. How had they got this address? Nobody except my family knew I was here. I picked up the phone and rang my contact, W.B., in the Federal Police. I told him I'd had a visit from two New South Wales detectives. Could he find out what Task Force Snowy was doing? He said he'd ring me back in ten minutes. Rattled, I paced the small book-ridden apartment.

Two hours and 45 minutes later the phone rang. 'I've had to pull in a lot of favours to get you this,' the Federal Police officer said. I had never met my contact, W.B., in the flesh but I guessed from his voice that he was in his mid-forties. 'Are you sitting down?'

'Why?'

'Because this is going to take some time.'

I grabbed a pen off the bookcase and tried to jot down everything I could. This is what he told me.

•

On 11 April 1994, registered police informant SS520 of the New South Wales Police Service was transferred from Goulburn Gaol to Unit 3, C Wing of the Special Purpose Centre at Long Bay Correctional Complex. A seventeen-stone heroin addict, Gary Trevor T— [*Subject under Witness Protection*], had 22 recorded convictions for assault, 'armed robs' and breaking and entering. Half of his 33 years he'd spent in corrective institutions. When told by the gaol superintendent he was to share a unit with another prisoner in protection, Gary asked, 'Who?' The superintendent wouldn't tell him.

'To my horror,' Gary said, 'when I opened the cell door I saw "Neddy" Smith.'

Arthur Stanley (Ned) Smith at the age of 49 was an imposing sight. Standing six foot four, weighing sixteen-and-a-half stone with snowy white hair, transfixing eyes and an uncontrollable twitching of his large head, Smith had a sinister appearance. Rated the best street-fighter to come out of the New South Wales prison system in twenty years, Smith's convictions included rape, armed robbery and the drunken murder of a tow-truck driver. Placed in protection after informing on New South Wales Police officers to the Independent Commission Against Corruption, Smith's reputation in the underworld was of an extremely violent man who would fly into murderous rages.

The minute Gary entered Unit 3, Smith fronted him, standing over his bunk, eyes burning. 'I've checked you out with the NCA,' Smith said. 'You're a dog. I will not be telling you anything about myself at anytime in the future.'

Smith made Gary sign a Statutory Declaration that he would not enter into any conversation with him about any of his legal matters or past crimes. That night the younger man heard grunting and puffing in his adjoining cell as Smith completed his nightly quota of 250 pushups in sets of 50.

During the day the doors to Cells 11 and 12 were left open and the two men exercised in the courtyard at the rear of Unit 3, the size of a small two-bedroom flat with a shared living area for cooking and washing at the front. The two cells, situated in the centre of the unit with their own toilet, shower, bed, table and shelves around the walls, were both locked every night at 6 p.m. and re-opened at 6.45 a.m. The two prisoners sparred in the cells. Even with Parkinson's Disease and fifteen years his senior, Smith was much stronger and quicker than Gary. For 30 years Smith had practised throwing king hits in gaolyards and backroom bars. He knew how to kill unarmed. He filled Gary's ears with stories of biting the cheeks off a man in a Sydney hotel and pulling blokes' eyes out with his fingers. Gary was overawed by the older man's physical presence and psychopathic charisma.

'We played Scrabble three times a day,' Gary said. 'Neddy used to win most of the time, but he was a bad cheat. Sometimes I'd beat him and he'd hate it.'

In the first few days Smith laid down the law: Gary was not to eat out of Smith's side of the fridge; he was never to go into Smith's cell alone. When he was in a mellow mood Smith played practical jokes such as putting rotting vegetables under Gary's pillow and tipping scalding tea in the younger man's lap. One day they were in the cells listening to the radio and 'Danny Boy' came on. 'Ned had tears in his eyes,' Gary said, 'because he had a son named Danny. Neddy was very strong on family.' The two men shared a similar taste in old-time music. 'I'll Take You Home Again Kathleen' was a favourite. As they grew closer, Smith handed Gary chapters from the manuscript he was writing on a Corona word processor about unsolved murders in the Sydney underworld.

'Tell us what you think, Gaz,' Smith said. Gary read the chapters, helping correct the older man's spelling and syntax. The truth about these killings, Smith explained, could never be revealed.

'In the first week Neddy said he'd tell me what really happened,' Gary said, 'but if I said anything to anybody he'd kill me.'

While they were exercising in the yard the next morning, Smith described shooting a brothel-keeper in a cellar. The man's last words were, 'I'd die for you, Ned.' And Ned had replied, 'You're about to, you cunt.'

'Ned started laughing and I started laughing too,' Gary said. When Gary returned to his bunk he discovered that he'd left his recorder running after taping FM music off the radio for his wife Carol. He waited until Smith was locked in his cell and, sticking his head under a pillow, rewound the tape and heard the faint, yet distinctive, voice of Smith detailing how he'd buried the man in Botany Bay.

All night Gary stayed awake, tossing and turning. He had his parole coming up. Maybe he could use it for that. But Smith was a maniac. He'd kill him if he even suspected what he'd done. Next morning Gary rang his case officer, Detective John Wilson. He had information he wanted to trade. Detective Wilson encouraged him to 'get more dirt on Smith'. Gary started leaving his tape recorder on in his cell while he and Smith exercised in the yard. Any time the conversation related to the killings, Gary was able to flick a switch and the cassette player would function. 'I had to make sure Ned didn't see the cassette player flashing,' Gary said, 'or hear the sound of it switching off.'

To disguise the contents of the Akai brand SX-90 tapes stored in his cell, he wrote on them, *Spiritual Growth, Songs for Caroline Vol 1, Carol's Music Vol 2.* Twenty minutes before they were locked down for the night was the best time to switch on the machine. His hands shook from nerves as badly as Smith's did from Parkinson's. On 14 July 1994, Gary taped four conversations with Smith as they paced up and down the kitchen area of the unit just outside his cell. Gary listened to the tapes and transcribed what he could. Much of it was inaudible but towards the end of tape 4 Smith boasted of one murder he'd committed. The one he'd enjoyed the most.

Sallie-Anne Huckstepp.

'Killing her was the most satisfying thing I ever done in me life,' Smith said.

The next morning, when Smith was receiving a visit, Gary handed the tapes over to Detective Sergeant Wilson who reported to his senior officers. On Monday, 18 July 1994, at South Region Command, Assistant Commissioner Peate of the New South Wales Police Service, Detective Superintendent Bull and Detective Inspector Laycock commenced Operation 'Snowy'. That afternoon Task

Force detectives went to the Supreme Court building and saw Mr Justice Allen who authorised the use of a Listening Device warrant.

The voices on the homemade tapes were so distorted they were virtually useless. On Friday morning Gary received a new computer in his cell. Inside it police technicians had installed a listening device behind the disk drive. Voice-activated, the concealed tape recorder began to whirr loudly the moment Smith walked into Gary's cell. 'What's that noise?' The older man moved towards the computer.

'Just the disk drive.'

'Lemme take a look.'

'No no, it's fine. Really.'

With his heart thumping in his chest, Gary managed to get Smith out of his cell and rang Wilson. They had a code worked out. If he needed to see his case officer urgently he'd send a message, 'Bring me more pens'. And Wilson would drive out to Long Bay. Gary blew up over the faulty device, accusing Wilson of trying to get him killed. The listening device was replaced. Over the following weeks, the younger man encouraged conversation with Smith on the subject of murder. But Smith grew suspicious. When Gary tried to steer the conversation back onto Sallie Huckstepp, Smith glared at him. 'What do you want to know about her for? You going to write a book you cunt?'

'No, no, I'm just interested that's all.'

'You'd better not be telling on me you weak cunt.'

Gary laughed. 'No, I'm not telling.'

'You been asking a lot of questions lately.'

'Yeah, well there's nothing wrong with that.'

'Depends on what you want to know for.'

Gary invented a story that he wanted to kill a man who had sexually molested his stepdaughter. He convinced Smith as they strode up and down outside their cells that he needed to know the best way to murder someone.

'Don't ever strangle any cunt,' Smith said. 'It's the hardest thing in the fuckin' world.'

'No.'

'You see 'em do it in the movies, it's just bullshit.'

'Yeah.'

'I'm pretty strong and I did it once, let me show you something.'

'Oh.'

'That's what you got to do, grab 'em like that.'

'Oh fuck!'

'Cuts 'em—'

'That cut me air straight off!'

'There's two lumps there. Just feel that. Feel that. Those little lumps.'

'Yeah I felt—'

'You just grab there and they can't, they can't move. They're paralysed once you do that.'

'Sorry.'

'Paralyse their whole body.'

'Yeah.'

'Double-barrel shotgun to the head. That's the best way of killing them.'

'Jesus . . . let's walk.'

[The sound of footsteps echo in the cell]

'If you shoot them in the eye they live longer. It's easy killing cunts, but don't get used to it.'

'No, I won't.'

'When you find out how easy, how good it is, you just want to kill everyone—'

'No, well I won't be that stupid.'

'Don't rush it mate. I waited three weeks for Sallie.'

'Yeah?'

'And she turned up right in the middle of the park, middle of the night.'

'Yeah?'

'Wobbling her arse she was.'

'Jesus.'

'If it's got to be done, it's got to be done.'

'Yeah.'

'Nothing you can do about it.'

'I'm a bit scared. That's all.'

'If you want to, I'll give you a hand, or I'll fuckin' do it for you.'

'Yeah well, no, no, no, you've got enough on your plate.'

'One more won't fuckin' hurt me.'

'I don't mind if you come up with me, but I want to do it.'

'Well, I wouldn't trust you that much, Gaz.'

'Oh, right.'

'I'd do it for you, but I don't want you near me. Christ no.'

'No mate, no, you got too much on your plate.'

'If anything . . . I'd have to fuckin' zot you too. I couldn't trust you.'

'No, I'd do it, you can just watch.'

'I couldn't trust you that much, mate.'

'Oh right. Fair enough.'

'I don't know you that well.'

'Well [coughs], I'll just do it myself you know, I mean, I'll be okay.'

•

First thing next morning Gary rang Wilson. 'Bring me more pens.' When his case officer arrived at Special Purpose, Gary handed him the tapes. 'This bloke gives me nightmares,' he said. 'I want out of here.'

'Don't worry, Gary, we'll look after you. But we need more details.'

Gary returned to his cell where he kept a computer log of his murder conversations with Smith and a diary.

•

Tues 27/9/94—'Today the screws had their annual picnic day, so we were both confined to the unit. I had hidden the microphone as usual last night before going to bed and had trouble setting the tape recorder back up today due to Ned continuously pacing in circles around the kitchen all morning. I got it set up about two and activated the tape. An hour later I managed to get Neddy onto his favourite topic, himself, and tried to steer it around to the topic of murders.

'Smith was very suspicious of me and wanted to know why I was asking about Sallie-Anne Huckstepp again. We moved out of my cell area. Playing to his ego is the only way I can get him to talk about the murders he committed, but it's not something I relish.

'I'm certainly taking a big risk. No-one else has put themselves out to stop him and if I slip up, I'm dead!

'Subject then came into my cell and conversed with me on the topic of murder. He gave excellent descriptions of how he strangled and drowned Sallie-Anne Huckstepp. Subject said he wanted his eyes to be the last thing she saw before she died.'

Wed 28/9/94—'Returned from work at about 10.50 a.m. and set up tape. Smith continuously talked through the tape how when he gets out he will kill people. Looks like I can add my name to his list when he finds out!

'As soon as I can, I'm getting away from the unit. There is something very wrong with Smith. He's satanic.'

Thurs 29/9/94—'Decided to ring Wilson to order some more tapes and diskettes for the computer. Loaded tape when Smith had gone to his cell.'

Fri 30/9/94—'Didn't activate tape at all today due to Smith's suspicion becoming aroused yesterday afternoon. Smith asked me why I wanted to know things he had already told me about. He said he would kill any person who informed on him, he said he would kill their family and the friends of their family. He knows my address and the address of my stepdaughter!'

Sun 2/10/94—'I'm fed up to the back teeth with sharing this unit with Smith. I want to move out of here this week.'

Wed 5/10/94—'I just can't tolerate one more day of Smith's selfishness. I'll ask nicely to be put somewhere else. It'll mean the end of the operation, but I've done the very best I can.'

Sun 16/10/94—'I am very happy to report that the subject has just moved out of the unit. He asked to see me in the pool room at 2 p.m. The subject loves games, particularly computer games where shooting and killing is involved.'

Mon 17/10/94—'Subject said that it was Superintendent [*name deleted*] who wanted Lanfranchi murdered and that he had Rogerson do it.'

Tues 18/10/94—'Subject talked to me of other murders in the pool room. I just have to get it on tape. I need to get my computer into the pool room somehow and get hold of as many shooting and war-type games as possible to teach Smith.'

Wed 19/10/94—'Smith has found out information that my parole is coming up through his NCA case officer. My life's in danger and the NCA are leaking information about me to Smith!'

Thursday 20/10/94—'Today Smith asked me, "How come you been asking so many questions lately?" I quickly changed the conversation and got him out of my cell but he threatened me quite strongly.'

The following day Gary Trevor T— was released into the State Witness Protection Program. Police assured him that his role in operation 'Snowy' would remain secret.

On Monday, 14 November 1994, Detective Sergeant Conrad Moores, after being comprehensively briefed by Detective John Wilson, commenced duties at Task Force Group State Command as senior investigator into the Huckstepp murder.

•

'Have you heard the listening device tapes?' I asked my Federal Police contact over the phone.

'I've seen a rough transcript,' he said. 'I'm trying to get hold of a copy now, but I warn you. It's chilling stuff.'

'Does Smith say why he killed Sallie?'

'He says he killed her because she tried to tape him and Rogerson to get evidence about crimes they were committing. Now some fool's leaked Gary's tapes to the media,' he said. 'He's terrified New South Wales Police are trying to bump him.'

'Why would New South Wales detectives leak their own evidence?'

'Everything goes back to the Lanfranchi shooting,' he said. 'You're dealing with the same players.'

•

Two days later, Sallie Huckstepp's photo was splashed across the inside of the *Sun-Herald*:

EXTRACT, 22 January

I KILLED SIX: NEDDY SMITH
Confessions rock police, underworld

Convicted murderer Arthur Stanley 'Neddy' Smith in a series of sensational admissions detailed the gruesome particulars of the strangulation of former drug addict Sallie-Anne Huckstepp and five other murders.

A prominent Sydney solicitor and columnist, Chris Murphy, had received an anonymous bundle of fifteen photocopied pages 'dropped off at his office' including excerpts from the Smith transcripts. I read through the alleged confession, looking for details on Sallie's murder that only someone present at the crime scene would have known. Smith claimed to have been lying in wait in the grass dressed in black when she arrived 'for a meeting with her boy-friend [*sic*] drug supplier'. After strangling Sallie-Anne, Smith removed a Federal Police identification badge from a plastic bag and dropped it near her body. He said it was given to him by Roger Rogerson.

The inclusion of the Federal badge bothered me. No Federal badge had been found at Busby's Pond. Despite the report in the *National Times* to the contrary, there was nothing sinister about Constable Bradley Conner's loss and subsequent retrieval of his collar number 8326. If Smith had lied about the police badge, then could the rest of his story be believed? Why had he included a false detail which could so easily be checked? Either Smith was stupid or he was extremely cunning.

According to the newspaper report he'd strangled Sallie-Anne 'because Roger Rogerson had said she was taping police who were supplying heroin to the drug trade'.

Did that mean Rogerson ordered him to do it? Or had Smith acted on his own initiative? Back in my flat I hunted through the owner's extensive collection of noir fiction for Smith's autobiography, *Neddy*, and spent the afternoon searching for a link between Smith and Warren Richards. On p. 229 I found it:

> I teamed up with a guy called Warren. He was strange, but a good earner. I made plenty of money with him. He used to have this thing about cop cars. As soon as he saw one, regardless of where he was, he would take off at 100 miles an hour. He once killed a girl accidently while escaping from police. We lasted until one of the charges he was on bail for came up and he was sentenced to a few years jail. We remained friends.

Sallie-Anne had taped Federal Police and she had taped Gary Adam Spencer attached to the Drug Law Enforcement Bureau of the New South Wales Police. At her inquest, Spencer said he had no knowledge that Sallie had taped him until after her death.

'No rumour had reached you that there was a tape recording?' Andrew Haesler had asked.

'No.'

'No-one from Internal Affairs contacted you prior to her death?'

'No.'

'When you say on the tape to Sallie-Anne, "My blue, my mistake, I did speak to him", what does that refer to?'

'I spoke to another detective in the Drug Squad,' Constable Spencer said, 'to find out if Sallie-Anne would supply information.'

'Was that other Detective Con Moores?'

'Yes.'

'You're sure that Sallie-Anne didn't say, "You can ring Con, he's my referee, he'll speak for me."'

'No.'

'Sallie didn't say, "Con'll tell you I'm reliable."'

'No.'

'And you say the next contact you had with her was on the day she died?'

'That's correct.'

'Do you recall the substance of that call?'

'She, Sallie-Anne, asked to see me, she gave no explanation, but I told her I was busy or I was unavailable and could she ring back at a later date.'

•

I sat down on a rickety chair and grabbed the phone book. Con Moores had worked in the Drug Squad with Gary Spencer; Con Moores had dealings with Warren Richards; and Con Moores had dealings with Sallie-Anne. Now he'd been appointed senior investigator into her murder. There was nothing untoward about that, but it was one hell of a coincidence. I rang the Task Force and spoke to Detective Moores. I asked if we could meet the next day and he agreed.

We met at a cafe halfway between the gay bars of Oxford Street and Task Force State Command in Goulburn Street. I was drinking fruit juice when Moores walked in partnered by a young, tanned detective wearing a lime-green tie, brown leather jacket, knife-creased slacks and slip-on loafers. 'This is Wayne Starling,' Moores said. Starling smiled in my direction, but it was a smile that gave nothing away. They ordered black coffees and Moores leaned across the table, his grey-white beard clipped close to his face. 'Did Kelleher talk to you out at the Bay?'

I shook my head. 'Tell me about these tapes.'

'Don't believe everything you read in the papers,' Con Moores said. 'What are you doing this for anyway?'

I told him I was trying to get to the truth; it sounded naïve when I said it.

'I used to see Sallie and Debbie up the Cross,' Con Moores said in a dry, flat voice. 'Standing up both ends of Darlinghurst Road and they wouldn't be talking to each other, but as sisters go they were close. Sascha was living by herself when she was fourteen. She used to get around the Cross when she was young with her mother living here and there, one guy after another. Sascha grew up fast. She had to. You get the word on Sallie-Anne that she was an informing junkie prostitute that would sell you out for the price of a fix. There were many people who despised her. On the other hand she was a very good mother. She used to let her daughter package the heroin.' Moores looked at me. 'Have you spoken to Gwen Beecroft yet? Beecroft knows much more than she's letting on.'

Con Moores stood up. He was tall and lean and there was a weariness in his eyes, the jaded look of a Major Crime Squad detective. I got the bill, standing at the counter beside Detective Starling who hadn't spoken a word to me. 'If Kelleher agrees to talk to you,' Moores said quietly, 'let us know.'

•

Walking home through Darlinghurst I realised how they had got my address. Long Bay. I kept thinking about Sallie-Anne's involvement with New South Wales Police. The names of half a dozen Kings Cross detectives were found in her blue and pink address book, and no doubt Con Moores' name was one of them. I did not believe Detective Moores had anything to do with Sallie-Anne's death, but from what her sister, Debra, had revealed to me only days earlier—when I flew up to Queensland to see her—it was fair to say he knew why she was murdered.

'About three or four months after Sallie died,' Debra said, 'I wanted to get out of the whole drug scene. So I rang Con Moores up because he'd looked after me at the Cross, then all of sudden it turned into a physical affair. Con treated me nice, he looked after me for about a year. I used to strap on his holster and run around the flat naked with his gun on. He paid my rent. I think he wanted to know exactly what I knew. I used to go and drink with them at the Bourbon and Beefsteak, all the Drug Squad detectives.

'And it was funny after the inquest because Gary Spencer walked in one night wearing a white jacket and he had on white shoes and all the other detectives were putting shit on him, and I said, "C'mon he doesn't look that bad." And Con turned around to me and said, "Don't you ever give him any pity, Debra! I'm telling you now."

'And just the way he said that,' Debra said quietly, 'there was an implication there that it was something to do with my sister's death.'

•

The answer machine was flashing when I stepped into the apartment and slipped the key from the deadlock. While I fried up some fish, I pressed the play button and let W.B. bring me up to date.

A team of five divers from the New South Wales Police Diving Unit had conducted a briefing at Centennial Park shortly before dawn this morning. Their instructions were to search for a six-starred Federal Police badge. At 7.00 a.m. they entered the water and commenced a wade search of the western bank of Busby's Pond. The bottom was packed hard with sand but further out the bottom of the pond consisted of one metre of suspended weeds and mulch. Divers then commenced diving in scuba gear in the north-west corner and at the mouth of the stormwater drain near the willow tree. They used underwater metal detectors but the large amount of metal debris in the pond hampered their usefulness. Five hours later they gave up the search. Task Force detectives then interviewed Peter Mark Parker Smith, formerly of the Australian Federal Police, and now a security consultant, at the Sydney Police Centre. In his statement Peter Smith said, 'I have never reported lost or stolen any of my police identification badges.'

It didn't surprise me. No Federal Police badge had been dropped at Busby's Pond. That part of Smith's story was a lie.

•

Frying fish in a small apartment is not a great idea. The smell still lingered in the flat when I rang W.B. the following evening.

'I've got something you might like to hear,' he said. 'Ned Smith's statement. Want me to read it out?'

'Go ahead.'

'I'm not very good at doing voices,' W.B. said, 'So you'll just have to imagine it's Smith talking':

> As soon as I was placed in Unit 3 with T— I told him I was aware of his reputation as a dog and that I would not be telling him anything about myself at anytime in the future. T— is a heroin addict and has been for many years. In Unit 3 he was receiving large doses of methadone seven days a week and valium twice daily. He was bombed out of his head most days. I knew exactly how Huckstepp had been murdered having been told by Rogerson and by following the inquest. Also the detective who was originally in charge of the Huckstepp murder had rang Rogerson the same day at the Iron Duke Hotel telling him about how she was murdered and the phone was bugged and the officer was taken off the case and had to front the police tribunal.
>
> I can't remember all the shit I told T— because I only ever spoke shit to him knowing that every word was being handed over to John 'Buckets' Wilson and then to Brian Harding that born-again Christian. T— had a code worked out with Wilson for when he wanted him to come over. He would ring Wilson and say, 'I need some new pens, can you bring them straight out.'
>
> Wilson would drop everything and drive straight out to Special Purposes to see him. As if a senior fucking detective would drop whatever he was doing to come out just to bring T— some pens. T— must have thought that I was a bigger fool than I thought. I was aware that T— was taping me with his twin tape deck that he had set up at the foot of his bed. The tape deck had flashing red lights when it was taping. It was impossible to miss them.

There was a long silence and then W.B. said, 'Well, he would say that *now*, wouldn't he? Something else you might like to know.

Con Moores and Wayne Starling went to Glebe Coroner's Court early this morning and collected three boxes of records. They spoke to the coroner, Greg Glass, who has issued a warrant to exhume Huckstepp's remains from Rookwood Cemetery.'

•

I drove out to Vaucluse around seven the following evening, the air filled with the honking of car horns. Traffic blocked the intersection on Ocean Avenue. My fingers tapped at the steering wheel. Why would Neddy Smith tell a prisoner he knew to be a junkie and a registered informer about murders he'd committed? Sallie said that Smith was a fool, but I wasn't convinced yet that he'd killed her. The big question was why? Why nearly five years after Lanfranchi? The reason W.B. had given me over the phone didn't stand up. Sallie had nothing to do with taping Neddy Smith or Rogerson. For a start they wouldn't have let her come within a mile of them. The only policeman she was known to have taped, apart from Peter Smith and Terry Muir of the Australian Federal Police, was Detective Constable Gary Spencer attached to the Drug Law Enforcement Bureau. Seven hours before Sallie was murdered she had rung Spencer and asked to see him. Spencer told her he was busy.

The traffic started to move and New South Head Road curved past the Golden Sheaf Hotel in Double Bay where Sallie had met Spencer eight weeks before her death at 6.30 p.m. and taped their conversation for 90 minutes. Was that the reason she had to go? Was he the police officer who inadvertently caused her death? If Neddy Smith did kill Sallie, who gave him the order? Was it Rogerson or was it someone higher up? The road climbed past Rose Bay Convent and then levelled out to meet the sea. I drove past elegant Vaucluse houses with white-framed windows that looked west towards Port Jackson, emerald-green BMWs and sleek black Mercedes secured behind wrought-iron gates. The pavements were spotless. I parked two streets away and walked down a slope towards a big block of units. The sun was sinking into the harbour.

Mrs Krivoshow was much younger than I'd expected. A tall,

handsome woman, smartly dressed. Meeting her made me wish I'd worn a suit. She directed me to a chair in the lounge room of her split-level apartment and a white fluffy dog ran down the stairs and sniffed at my big scuffed shoes.

'Here Ziggy, Ziggy, Ziggy. No.'

The little white dog skittered back up the polished staircase, paws scratching on brushbox. I knew nothing about Mrs Krivoshow except that she was Sallie's second stepmother and Jack's third wife. 'So when did you first meet Sallie?' I started.

'I met Sallie when Jack came down to Melbourne with her in 1970,' Mrs Krivoshow said, 'and she was really nice but there was something underneath, I guess. Sallie was fine, she was pleasant, she was intelligent, she was obliging, she was all those things, but I think in retrospect, it all goes back to a dysfunctional childhood.'

When Mrs Krivoshow came up to Sydney to live with Jack she didn't see anything of Sallie. Sallie had run away from home and was living with the manager of Billy Thorpe's band.

'Jack and I bought a flat at Drummoyne and Sallie went to Minda Juvenile Centre and when Sallie was released she came to live with us for three months. Because Sallie had had all this freedom and so forth, all I asked was for the place to be kept clean and Sallie was only fifteen, and I said to Jack, Sallie should be home at a reasonable hour, but no, Sallie wasn't responding, so I thought maybe it's best Sallie goes to somewhere she can. I didn't see Sallie for the next seven years. It was 1980. We were living in Queensland and I just didn't want to know. Sallie was going through a bad time and when we came down we visited her in Woollahra and from then on we had a very good relationship and Sallie wrote me a beautiful letter and thanked me for coming to visit and Sallie said that she knew it was hard and that she was jealous of me.

'I think Sallie would've been jealous of any woman around her father,' Mrs Krivoshow said. 'The day we met after the seven-year period, we all went to have coffee and Sallie said to me, "Oh, isn't Dad good-looking. If he wasn't my father . . ."

'And I thought, oh, maybe she's got one of these fantasies about her father. And I said to Debbie, I was a bit concerned about Sallie's comment. I was trying to get in deeper, to see maybe she was just jealous of anyone coming into his life. She was only five when her natural mother left. Jack was very proud of the girls. He married his second wife to provide a mother for them. Estelle used to put a cardboard sign around Debbie and Sallie's necks and parade them up and down the street in Bondi if they were bad. But Sallie would have had a problem with anyone who came into Jack's life. It's possible she felt like the little mother in the home, the little lady in the house and she didn't want another woman coming in.

'When I first got with Jack,' Mrs Krivoshow continued, 'I thought isn't this nice, I'll make a nice little home environment with Jack and the two girls, but it wasn't to be. They knew more than I knew. I didn't know about drugs, I'd never seen drugs. I didn't know what marijuana was. They just knew so much more. They were quite street smart. They used to have strip shows and charge the local boys twenty cents and all this jazz. Sallie used to say, "I wish I could find my real mother." But I couldn't play mother to Sallie. I was only eight years older. I just couldn't do it.

'One night, it would've been in '85, I read about this visiting clairvoyant up from Tasmania and I made an appointment and I arranged to meet Sallie beforehand and then Sallie was going to see this clairvoyant after me. I said to Sallie what did the lady say to you and Sallie said, "She told me I'd be having a lot to do with the police."

'Sallie brought all this corruption to light, it was Sallie-Anne who alerted everybody to Rogerson and all the rest of what's gone on in this city. But the press are very cruel and unrelenting here. The way they always referred to her as Sallie-Anne Prostitute and Drug Addict. Sallie was forced into prostitution. She had an excellent personality, she was really a communicator. She was very charming, a lovely girl, well-spoken, she wasn't like a lot of the poor unfortunate girls you see on the street. She was articulate, she was extremely intelligent. She really had everything going for her. It was an absolute tragedy. Sallie never asked for help from her father. She had honour in many respects, she had a lot of honour. She was straight up and down. Sallie had backbone. She would fight her own messes.

'I must say,' Mrs Krivoshow said on her doorstep, 'both girls always had excellent dress sense. Sallie always looked a million dollars. She was a classy girl. Absolute class. She just had it. When she came up to Queensland with Sascha to visit, I said to her, ' "Why don't you go straight, Sallie, meet somebody decent, have a nice normal life."

'And she said, "Oh no, I couldn't."

'Sallie wasn't interested in having a nice suburban life.'

•

Seventeen kilometres west of Sydney in the heart of the working-class suburb of Lidcombe lies the largest necropolis in the southern hemisphere. More than one million people are buried within the boundaries of Rookwood's 777 acres. Gothic tombs, gargoyled urns and giant Celtic crosses keep watch over the remains of the dead.

The temperature was climbing when I arrived at the Jewish sector at 7.45 a.m. and saw that Sallie-Anne's black granite headstone had already been removed. A team of overalled police officers was erecting a hessian screen around gravesite 684. White vans, a back-hoe and special police wagons encircled the tent-like barrier and members of the press were being kept back behind a rope. I stood on a rise and watched, through a gap in the hessian screen, as rescue-squad officers struggled to unearth Sallie's coffin. Water had seeped into her grave and the officers worked with great care, trying to prise the rotting wooden casket from its plot.

I heard shouts of frustration as Sallie's coffin flexed and creaked, resisting their efforts. Overalled policemen wiped sweat from their brows and scraped wet clay from the soles of their boots. The sun burned the backs of their necks and the air smelled of disinterred earth. Whatever could be said about their treatment of Sallie-Anne when she was alive, there was no doubting the pains New South Wales Police took when she was dead.

For three hours they worked without break. At 11.05 a.m.,

amidst loud murmurs of relief, her pine coffin was brought to the surface in one piece and laid gently on plastic sheeting. A bunch of detectives stepped forward; Crime Scene Officers took soil samples and photographs. The lid of the coffin was eased open under the supervision of Professor Hilton from the Institute of Forensic Medicine, and the remains of Sallie-Anne Huckstepp were carefully placed in body bags in a fresh coffin which was finally lifted into the rear of Flanagan's Mortuary ambulance.

A young plainclothes detective whom I recognised as Wayne Starling climbed in beside her, and under tight security, the ambulance backed out between the white police wagons and drove at a steady 25 kilometres an hour towards the Barker Street gates.

At 2.10 p.m. on 13 February, I would learn in the days to come, the skeletal remains of a human on trolley number 55 were wheeled into the main autopsy room of the Glebe Mortuary. Professor Hilton, Dr Oettle, Detective Sergeant Con Moores and Detective Wayne Starling from Task Force Snowy, forensic assistants and other police officers watched as the blue zippered body bag was opened.

Inside was a clear plastic sheet folded in envelope fashion, and written on the plastic in indelible red ink was the word, 'Huckstepp'.

Assisted by Dr Oettle, Professor Hilton made a preliminary examination of the body fluid and skeletal remains. Sallie-Anne's bones were X-rayed while still in the body bags.

The following morning the examination continued. Two portions of her hyoid were retrieved by sieving and were then washed. Professor Hilton inspected the hyoid closely, a small horseshoe-shaped bone found in the throat between the thyroid cartilage and the base of the tongue. Under magnification of the dissecting microscope, the appearance of the hyoid suggested an incomplete fracture with no displacement. Her right forearm showed a healing fracture; a surgical plate with six screws was present, bridging the fracture line. Sallie's skeletal remains were cleaned and photographed. Her skeleton showed appreciative demineralisation. Fifteen finger and toenails were recovered along with a container of fluid taken from the casket, a sample of head hair and three bones including her left femur.

Mortuary staff placed the exhibits in two large resealable plastic bags and handed them to Detective Wayne Starling who conveyed them under escort—along with two jars of Sallie's fingernail clippings found in a brown paper bag labelled F587/37 at the Inner West Crime Scene Unit—to the Lidcombe Analytical Laboratories where they were DNA profiled.

At seven o'clock the next morning the radiographer, Mr Ian White, took twenty radiographs of Sallie-Anne's skull and skeletal remains using the highest quality X-ray film. The X-rays showed a fracture on the greater horn of the hyoid; no observable fracture had shown up in the radiographs taken ten years earlier, although there was a chance that the hairline fracture had been missed.

At 12 p.m. on the following day Detectives Moores and Starling from Task Force Snowy went to the WITSEC [Witness Security] area of the Sydney Police Centre and spoke to registered informant SS520, Gary Trevor T—, about particular details from the listening device tapes. At 3 p.m. Dr Oettle was called to the sixth floor of the Sydney Police Centre and shown photographs of marks to the neck of Sallie-Anne from the 1986 post-mortem. The discovery of the fractured hyoid was now considered to be an important breakthrough. Sallie's skeletal remains were returned to the body storage room of Glebe Mortuary on trolley number 55 and, at 9.40 a.m. on 14 March, they were placed in a casket and sealed while the police video unit taped the process.

The casket was then conveyed to the Northern Suburbs Cemetery for cremation. At 5 p.m. Task Force Snowy detectives attended the Downing Centre Court Complex where they held a conversation with Mr Barnett SM who granted police a warrant to search Unit 7, Cell 19, 'C' Block, Special Purpose Prison, Long Bay Correctional Complex.

•

I returned home from Rookwood Cemetery, knowing nothing of this. Exhausted from standing in the sun, I lay down on the bed, with the red light of the answer machine flashing at the edge of my vision. The stark image of Sallie's opened grave, and the grunts of police as the casket was raised from its damp tomb, stayed with me.

For a week I remained in bed, feverish, my chest weighed down with some strange viral infection that was exacerbated by the dust from the thousands of books in my borrowed apartment. The only sounds were the ticking of the fridge, the short sharp ringing of the phone and the click of the answer machine.

I didn't know why W.B. was risking his career to bring me information. The reason he gave was unconvincing and I suspected that he had known Sallie-Anne more personally than he admitted. He never left a name when he called and his voice sounded distorted as if he'd gone out of his way to disguise it. I don't know if he would have lost his job for what he was doing but, like all senior police, he had learned to be cautious. DNA tests carried out at the Forensic Laboratory, he said, had confirmed that the major DNA component from the fingernails of the left hand belonged to Sallie-Anne as determined from the profile obtained from her left femur. The minor components of DNA under her fingernails were foreign to her but the Forensic Biologist was unable to derive a DNA profile for the individual sources of the minor components. Task Force Snowy were now concentrating all their efforts on the correlation between the fractured hyoid and Smith's description of the murder on the legally obtained digital audio tapes. Developments were happening so rapidly over there that he could barely keep up with them. W.B. never explained exactly who at the Task Force was feeding him his information but it was obvious that it came from a very high source in State Command.

'Listen,' I said, when I had finally recovered enough to get to the phone. 'I really need to get hold of that DAT transcript.'

'Do you want to hear what I've got to tell you?'

'Let me grab a pen.'

•

At 10.07 this morning Task Force Snowy detectives, led by Superintendent Laycock and carrying video cameras, still photographic equipment and silver steel suitcases, had arrived at C Wing Special Purpose Unit, Long Bay Prison Complex. The moment they arrived, Prisoner 136 requested to make an urgent phone call to the Independent Commission Against Corruption.

'G'day Ned, I'm Detective Superintendent Laycock and we have a warrant to search your cell. Do you understand?'

Smith was chewing on a paper clip. 'I'm not saying nothin' to you without my solicitor.'

'Will you give me permission to take a blood sample—'

'No,' Smith said.

Detectives began to search Smith's cell. Watched by Prison Officers, they picked up articles belonging to Smith and showed and described them to the video camera. Some of the articles were put in brown paper bags and some in plastic bags. Pubic hairs were collected from Smith's toilet seat with sticky tape, an apple core was retrieved from the bottom of a wastebasket and a bloodstained handkerchief and dirty underpants were removed from a clothes receptacle. Every detail was recorded. Among documents seized in a wardrobe by Task Force detectives was the manuscript of Smith's second book, *Catch and Kill Your Own*, a fictional account of Sydney's unsolved gangland murders. Detective Sergeant Moores picked up another document and asked Smith what it was.

'That's a corro course.'

'For what?'

'Writing,' Smith said.

Detectives removed disks and printed out the pages of a first draft novel on Smith's Corona word processor. One of the detectives read a few paragraphs and laughed.

'Take your pants off please, Ned,' Superintendent Laycock said. 'We need to photograph you from the neck down.'

Smith lowered his prison track pants to his knees exposing his underpants and he was photographed. Smith then removed his

T-shirt, green track pants and underpants which were placed in a paper bag.

'You finished?' Smith said.

The paper clip that Smith was chewing on was snatched from his mouth by a Crime Scene Unit detective, whisked into a plastic bag and sealed. At 12.59 p.m. detectives left the gaol complex and entered the exhibits in the TASK FORCE SNOWY exhibit book.

•

Like all good detectives, W.B.'s eye for detail was so precise that I could picture Smith prowling up and down his cell, working a paper clip between his teeth.

'So they're going to charge him?'

'There's more,' W.B. said. 'At 4.10 this afternoon Task Force Snowy detectives interviewed Warren Austin Richards in the presence of his solicitor on the sixth floor of the Sydney Police Centre. Richards was not prepared to answer any questions in relation to the murder of Sallie-Anne Huckstepp, but he did supply police with a blood sample. One of the detectives told me that Richards' biceps were the size of his thighs. They broke two needles taking 20 millilitres of blood from him.'

'And Rogerson?'

'Starling and Moores interviewed him at Berrima Correction Centre. Rogerson denied handing Neddy a Federal Police Badge. Rogerson's still clinging to his alibi of being at the Merrylands Bowling Club the night Sallie-Anne was murdered.'

'That's no alibi.'

'Half an hour ago Con Moores flew to London carrying a jar of fingernails belonging to Sallie-Anne in a locked briefcase. Tomorrow he catches a train to Birmingham to have DNA extracts from Sallie-Anne's fingernails and her femur bone analysed along with Smith's bloodstained handkerchief, his toothbrush and pubic hair.'

'Why England?'

'The turnaround time there is the quickest for receiving exhibits,' he said. 'Task Force Snowy are in a hurry. I can tell you now that

Smith will be charged with Sallie-Anne's murder along with five, possibly six, others regardless of what the Forensic Service Lab in Birmingham comes up with.'

'They're sure it's Smith?'

'He did it alright, you only have to listen to the tapes.'

'Right,' I said. There were still pieces missing. Even if Smith had murdered Sallie-Anne I wanted to know who else was involved. Whose orders was Smith acting on? Was it New South Wales detectives? Why did underworld figures feel so threatened by a 31-year-old single mother of no fixed address that they would have her strangled and dumped in the city's largest public park?

'When all the drama settles,' W.B. said, 'I'll get you that transcript.'

'Why are you doing this?'

'I told you before. I owe Sal a favour.'

'Is it something to do with the furs?'

'Nothing to do with police work,' W.B. said. 'I grew up in North Bondi. My family lived in a block of flats just down from the Krivoshows in Ramsgate Avenue. I used to see Sallie-Anne and her little sister and her aunt Rose. Her aunt was a beautiful looking woman, absolutely stunning. Dark Jewish look. I used to see her walk up from Bondi beach in a bikini and I'm talking late sixties and she'd be turning heads, cars stopping. Sallie-Anne had the same look, she was very much like her aunt, except she was blond. I got to know Sallie-Anne well before she went to Kalgoorlie.'

'What was she like?' I said.

'Very mature physically, very vivacious. She had a quality, a lot of charisma. She was the girl in North Bondi that every boy wanted.'

12

Kalgoorlie

Two months after her seventeenth birthday, Sallie-Anne flew to the remote gold mining town of Kalgoorlie to work as a prostitute. Her future husband, Bryan Huckstepp, had convinced her that for the sake of his freedom and their future happiness a short stint in the famous brothels of Hay Street wouldn't hurt her. Desperate to escape New South Wales Police and a certain prison sentence, Bryan persuaded Sallie to fly on ahead to earn them a thousand-dollar stake and then he would join her.

'I felt I owed him,' Sallie-Anne wrote in *Penthouse*. 'I'd met Bryan as a screwed-up sixteen-year-old, insecure and with terrible emotional problems. He was the first man to really care for me—my first emotional security—and if holding onto that meant becoming a hooker, then so be it.'

Arriving in Kalgoorlie late at night Sallie-Anne was met at the airport by the madam of the house she was to work in. 'Though we'd never met,' Sallie wrote later, 'she could hardly fail to recognise me, as I was the only woman on the plane.'

'What's your name, dear?' the madam asked.

'Samantha.' She had chosen the name from her favourite TV show.

'Where are you from?'

'Adelaide,' Sallie-Anne said quickly. Her plane had refuelled in Adelaide. Carrying a small suitcase containing one change of clothes, her diary and Errol Flynn's autobiography, *My Wicked, Wicked Ways*, Sallie followed the madam out to the car. The dry heat of the tarmac baked the soles of her sandals and she slipped off her yellow cardigan, slinging it over one arm. In the big roomy Valiant she let the softness of the brown sheepskin seat covers embrace her bare shoulders as she gazed out the window at the flat red landscape. The streets of the town were wide enough to turn a road-train around, the iron-roofed sheds hugged the earth.

'Never before or since have I been so frightened,' Sallie-Anne wrote in *Penthouse*. 'I saw all these other brothels made of corrugated iron and fibro. I had these images of rough gold-miners covered in mud and silt, stinking of beer and sweat. I went to the house and there's these huge fences, bars on the windows and I thought my God. I thought it was like a gaol. It was dark and hot and I couldn't see the rest of the street or the other houses, we just drove straight in, I didn't get a real look at the place.'

Expecting the worst, Sallie-Anne was led into the portable fibre house that would be her home for the next three months. 'I was really surprised,' Sallie told Michael Willesee years later. 'I thought it would be dark and dingy and tattered and horrible and I walked into this spotlessly clean little house.'

Sallie had never met a prostitute before and she had no idea of what to expect. In her imagination she pictured sleazy, tough harpies with teased beehives and stiletto heels. Her surprise was enormous when she was introduced to the girls of the house and instead of hostility she found warmth and friendliness. 'Maybe they looked a little hard around the eyes,' Sallie wrote in *Penthouse*, 'and their dress was provocative for the times, and they swore like troopers—but basically they were no different from other women.'

'This is Samantha Krivoshow from Adelaide,' the madam announced.

'Lane,' Sallie said, 'Samantha Lane.'

'Okay dear.' The madam was accustomed to pseudonyms; she had been in the business for 34 years. She introduced some of the other girls: Amber, Ricki, Ceylon, Sabrina, Melissa. Big-boned country women from the sheep stations; suburban housewives who were saving for their own homes with husbands waiting for them in the eastern cities; barmaids from Perth and Fremantle; women who were working to send their children to private schools.

'Every girl had a story to tell,' Sallie wrote in *Penthouse*, 'about her reason for winding up in "Kal", none were exactly alike, although there were a lot of similarities.'

Sallie spent her first evening in Kalgoorlie interrogating the older women, trying to learn what to expect the next day, what went on in the rooms between a hooker and her client, besides sex. What do you say to them? What if they're ugly? What if they've been drinking or they're diseased? What if they refuse to pay?

'Seventeen years of conditioning told me that prostitution was the most degrading level a woman could reduce herself to,' Sallie wrote that evening when the rest of the house was asleep. 'My own shame at what I am about to become is the main reason I've travelled all the way here to Western Australia where I can't possibly be recognised. What will it feel like to let a stranger touch me in the most intimate ways? Who will they be? What will I feel?'

The housekeeper woke her at nine the next morning and Sallie showered and picked at her fried sausages and eggs. While she chain smoked, the madam of the house fussed over her, allaying her fears, showing Sallie where to secure the money and how to record what she'd made. On the workbench beside the bed, the madam demonstrated how to check a client for venereal disease by gently massaging his testicles and squeezing the glans of his penis to see if any discharge was visible. The madam warned her to wash the man's genitals thoroughly before sex.

'You'll be fine, Samantha, you'll be fine.'

Sallie-Anne sat on the edge of the bed in a pair of red and black knickers and a matching lace top, staring up at the whirring metal fan. The temperature outside was climbing and she could feel sweat gathering on her brow and between her breasts. She couldn't do this. No, she was sorry, she just couldn't. She opened her bag and counted her change. Everything she owned had gone on the one-way ticket to Kalgoorlie. Bryan was depending on her to make good.

Knuckles tapped on the door and Sallie jumped. The madam poked her face around. 'Samantha, come and meet one of our regulars.'

She had to think of Bryan. He was crazy about her. She didn't want him to go to gaol.

'He's very gentle, dear,' the madam whispered in her ear.

Sallie walked out into the hall and came face to face with an enormous miner, his muscled arms bulging out of a buttoned-up Wrangler shirt, his golden hair parted and slicked down with water. She led him back into her room and took his money, careful to avoid his eyes. They undressed and she washed him at the work-bench, squeezing the head of his uncircumcised penis like she'd been shown.

Silence building between them.

Sallie started to panic. Everyone had given her so many instructions, but no-one had explained what to do next. Overcome with shyness, she lay down on the bed with her eyes closed and her legs parted and breathed in. Within seconds the big blond miner had lowered himself on top of her and before she had time to think he was bucking and rearing.

'I bucked and reared with him as I thought it was the polite thing to do,' Sallie wrote in her autobiography, 'too naïve to know that every other girl just lay there like a slab.'

Satisfied, the miner dressed and left her staring up at the whirring fan. Sallie checked her money. Ten dollars for fifteen minutes. Half of this went to the brothel, so in fact she was being screwed for $5 a time, and whenever she bought anything in Kalgoorlie over the following months, she measured its cost not in dollars and cents, but in numbers of screws. A thousand dollars divided by five was 200. She had 199 men to go, and that was without cigarettes, cosmetics, clothes, bourbon. She heard footsteps and a confident knock. Sallie rose to greet a line of men waiting outside her door. Word had spread in town of the fresh new seventeen-year-old.

The job was draining and the hours were long. At ten in the morning Sallie started work and she would service up to four clients an hour for fifteen minutes each. At noon she had an hour off for lunch and was back working until five o'clock, staring up at the spinning blades. Another hour off for dinner and promptly back at six working through until three or four in the morning. The next day she would have free, starting work again at 6 p.m. If she worked particularly late then she wasn't woken until 10 a.m and wouldn't be at her door until eleven. Every girl in the house worked seven days a week, with one day off a month for the first day of their period. Apart from the physical strain, the work was emotionally draining. She learned how to use tricks of the trade, to apply creams to stop her chafing, to placate the drunks when they became abusive, never showing her revulsion at the unwashed miners who dripped sweat over her, or those who belched in her face. The temperature in Kalgoorlie in February hovered around 35°C, sometimes breaking through the 40°C mark. For comfort Sallie wore as little as possible, usually a tiny pair of knickers and a skimpy top that showed off her young full breasts to best advantage.

Pleased at seeing her bank account grow day by day, Sallie became kinder and more attentive to her clients. She put more energy into her work than any of the experienced hands. Young and enthusiastic, she learned of positions she had never believed possible, or never realised could be so physically uncomfortable. She began to understand the true function of a prostitute in society. Sex was only a small part of it. Many of the miners who came to see her just wanted her to listen to their problems, their desires, their wild dreams of striking it rich, of finding that big gold nugget that would change their lives and propel them into a fantasy world of Lear jets and stretch limousines.

Her reputation spread in the golden mile. Sitting by the door of the small portable fibro house each morning she faced a pretty courtyard and a long queue of married and unmarried clients.

'I became the most popular girl in Kalgoorlie,' Sallie told a journalist years later. 'It became very satisfying to have a man return to see me time and time again, and to know he was seeing me as a person, not just a lump he was using to satisfy himself.'

Many of the miners who passed through town had spent months working in the deserts of northern and central Western Australia prospecting for gold, nickel, iron ore and uranium. Deprived of social contact they would hit Kalgoorlie for a huge splash-up, blowing a fortnight or even a month's wage in one night. The resident families and shopkeepers turned an economical eye to the brothels in Hay Street, but Sallie-Anne soon discovered that the working girls had few rights and that the hypocrisy of Kalgoorlie's respectable citizens was appalling. Like every prostitute in town, Sallie had to be off the street by 5 p.m. She wasn't allowed to enter any of the hotels for a drink unless she was accompanied by the madam of the house. She wasn't allowed to chat to a man on the street or enter into any personal relationship outside the brothel. No boyfriends were allowed in the rooms. Using the public swimming pool, the racecourse or going to the picture theatre was forbidden by Kalgoorlie's civic leaders.

'On the social ladder we were right at the bottom,' Sallie wrote in *Penthouse*, 'except for the Aborigines. The Aborigines were just below us.'

She became concerned with her public image in the town and worried about her appearance. Everyone knew who she was and where she came from and what she did, and when she went shopping she saw the way the married women looked at her and the way their husbands avoided her eyes. 'In a sense,' Sallie wrote, 'I was invisibly marked and that feeling stayed with me right through my working life.'

Every now and then the Vice Squad arrested a batch of girls to maintain their arrest rates. On 17 March 1972, Sallie-Anne was charged with soliciting and fined $30 or, as she put it, 'six screws'. An hour later she was back working at the house, when a pit manager from Boulder came in and paid his money. They undressed and the man removed his glasses and lay down first. When Sallie climbed on top, he asked her to urinate on him. 'Pardon?' Sallie said. The man repeated his request. 'Piss on me.'

Sallie stammered out a refusal. With his head thrown back, the man started hissing at her to swear at him. Sallie tried to oblige, but she kept running out of words, feeling silly. 'Swear at me, you little bitch!' He closed his eyes. Sallie tried to swear, but she was too inexperienced to do it in the right tone. Finally the man climaxed, but never returned to her door again.

Her experience with fetishes had been non-existent, most of her clients were fit young miners who were into straight sex. 'Oral sex was totally out of the question then,' Sallie wrote in *Penthouse.* 'Personally I would have felt violated, and considered it as a gift that I gave to my man only.' When she spoke to the other women in the house, Sallie was surprised to find that they all preferred to satisfy a client orally, since they found it less intimate than having a stranger invade their womb.

After a while Sallie began to forget the names and faces. Some nights she went with ten men. But she never forgot the heat, or the fans going all the time, or the water pail in a corner, or the bars on the windows. Once a week she visited the town doctor to be checked for disease and have her medical book signed. Condoms were the exception rather than the rule. There was no entertainment, nowhere she was allowed to go to relax. Her only real source of pleasure was the young men who hung around her door at night when she had a quiet spell and talked to her of their own dreams. Carl, a young explosives expert, dropped in every night to see how she was and whether she needed anything. He never came into her room, never approached her sexually. Finally Sallie had to stop him coming around because she realised he was falling in love with her and rather than hurt him more by feeding his fantasy of 'taking her away from all this', Sallie cut him off gently.

Three weeks after she'd arrived in Kalgoorlie, Bryan Huckstepp rang. He had been arrested in Sydney for breaking and entering and needed bail. Without hesitation Sallie wired him five hundred dollars.

•

A short, fine-boned young man, Bryan Roger Huckstepp was studying art at East Sydney Tech when Sallie first moved into the same block of apartments on Bayswater Road. He showed her his drawings. Sallie saw him as an intellectual. Handsome and beautifully dressed in Carnaby fashion, he wrote poems for her and witty letters. Laughing, Sallie used to read them aloud to her sister and friends. She admired Bryan's manners and being with him gave her a confidence she lacked. 'It was not one of those meetings that produces a bolt of lightning,' she wrote in *Penthouse*, 'yet after a time he made it possible for me to invent a different Sallie-Anne, a person people found more interesting.' To make ends meet Bryan was selling grass and bullets—marijuana heads that looked like a bullet in brown paper. He shared his dope and his money with her and took her to the trendy haunts and nightclubs around the Cross.

One night Bryan came down to her apartment with a mad painter friend who had just done a drug run to Penang. Sallie had taken ludes and tickets and mandies and tueys before but when she and Bryan started snorting the white powder she felt a warm glow in her stomach that spread through her bloodstream as if her whole body was wrapped in silk. She fell into a soft dreamy sleep on her sofa and all her pain slipped away. And then Bryan asked her if she wanted to inject and she said yes. She watched him take her arm, turn it over and run his index finger down between her two blue tram lines.

'You've got lovely veins,' Bryan said and tied the knot. When he plunged the spike into her arm Sallie said, 'Now, I'll do you.'

While Sallie-Anne was dabbling in heroin, Bryan got into debt with his new supplier. The original drug sub-culture that Bryan Huckstepp belonged to consisted of musicians, artists, builders' labourers, bohemians and middle-class kids from the North Shore and Eastern Suburbs who would bring in gear to pay for their overseas trip. By the late 1960s and early 1970s Sydney's old-style gangsters, men like Lennie McPherson, had seen the money to be made in cannabis and heroin, and had moved to take over the drug scene. No longer could Bryan score on tick. His new supplier tightened the screws. Bryan started doing B&Es to pay his growing drug debt, but there was a problem. He kept getting caught.

'Bryan was a bit of a loser,' Debra Krivoshow said. 'He didn't have the go in him that Sallie-Anne had.'

'He was a hopeless spineless creature,' Jack Krivoshow added. 'A deadbeat.'

'She was the strong one,' Debra said. 'I can remember going to visit them when they were first living together in the Claridge. Sallie had on this black mini dress with a round neck, tight fitting in the sleeves and at the waist and she had real snakeskin boots on, grey snakeskin and this black dress, it had four yellow stars down the front and she walked down Bayswater Road and she was a knock-out. She was so beautiful.

'Bryan would do a break and enter and he'd run around the Cross with a microwave. It got to the stage where if he got caught again he was going to do serious time. I didn't like what he was doing to Sallie and what was happening. There were two girls that Bryan had shared a flat with upstairs before he moved in with Sallie. One night Bryan put a whole lot of Mandrax in her drink and Sallie crashed out and when she woke up he wasn't home and she went upstairs to the girls' flat to ask where he was and there was Bryan fucking both of them.'

•

The night Bryan arrived in Kalgoorlie it was so hot the town appeared deserted. He lugged his black canvas bag down Hay Street, his mouth dry from the train trip, dust irritating his eyes. Sallie-Anne was standing in the doorway of a blue fibro house, a naked bulb burning above her head, wearing tiny black panties and a white satin slip, her blond hair brushed off her face so that she barely looked seventeen. Bryan jumped the gate and ran up to hug her. 'I've missed you, Sal,' he said. 'Missed you bad.'

When he released her, Sallie looked over her shoulder.

'Aren't you going to invite me in?'

'No boyfriends allowed in the rooms,' Sallie told him. Rather than tell the madam about Bryan, she wrote his name in her client book. This meant that she had to pay the house for half the time Bryan spent with her. He followed her inside and no sooner had he rested his bag on her workbench than he was kissing her on the neck, rolling up her slip. 'I love you baby.'

'No, Bryan,' she said.

'What's eating you? I've travelled 2000 miles.'

Sallie shook her head. She couldn't stand him touching her. She didn't want him in her room. 'Look you'll have to stay in a motel tonight.' She grabbed her purse. 'It's been a hot day and I'm exhausted. I've been working since six.'

Bryan took the three notes she was holding. 'I don't know what's the matter with you, Sal,' he said. 'I thought you'd be pleased to see me.'

'Tomorrow,' she said.

'I love you. You know I love you. You know that.'

The next morning Sallie went to see him. She sat on his bed while he shaved and then Bryan came out of the bathroom with two fat rolled joints. 'Moroccan gold,' he said. They lay side by side on the bed smoking with a bath towel rolled up against the bottom of the motel door. Bryan gave her a gold-plated lighter he'd bought in Kalgoorlie. 'That's for you, baby,' he said. 'A gift.'

He undressed and made love to her, Sallie lying on her back, staring up at the ceiling. When Bryan finished, she went into the bathroom and locked the door. 'I suddenly realised things had changed between us,' Sallie told her sister years later. 'All the passion had gone, lost in a blur of bodies and faces and penises.'

That afternoon when Sallie returned to Hay Street she sought out the madam of the house, a fleshy woman in her late fifties who had acquired a formidable reputation in the goldfields ever since she had broken a drunken miner's jaw in a fist fight. She didn't smoke, drink or gamble. Her only indulgence was the cast iron bath she'd had trucked in from Perth and in which she would lie for hours in the heat of summer. None of the girls was allowed to use her bath. Water in Kalgoorlie was more precious than gold—all the town's fresh water was pumped 600 kilometres east from Perth.

Sallie found the madam up to her neck in foam, white doughy

arms dangling over the edge of the bath, a small dish of dark chocolates within reach. 'I need to go to Perth,' Sallie said.

'You're coming back dear, I hope?'

'Yes,' Sallie said. 'I want to.'

'I'll keep your room vacant for one week.'

Sallie left her soaking in the bubble bath, the fan whirring overhead, windows open.

Outside, the temperature touched 42°C. Sallie and Bryan kept to the shadows of the corrugated iron buildings as they hurried to the train station. When they reached Perth the following evening they booked into a hotel. It was wonderful to walk around the shops, to go freely into restaurants and lounge bars. Without worrying who might see you.

At least three times a day Bryan pestered her to make love. She had become much more desirable to him since she had begun working in the brothel. Their lovemaking wasn't as bad for Sallie as it had been in 'Kal', but nothing like it had once been. She caught the glint in his eyes, felt his hands stroke the nape of her neck, heard his whispered words and knew she was part of some fantasy he had spooling through his head. In the past month she had got to know men well.

Lying on the bed with him, and a bag of white powder. 'You like that, huh? You like that?'

She did. It made everything so much easier. Melting the sharp edges of the room. Her toes wriggled with pleasure. Bryan was talking, making plans, always making plans, he was looking for a house, he was getting a job. Things were about to happen. Big things. Her money was nearly gone. In her heart she knew she would return to Kalgoorlie, finish up the three months. If she could handle Hay Street then she could handle anything the world could throw at her.

'I'm going back,' she said.

Realising he was losing her, Bryan begged her to stay on with him. 'I love you, Sal. Here, you have the last taste.'

The next day she returned to Kalgoorlie. The madam was delighted to see her. Seventeen-year-old attractive blondes were rare on the goldfields and Sallie was a good worker. 'I've had a lot of inquiries for you, Samantha,' the madam told her from the bathtub. All the girls in the house greeted her with warmth, hugging her as if she'd been away for a year. They were like her family and the young guys who hung around her gate at night brought her a bunch of yellow and green native wildflowers that lifted her room.

For the first week she was flat out. One night she went with thirteen men. She was so sore the next morning she could barely walk. In a strange way Sallie was happy in Kalgoorlie. For the first time in her life she had a real home.

'I felt stable there,' Sallie told the journalist Michael Willesee ten years later. 'I was so young. At seventeen you don't know anything about anything. What a realisation to think that I found my stability in a whorehouse!'

On her visit to the town doctor Sallie discovered she had gonorrhoea. When she confronted Bryan on the telephone he denied 'passing it on'. 'You must've given it to me, babe,' he said. But she knew that Bryan's was the only penis she hadn't checked.

Every day he rang from Perth, urging her to finish up, to join him. He had found a flat, a job, some secondhand furniture. His calls depressed her. Out of action for a fortnight, she went for long walks to the edge of town, watched the road-trains rumble in, chewing up the fine red dust. She made friends with an Aboriginal woman who sat in the shade of the same scribbly bark every morning with her baby. They shared cigarettes and Sallie watched her breastfeed, batting the flies from the child's nose and eyes with her hands. There were very few women in the mining camps and those few were married. Outside of working hours Sallie found that the Aboriginal women were the only people in the town who accepted her.

At the end of three months she said goodbye to Hay Street and the other girls. Her feelings towards Kalgoorlie were ambivalent, but she realised that her experiences here had made her a survivor. She flew to Perth and moved in with Bryan, found work in a hotel pulling beers to support them both. His habit was growing, but Sallie controlled her usage, only shooting up on weekends. Sexually, she was cold towards him. She realised that the relationship had ended the day she went to work in Kalgoorlie, but he'd come to rely on her and she didn't have the heart to dump him.

'I don't know when she split up with Bryan,' her sister Debra said. 'They'd split up and then he'd come back for a while and then they'd split up. He had become a liability. She was tired of carrying him.'

Six weeks after she arrived in Perth, Sallie discovered she was pregnant. She'd saved up enough money, and she and Bryan flew home to Sydney.

•

When Debra went to Bali she brought Sallie back a sarong. 'No-one was wearing sarongs then,' her sister said, 'and Sallie was pregnant, heavily pregnant. It was the middle of summer and she just used to wear this sarong everywhere. Sallie'd go down to Bondi and she could lie on the beach in the sarong and then just go in the surf in the sarong and everyone used to look because it was quite different but sarongs were great when you were pregnant, she didn't have to wear underwear or anything. They moved into this funny little unit in an old block of flats in Bondi and they lived there for a while. They were doing it really hard.'

On 23 March 1973, at the age of eighteen, Sallie-Anne gave birth to a daughter, Sascha Michelle. Her father refused to accept Sascha as his grandchild. 'Dad came to the hospital,' Debra said, 'and put shit on Bryan, called him a hopeless bloody idiot. He went on and on about Sallie not being married. Crazy stuff.'

By now Bryan Huckstepp was hooked on heroin. He lived partly on Sallie-Anne's generosity, partly doing B&Es, crawling through hotel windows trying to steal guests' wallets. When Sallie came out of hospital Bryan was nabbed in the airconditioning vent of a block of apartments in Macleay Street. This time Bryan went to gaol. Alone in Sydney, with a new baby and no money, Sallie found work in Bondi Junction as a barmaid. Her self-esteem had dropped to rock-bottom. She worried about the image she projected. The fear that customers could tell she had worked as a prostitute. But even with a baby there was no shortage of male admirers. For a while she hung around with Billy Thorpe and the Aztecs, Max Merritt and the Meteors. She called herself 'an orchestra lady', rather than a band moll. A lot of men were taken with her beauty. Sallie-Anne started going out with a friend of Bryan's, whose wife, Vickie Barley, ran a brothel called the Pink Flamingo.

One afternoon, Vickie Barley found her husband and Sallie-Anne parked in New Beach Road and rammed her red Mercedes into the back of his ute. Sallie got away. The next morning she was feeding Sascha in her flat when Vickie Barley burst in through the glass doors accompanied by a tough street prostitute from the Cross.

'You little tart,' Vickie Barley yelled, 'I'm gonna fix you!'

'It was wild,' Debra Krivoshow said. 'Vickie Barley was spitting in Sallie-Anne's face and abusing her. She had Big Tits Anne there to back her up. Vickie Barley pulled a revolver out of her purse and was going to kill Sallie-Anne on the spot. I was going please, please, don't do this to my sister, she's got a new baby. Sallie just stood there and took it. If Sascha hadn't been on the bed I'm sure Vickie Barley would have shot her.'

Disillusioned with married men, Sallie-Anne quit the hotel business and found work in a Double Bay massage parlour. The owner of the parlour assured Sallie-Anne she wouldn't have to have sex. This was a different type of business altogether. 'We specialise in bondage and fetishes,' the woman told Sallie. 'You'll discover that people who want to indulge in unusual pleasures usually have the money to pay for it.'

At $500 an hour, Sallie found the work rewarding. 'It was fun actually,' she told Michael Willesee. 'I loved it. I had two clients I used to dress up as babies. I used to put them in the bath and put the rubber duckie in the bath with them, bathe them and wash their hair in baby shampoo. I had special towels for them and I used to put nappies on them and have the formula ready, feed them bottles. They were great.'

Most of her privileged clients simply liked to be tied up or scolded, but there were others who had more involved fantasies.

One 40-year-old advertising director liked to have a knitting needle stuck down the eye of his penis, and another man, a bank manager from the Eastern Suburbs, liked to have his balls burnt with a Bic cigarette lighter.

'Why does he want me to do that?' Sallie asked.

'Guilt,' the parlour owner told her. She was counting the evening's takings in the perfume-scented reception room. A slender woman with a perfect bob of platinum-blond hair, lightly powdered skin and a touch of gold on her wrist and wedding finger, Jillian had built her boutique business up from scratch, catering to the cream of Sydney society. Sallie-Anne admired her confidence, her clothes, her thespian background.

Jillian inquired about Sallie's daughter. Where was she staying tonight?

'Sascha's with her grandparents,' Sallie said.

'Would you like to see my view?'

They drove in Jillian's racing-green E-Type to a penthouse on the tip of Darling Point. They drank pink champagne and swam in the heated pool. Sallie stared at the white and yellow lights strung out across the flat black harbour. Leaning over the guard rail in her bra and pants, arms stretched wide. 'One day I'll have a view like this,' she boasted.

'Careful, Sallie!'

Rocking on the heels of her small bare feet. 'I'm going to be an actress or a famous writer!'

'Never trust a man,' Jillian told her later that evening. 'They will always knife you in the back.'

'But you're married?'

Jillian slipped the ring from her finger, let it clink against the stem of her glass. 'That old goat.'

In the morning the Filipino maid brought them coffee and hot croissants smeared with fresh strawberry jam. Sallie was sprawled across the water bed painting her nails. 'Do you think I wear too much make-up?'

'No,' Jillian said. 'You're a very attractive girl.'

Sallie didn't let on that she used. Jillian was a woman of a different generation. Cocaine and champagne were acceptable in her circles (coke had been fashionable in Sydney since the 1920s), but heroin was for low-life. Jillian grew fond of Sallie-Anne. She lent her books, Flaubert, Artaud and Strindberg. She reserved the elite of her clientele for her young protégé, men who held significant positions in Sydney society. No names were used. Sallie tried to guess at the occupations of the clients she saw. Once she recognised a cabinet minister. She rubbed bottoms with a Supreme Court judge and undressed captains of industry. Working in the parlour was like working in the theatre, Jillian told her. You had to keep the fantasies exciting, you had to make each performance resemble an intense one-act play.

'It was hard work,' Sallie told Michael Willesee years later. Catering to the whims of the rich and powerful exhausted her creativity. To relax she began 'speedballing', mixing a cocktail of coke and heroin. At eighteen years of age she was earning $4000 a week. Money was like heroin. It changed reality, it changed everything.

'Sallie loved to go into luxury shops and lay-by,' her sister Debra said. 'She went into Cornelius Furs in the city and she had something like $300 and she went and put $250 on a fur coat, a silver fox fur coat that was like $3000, and she was never going to go back for it. There was $250 thrown away.

'She was not a house person. She wasn't a cook. She could make a reasonable macaroni cheese and tuna casserole and a great goulash, but she was the type of person who would ring up a cab to go and pick up the take-away. She loved to do things for Sascha. She always made sure that her daughter never went without.'

'I'm not a very good mother,' Sallie-Anne told Michael Willesee. 'I'm not maternal. I do what I think is best and poor Sascha has always had to follow along behind me.'

•

One Friday evening, five weeks after Sallie had begun working at the parlour, she was walking home from Rushcutters Bay with her sister. Turning into Darlinghurst Road, Sallie kept Debra close to her side. The smell of spit-roasted lamb and charcoal chicken drifted out of a hot bar window. Cars cruised bumper to bumper along the strip, tattooed arms sticking out of rear windows, engines and audio systems blaring.

'Don't walk like that,' Sallie said.

'Like what?'

'Don't wiggle your hips.'

A spruiker in a dinner suit worked the pavement outside the Pink Pussycat, rolling his shoulders, yelling out 'girls girls girls' in a gravelly voice. Liquid neon spilled down the sides of buildings. Sallie took Debra's hand to guide her through the maze of red-eyed men. A woman in a tight black vinyl skirt and a tank top leaned in a bank doorway, rubbing her bruised heels with her fingers.

'Keep your eyes down,' Sallie said. 'Don't walk like a tart.'

'I'm not,' Debra said.

Uniformed police milled outside the ice cream parlour licking chocolate cones. The back end of their wagon jutted out into the traffic. They watched Sallie-Anne hurrying along Darlinghurst Road with her school-aged sister in tow. When Sallie reached the corner she stopped and dug her nails into Debra's wrist.

'What is it?' Debra said.

Sallie was staring at a thin, blond woman in her mid-thirties coming out of a restaurant on the other side of Macleay Street. The woman was wearing a full-length electric-blue dress and pearls. Her eyes met Sallie's and then, hoisting her dress to her knees, the woman turned and ran down a sidestreet. Sallie chased after her. Tyres squealed on the road; a car horn blew. The woman ducked into an apartment building flinging back the security door. Sallie tore after her, Debra running behind yelling, 'No, no.' When Sallie got into the carpeted foyer of the apartments the woman was gone. Sallie leaned on the lift door, jabbing her thumb at the triangular button, sniffing the faint scent of expensive perfume that lingered in the air. Debra came up behind and laid a hand on her eighteen-year-old sister's shoulder. 'If she doesn't want to see us,' she panted, 'who cares.'

'That's my mother,' Sallie said. 'That's my mother!'

•

'Sallie-Anne was much more emotional and let things affect her a lot more than me,' Debra Krivoshow explained twenty years later. 'She had this armour, this big bravado, but underneath it all she could never understand how our mother could walk out on us in the first place. I mean you could understand it if we were deformed or mentally disabled, but we weren't, we were beautiful children.'

'My mother left when I was three years old and my sister and I were brought up by my father and his girlfriends and wives,' Sallie-Anne wrote. For the next eleven years Sallie received no news from her mother other than rumours that she had moved to America and re-married. When Sallie was sixteen her mother, Pat, wrote her a letter signed *love mummy*. She was staying in the Cross with friends and wanted to meet her daughter. Sallie-Anne had been released from Minda children's home and her father and his third wife had refused to have her under their roof a moment longer.

'Sallie-Anne moved into the Claridge in Bayswater Road,' Debra said. 'They were units then, little bedsitter flats. She moved in there with Pat. That's how she met Bryan. Bryan was living in the flats too. I was at boarding school in Moss Vale. Sallie came to visit me at SCEGGS (Sydney Church of England Girls Grammar School). We were in the dining room having Sunday lunch and it was formal and she walked in and stood in the doorway and she had this dress on, it was like a leopard print, but not leopard print, like a giraffe print and cut nice and these beautiful boots on from Raymond Castles, and the whole dining room stopped eating and stared at her and I remember I was so proud of her. She was beautiful, God she was beautiful.'

When Debra travelled back that night on the train, Sallie took her upstairs to meet their mother. A thin elegant blonde with a faint English accent.

'"Oh my darling daughter!" she went,' Debra said. '"Oh my baby!" It was too much for me. I never bothered going back. I never saw her again. Anyway Sallie-Anne got really close to her. For four or five months Pat and Sallie-Anne lived there. Pat made her all these promises, "I'll make it up to you, darling, I'll take you to America, sweetheart. We'll be mother and daughter again." And all this stuff.'

Sallie-Anne found work in a Kings Cross pharmacy. She wore a crisp white uniform and helped the Polish-born chemist make prescriptions for methylamphetamine and barbiturates. Pat suffered from insomnia so Sallie procured her mother's tranquillisers cheaply. At nights they listened to the collection of jazz records Pat had bought in New York, Miles Davis, Charlie Parker. One afternoon Sallie came home from the pharmacy and found her mother gone. 'No note, no nothing.' A shadow of dust marked the ledge where her turntable and jazz records had stood.

'When Pat dumped Sallie-Anne the second time, I mean that really fucked her up,' Debra said. 'Sallie sort of fell in love with Bryan on the rebound, and that's when she went to Kalgoorlie. Bryan was like her pimp in a way, but when your own mother makes a habit of walking out on you it doesn't do a lot for your self-esteem. Sallie used to say to me, "If only I'd had my mother it would've been different."'

•

Obsessed with the fact that her mother had abandoned her, Sallie-Anne hired a Kings Cross private detective in the winter of 1973 to track her down. She would make her mother rue the day she had run out on her. The P.I., a former Consorting Squad detective sergeant, phoned back information. Pat had re-married five times, he said. She discarded husbands like other women discarded hats. He had word that she was living in South Perth. For $1000 he would fly over, check it out. Sallie paid him in cash, money she had saved from the massage parlour. The P.I. returned, wiping his tan shoes on her doormat, removing his porkpie, shaking his head sadly. Pat had left the country; she was living in Los Angeles. For $3000 he'd fly over, check it out.

'The man's milking you,' Jillian said. 'Forget about her. You've got your own daughter.'

Sascha was everything good in her life. But there was something missing inside. Waves of depression rolled over Sallie. She stayed in bed for days. Up until now she had kept a lid on her drug use, but when she paid off the private dick she made a conscious decision. 'It was like jumping out of a plane,' she told the journalist Graham Gambie years later. 'You know what you're doing is dangerous, but it's wonderful to let go.'

Eyelids drooping and slurring her words, she turned up for work. A silver Rolls was parked outside the parlour and Marsha, a twenty-year-old part-Maori prostitute, whispered in her ear that the son of one of the richest men in the country wanted a threesome.

Sallie told her she didn't have sex with clients.

'I've had [*Name deleted*] before,' Marsha said. 'He doesn't want to fuck, he just likes to whip you. He's very generous.'

Sallie followed her colleague into the bedroom where a big fat fellow with a puppy-dog face was waving a pair of tailor's scissors. He cut the bottom out of Marsha's panties and snipped her bra straps and then Sallie and he undressed. All she had to do was watch and stroke his testicles. She stared at his big white back while he secured Marsha's arms to the bedhead, fastened a gag in her mouth and, with a hand-carved stock whip, began lashing her, lightly at first, on her thighs and buttocks. The blows grew in intensity. Marsha flinched then bucked as the leather cut into her flesh, blood streaming down the backs of her brown legs, the son of one of the richest men in the country wading into her with all his strength. Naked, Sallie crouched in a corner and began screaming and wouldn't stop.

Next morning Jillian rang her at home and asked her to come in. 'There's nothing I can do, Sallie,' she said. 'I'll have to let you go.'

'But you own this place.'

'No,' she said, 'I only manage it on behalf of a consortium.'

At least in Kalgoorlie, Sallie said, the women controlled the brothels. In Sydney the industry was run by criminals and prominent businessmen. 'What about Marsha's stitches?'

'Marsha received two dozen red roses and five thousand in cash this morning,' Jillian said. 'She's taking a holiday to Greece. The client doesn't want you working here again. He said you were high on drugs.'

Sallie threw back her chair. She punched a hole in the wall. She threatened to go to the papers, she threatened to go to the police.

'Don't be so naïve!' Jillian said. 'How do you think we operate here? For an intelligent girl sometimes you lack commonsense.'

That night Sallie sent her daughter to stay with Bryan's parents. She leaned back on a chair with her arm resting in the dishes, the eye of a needle glistening in her small sore fist. She felt the breeze float through the curtains and imagined the sensation of tumbling three floors, the smack of flesh and bone on concrete. The curtains moved in and out. She listened to the city breathing outside her window. Hypocrites. One day she would expose them all. She went downstairs and wandered the streets of the Cross, stood near the dried-up fountain where she had seen her mother in evening dress. 'I'll make it up to you, darling, I promise!' Her mother had deserted a string of families. Maybe these other girls she saw standing awkwardly in doorways were her half-sisters, her womb mates.

She laughed to herself and lit a cigarette. She went into the Bottoms Up bar of the Rex Hotel, sat on a stool and downed bourbon after bourbon staring at a deep-voiced trannie with ringed fingers. A mob of Aboriginal women watched her from a far corner, brown eyes drinking in her shimmering stockings. A Koori woman came over, cropped hair, a razor-fine scar running from the corner of her mouth to her earlobe. She picked up Sallie's gold Ronson from the bar, lit a cigarette and thumbed the lighter down the front pocket of her jeans. 'I hate rich bitches,' she said.

Sallie got off her stool and the barman hurried over.

'They hassling you, miss?'

Sallie pointed at the mob of Aboriginal women, opened her purse and shook out two notes. 'I want to buy my sisters a drink.' She sat down on her stool and a black hand reached out and dropped Bryan's gold-plated lighter on the bar runner. The Koori's fingers were tattooed with crude blue letters across the knuckles, her toes poked through the canvas of her dirty Dunlop sandshoes. 'I like you,' she said. 'You're not scared.'

'No,' Sallie said.

'I'm Debbie Ryan. You got beautiful hair.'

Sallie handed her the gold-plated lighter. 'Take it,' she said. 'It's a gift.' Debbie Ryan clicked the Ronson on and off. She looked into the flame and then at Sallie swaying in the dim yellow light. 'Wanna score?'

On Macleay Street, Sallie struggled to keep up with Debbie Ryan striding ahead in her Dunlops, bumping into tourists, her port-red windcheater bunching between her bony shoulder-blades. At Fitzroy Gardens, an old Aboriginal woman waved at them from the shadows. 'That's where we live,' Debbie Ryan called into the wind. 'A whole mob of us.' She turned into Lankelly Place and banged on a steel roller door. A short muscled man came out of a side hatch; thick eyebrows above a broken nose. The man looked up and down the alley. He snatched the notes from Debbie Ryan's hands and slipped her a foil, his small dark eyes fixed on Sallie-Anne under the streetlamp. 'Come back soon, sweetheart.'

'Who's that?' Sallie said.

'Wozza. He's a world champion, judo or somethin'.'

They went back to Sallie's flat and shot up in the dark, Sallie rubbing her arm from the sharp bite of the needle, Debbie Ryan bent over by the window injecting a vein between her toes. Cars whooshed down below. Sallie sank back on the couch, heels off, feeling the hit pumping through her bloodstream. Locking out the pain. She had no money left now, but she didn't care.

'You've got lovely eyes.' Debbie Ryan leaned in close. Sallie's head lolled against the arm of the couch, breath slowing down, eyelids closing. She felt Debbie Ryan's spiky hair brush against her mouth, the moist touch of her skin. 'How come you like black women?'

'Kalgoorlie,' Sallie whispered. 'I was happy there.'

•

'That's when Sallie-Anne was going through real rock-bottom,' her sister Debra Krivoshow said. 'She moved out of her flat and started having this lesbian affair with Debbie Ryan who was notorious. They were living in the park. Debbie Ryan carried a knife in her bra, she had scars on her face from street-fights. One night her gang took on the bikies up there, throwing people over cars, slashing tyres. I mean they were very scary girls. They would stab you. You didn't answer the blacks back in the Cross. Sallie started behaving as if she was one of them.'

'Only Aboriginal women can understand what I've been through,' Sallie told friends.

'Sallie-Anne had this wild streak in her, totally reckless,' Debra said. 'Sallie was a highly sexual person who liked both men and women. She didn't look down on anyone.'

When Bryan Huckstepp was released from Long Bay he discovered Sallie was sleeping on a bench in Fitzroy Gardens.

'How's Sash?' she asked.

Bryan showed her the children's book he'd written and illustrated in gaol. A gift for his daughter. He was keeping it for her until she was old enough to read. The little girl's name in the story was Sascha and everything was wonderful in her world.

Sallie started crying. The skin on her face was inflamed from adulterated speed and she was so skinny her breasts were flat. 'I want her back, Bryan.'

'Welfare won't let you. Not until you pull yourself together.' In gaol Bryan had learned a new skill. He told her of his plan to make big money forging numberplates.

'Go straight,' Sallie told him, 'sell your drawings. You're not cut out to be a crim.' She couldn't believe Bryan's schemes had once impressed her. She stared at her ex-lover. She didn't feel anything for him anymore. She only cared for her daughter.

Gripped with fever, Sallie moved out of Fitzroy Gardens and took refuge in a halfway house. Sweating, her nose running, the joints of her knees and ankles swollen, she lay prostrate on her bunk. Her skin grew cold, goose-bumped. Shivering, she drew four Salvation Army blankets over her shoulders. She swallowed six Serepax and eight Doloxene dry. Her body shook, feet kicking at the iron frame of the bed. She began to convulse, clutching her abdomen, howling until the night staff came running in and she was transferred to Bourke Street Clinic.

On methadone, Sallie roamed the streets of the Cross looking for cheap accommodation. She found a room above the Lido. All she needed was a job. She had promised herself that she would never work in the massage industry again. She caught the train to Dundas. Bryan had been arrested 48 hours after his release for selling forged numberplates to an undercover detective. His solicitor suggested that if she were to marry him, perhaps he might cop a lighter sentence. Sallie agreed to change her name to Huckstepp.

On Christmas Eve, 1973, twelve days after her nineteenth birthday, Sallie brought her nine-month-old daughter home to the Lido. It was wonderful to have her back. She attached the child to her breast, but her milk had dried up. Never again would she desert Sascha. She was going to make something of their lives. Turn it all around. She dressed Sascha in her new cherry romper and bunny socks, rocked her to sleep in the portable cot and waited on the bed for the fourteen-year-old babysitter to arrive.

Two hours later Sallie went downstairs and wandered along Darlinghurst Road through the crowds of late night revellers. She stopped outside the pharmacy where she had once worked. Streamers and red paper-reindeers festooned the window; snow-capped letters spelled out festive cheer. The pharmacy doors were bolted and padlocked. Sallie stood in the shadows of the doorway with the small of her back pressed against the armour glass. She was safe here. A police car cruised past. She watched a bunch of men in suits stumble out of a strip club, clicking their lighters and blinking up at the flickering neon.

Sallie stepped out of the shadows and spoke to them.

13

Committal

A side door bangs open and all eyes in the courtroom flick to see Arthur Stanley (Ned) Smith, in a pale grey suit and garish tie, stride into the dock flanked by three corrective services' officers, Smith rolling his large head from side to side like a heavyweight contender. He grins at his wife, Debra, in the public gallery and his daughter, Jamie, a striking girl with her father's strong features and large hands weighed down by gold jewellery. Handcuffed, Smith whispers into the ear of his solicitor, David Giddy, a thin man with boundless energy who nods at his client's request then rifles through a bunch of folders on the defence table labelled 'Brown Dog'.

The public doors swing open as more spectators try to cram into court no. 2, but are turned away by the sheriff and his deputy. A young woman shakes her head, refusing to budge. One of the reporters says in a hushed voice, 'That's Sascha Huckstepp.' The young woman bears a faint resemblance to her mother. A Task Force detective approaches and shepherds Sascha past the Smith female clan to a seat behind the prosecutor's table.

At 10.23 the sheriff calls out, 'All rise!' Dressed in a lilac suit with a white blouse, the magistrate enters from a side door behind the bench, bows slightly to the packed courtroom and sits in a high-backed wing chair. Journalists start scribbling in Spirax notebooks.

Neddy Smith watches her intently. A small dark woman, Pat O'Shane is the daughter of an Aboriginal mother and an Irish-Australian father. By law her identity was established as Aboriginal and she has written that she does not wish it otherwise. Her reputation in conservative circles is of a magistrate who is anti-police. 'The DPP didn't want her hearing this case,' the grizzled female police reporter next to me whispers. Pat O'Shane glances in our direction, and then says warmly, 'Mr Maxwell, are you ready?'

'Your Worship, the defendant is charged with seven murders. Now in relation to the murder of Sallie-Anne Huckstepp, the defendant on the listening device tapes speaks of his deep hatred for Sallie Huckstepp and goes into chilling detail of how he killed her. Forensic evidence will be of significance in this case in the way it dovetails with the admissions from the listening device tapes. Both post-mortem doctors asked to comment upon the details given by the defendant on the tapes have found six criteria.' The Deputy Senior Crown Prosecutor slipped on a pair of gold-rimmed glasses.

'Speak up, Mr Maxwell.'

'Sorry, your Worship. Six criteria were extracted: (1) that he held her by the throat so that her feet were off the ground (2) that he punched her four times (3) that he snapped her neck (4) that he tried to choke her with an object (5) that he and Warren Richards dragged her into the water (6) that he held her under water. There will be some evidence that DNA testing of material found under the left fingernails of Sallie-Anne Huckstepp could have come from Smith, but DNA will not figure prominently. There will be two witnesses of significance who will say that the defendant spoke on many occasions about this felonious and malicious killing.'

Winston Terracini, counsel for the defence, then rose and launched a blistering attack on the motives of New South Wales Police in charging his client with these seven murders. A short, black-bearded man with a button nose, Terracini was an effective speaker with an aggressive walk-up manner. His voice echoed off the wood panelling. Word among the court reporters was that if you needed a barrister to save your neck you could do far worse than Winston Terracini.

At the morning interval, members of the public clung to their seats in case they might lose them, but the sheriff insisted that the court be cleared. Spectators milled outside the locked glass-panelled doors, jostling for position. 'Ned's got too much on New South Wales Police to ever be let out,' an old wrinkly woman declaimed in the queue. 'The coppers have loaded him up to clear their books.'

'You think?' I said.

A retiree who told us he was from Woy Woy chipped in. 'Smith killed her and them others. He's a low evil bastard who would slit your throat for a schooner.'

Re-seated in the court, I stared at the accused's broad shoulders and the pink dome of his oversized head as his nineteen-year-old daughter hugged and kissed him in the dock. Sascha Huckstepp watched from the prosecutor's table. There was no doubting Neddy's physical size and menacing aura despite the way his head lolled and his facial muscles twitched. His waxen skin looked as if it had been deprived of sunlight. With a tattooed hand Smith grappled at his wire glasses, removing them to scan a document from his solicitor.

Codenamed Mr Green, the first witness called by the Crown was a former seaman and drinking companion of Neddy Smith. With a hooded jacket concealing his face, he bumped into two large screens that had been erected around the witness box to conceal his identity.

'I used to drive Mr Smith around,' Mr Green said from behind the screens. 'I looked up to him.'

In February 1986, Smith rang Green at home and said, 'I'm going to get rid of that Sallie. I want you to bury her for me.'

'I knew he was referring to Sallie Huckstepp,' Mr Green told the court, 'because he often used to talk about her and say she was no good. When I refused to be involved, Smith abused me. As soon as he hung up, I unplugged the phone. I never saw or spoke to him after that. A few days later I read in the papers that Huckstepp had been found dead in the park. I was very fearful of Mr Smith. Deep down I was petrified.'

The Deputy Crown Prosecutor then said to the bailiff, 'Call Roger Caleb Rogerson!' Heads turned in the public gallery. Dressed in a grubby wind-cheater, work jeans and a striped butcher's shirt, the former detective sergeant, dismissed from the New South Wales Police Service in 1986, and now a factory worker, marched into the witness box and took the oath. When asked by Chris Maxwell to describe his relationship with Neddy Smith, Rogerson said, 'I wouldn't say I was a close friend of his. I haven't seen him in years.' Rogerson agreed that he had a conviction in 1990 for conspiracy to pervert the course of justice for which he had served three years of an eight-year sentence.

'Where were you on the night of February 6, 1986?'

'From memory it was the Merrylands Bowling Club.'

'Did you hand to Arthur Stanley Smith a Federal Police Officer's badge?'

'No, no, I never handed Smith a Federal Police Officer's badge.'

When Winston Terracini stood up to cross-examine, Rogerson glared at Smith who concentrated on his drink of water. Terracini began softly, 'Did you ever provide any police information to Mr Smith?'

'No,' Rogerson said. 'He was my informant, I was never his informant.'

Smith rotated his neck slowly in the dock, pulling at his collar with a finger.

'Did you ever take any money from Mr Smith?'

'I never received one cent off Neddy Smith.'

'You said that on February 6, 1986 you were at Merrylands Bowling Club with Keith Malcolm Spence and other detectives. Can you remember any of their names?'

'No, well, there was a big fellow there Dave ... I can't remember.'

'Mr Rogerson, your memory has deteriorated dramatically?'

'It has, it really has.'

Winston Terracini smiled. 'I would like to put to you a further allegation which was made by Martine James that on the night of February 6, 1986, she saw you in Lang Road, Centennial Park.'

'I wasn't there,' Rogerson said.

'So why is Martine James telling untruths about you?'

'Because the woman is off her head, she's a complete rat.'

'Have you found her to be unreliable?'

'She's a rat, yes, she's a rat.'

'In relation to Sallie-Anne Huckstepp's—'

'Mr Terracini,' Pat O'Shane interjected, 'Mr Smith appears to be in some distress.'

'Your Worship, pardon me a moment ...' The defence team rushed over to the dock where Smith sat slumped, his large head resting on his chest. Pat O'Shane adjourned the court while corrective services officers rang an ambulance. Outside, the corridors buzzed with excitement. Court spectators argued over Smith's 'sudden turn' and Rogerson's 'frustration in the box'. State Police in black leather jackets surrounded the Crown Prosecutor while members of Smith's family gathered at the gold pay phone. I walked out into Liverpool Street behind Winston Terracini. When he inquired who I worked for, I told him I was investigating Sallie Huckstepp's murder.

'Is this for a newspaper?'

'No, it's for myself.'

'Ned didn't do it, I can assure you,' Winston Terracini said. 'I have that information from a very reliable source.'

'Your client?'

'No, no. Someone else. Someone who knows.'

'Who?'

'I can't tell you.' Terracini shook his head. He was clasping a wide-brimmed leather hat between the thumb and forefinger of his right hand and a sleek digital phone in his left. 'Rogerson set it up,' Terracini said, 'he paid for someone to kill her. Why was Richards not picked up, not questioned? Because the New South Wales Police were protecting Richards and someone higher up. There are very high allies of Rogerson's in the New South Wales Police Service. Superintendents. Men far more dangerous than Rogerson.' And Winston Terracini disappeared into a Liverpool Street restaurant.

At ten o'clock the next morning he continued his cross-examination. When Rogerson refused to answer a question, saying,

'I believe it's contrary to the Evidence Act', Terracini yelled at him, 'You're not a QC, you're a convict!'

'Just answer the questions, Mr Rogerson,' Pat O'Shane ruled.

'Now yesterday you told the court that on the night Sallie-Anne Huckstepp was killed you were drinking with Mal Spence at the Merrylands Bowling Club?'

'That's correct.'

'And a witness has said that she saw you near Centennial Park that night.'

'Yeah, the rat.'

'Yet you told the ICAC in 1992 and I quote: "I've never been to any function with Mal Spence other than an Armed Hold-Up Christmas function." Did you give that evidence?'

'It appears . . .' Rogerson fumbled with his glasses. 'I mean . . . it does appear from the transcript that way.'

Throughout the five-hour cross-examination of Rogerson, Smith avoided eye-contact with his former partner in crime. Rolling his head from side to side and swallowing his daily dose of seven Sinemet tablets, 5 milligrams of Eldepryl and 10 milligrams of Parlodel, Smith and his illness replaced the inclement weather as the main topic of conversation in the press box. Described as 'debilitated' and 'a shell of a man', his condition was regarded by many journalists as an exaggerated ploy to attract public sympathy.

When Gary Trevor T—, codenamed Mr Brown, entered the witness box and took the oath, Smith's shoulders and backbone stiffened, his knuckles whitened on the wooden rail and corrective services officers moved closer as if Smith was about to spring from the dock. 'Ned still looks to have plenty of punch in him,' a police officer whispered.

Despite a weight-lifter's physique, a crew cut and 22 convictions including armed robbery, Mr Brown struggled to keep his voice from quavering in the box. His hands shook on the rail.

'How do you know the defendant?' the Deputy Senior Crown Prosecutor began.

'I . . . I shared a cell with him from April to November 1994.'

'How did you activate the tape so that the defendant would not be aware of it?'

'What I d-did was at t-twenty to six I'd activate it and I had to make sure that um, that, Ned didn't see the cassette player flashing. We used to get locked in at six, so I just had to chance it . . .'

'Was there anything unusual in the way he spoke about these killings?'

'With Sallie Huckstepp he was more emotional. He described how he strangled and garrotted her and when he said it was the most satisfying thing he's ever done, I think he meant it.'

Smith watched him from the dock, unblinking, like a crocodile. Winston Terracini stood up. 'Mr Brown, did Mr Smith say who else was present when he killed Miss Huckstepp?'

'Warren Richards and a third man. He said Richards couldn't sink him for it because he lured her there and Ned knocked her.'

'You say that Mr Smith told you he lifted Miss Huckstepp off the ground, grabbed her by the throat, and snapped her. What does that mean to you?'

'Her voice box.'

'Is that right?'

'Yes.'

'Then what?'

'Well he said he dragged her over to the water and stood on her.'

'Any particular part of the body, the neck or the chest—'

'Objection!'

'Just stop there, Mr Terracini,' Pat O'Shane said. 'It's simply not to the point whether he stood on her neck or her chest. It is not of substantial probative value. The evidence that is contained in the transcript is clear.'

Terracini pressed on, trying to expose some discrepancy with Mr Brown's recorded account. Time and time again Chris Maxwell objected to his line of questioning on the grounds of interpretation, hearsay, relevance.

'Where are you taking this, Mr Terracini?' Pat O'Shane asked.

'We have compelling evidence that the conversation is about things that did not take place.'

'Mr Terracini, nothing in what you have said persuades me to a different view and the Prosecution's objection is upheld. Move on.'

'But your Worship!'

'You have my ruling, Mr Terracini.'

Relations between Terracini and Chris Maxwell grew so discourteous that twice Smith's solicitor, David Giddy, pulled at the sleeve of defence counsel when he questioned Maxwell's ethical approach to this case. Tension in the courtroom was electric. The enmity that had existed between Sallie Huckstepp and Neddy Smith was now being displayed by proxy.

When Detective Sergeant Quinlan of the Fingerprint Crime Scene Unit was called to give evidence that an unidentified male palmprint had been lifted from the boot of Sallie Huckstepp's white Ford Cortina, found parked outside Centennial Park hours after her murder, Terracini sprang to his feet. 'Was Rogerson asked to provide a palmprint?'

'No, sir.'

'Was Rogerson fingerprinted when he was charged with a series of offences in the eighties?'

'No sir, he wasn't.'

'So despite being charged with a number of serious offences and being convicted of one major offence, Rogerson has never had his palmprint taken?'

'That's correct.'

'No further questions.' Terracini sat down with a thump.

On the courthouse porch I caught up with the defence counsel, his face flushed, his jaw resolute. 'Hard yards,' I said.

'She's the most appealed-against magistrate in New South Wales. Wait until we get this to a real court.' And with his coat flapping in the breeze, Winston Terracini trailed down the steps of Central courthouse accompanied by the busy Mr Giddy.

In a Liverpool Street cafe, I took coffee with Sascha Huckstepp. It was easy to forget that the purpose of this committal hearing was to determine whether a jury, if properly instructed, would be likely to convict on the evidence presented by the prosecution. It seemed the trouble with the law was that the truth got sidetracked. Two crucial questions needed answering: Did Smith murder Sallie-Anne? And if so, why?

I stared across the table at Sallie-Anne's 23-year-old daughter in her red and black dress. Sascha's blond hair resembled her mother's. She lit a cigarette. We talked a little of the case and her mother. 'Mum had a lot of fight in her,' Sascha said. 'One day people will appreciate what she did.' She seemed remarkably free of bitterness.

We walked back to the courthouse and Detective Starling approached her with the witness list. I asked him what had happened to Detective Moores.

'Con's been suspended,' Wayne Starling said, steering Sascha away.

In the press box I grabbed the paper from a dozing journalist and flipped through the court pages until I came to the headline: 'Crime squad sergeant rejects "corrupt" label.' Underneath a photograph of Detective Con Moores entering the Royal Commission hearings was a reference to Warren Richards who had known Sergeant Moores of the Crime Squad's Drug Unit since 1984. 'Suspended detective sergeant Conrad Moores is alleged to have accepted tens of thousands of dollars in bribes.'

I sat there with the broadsheet spread open on my lap. A witness was being sworn in by the sheriff but I paid no attention. Two days earlier, Sergeant Neville John Scullion, described as a big beefy detective with jug ears, was dismissed from the New South Wales Police Service after 'Scully' admitted receiving regular bribes from drug dealers while serving at Kings Cross. I kept thinking of the words a young constable in the Police Diving Unit had used earlier to describe the unsuccessful search of Busby's Pond, 'The further you went in, the murkier it became.'

When I finished the article for the second time, I went home. There was a message on the machine from W.B. Despite several attempts, he had been unable to secure a transcript of the listening device tapes. Without the transcript it was impossible to double-check the details of Smith's confession. Rumours were circulating in the press box that he had been set up by senior police.

'I find the allegation that Smith killed her very curious,' a solicitor who knew the milieu had confided to me in his chambers. 'Ned and Sallie never crossed paths.'

•

At 9.57 next morning I ran into Detective Wayne Starling drying his hands in the Gents. 'I want you to know,' Starling said, 'that the whole time I worked with Con, he never did anything wrong.'

'Maybe in some squads you don't have a choice.'

'No.' Starling looked me in the eyes. 'You've always got a choice.'

I went and sat at the rear of court no. 2, thinking Detective Senior Constable Starling was a straight-shooter.

According to Dr Staraj, the bruising on Sallie Huckstepp's face was consistent with 'at least four blows'. Markings on the right side of Ms Huckstepp's throat were consistent with a thumb print.

'You were the first pathologist to examine the body?' Terracini asked.

'I believe so, yes.'

'Would you agree that one of the problems you had determining whether this woman had been strangled was because there were no obvious signs?'

'There were no gross lesions.'

'Did you see evidence that would persuade you that this woman was lifted from the ground and held in the air for five or six minutes with one hand around her neck?'

'No.'

'And did you notice any trauma to the hyoid bone?'

'No, I didn't.'

'No trauma at all in the throat?'

'No.'

When Chris Maxwell objected to Terracini's next question and the objection was upheld, defence counsel said to Pat O'Shane, 'The problem that we have is that you do not listen!'

'That is completely inappropriate conduct by counsel!' Maxwell interjected.

'My friend was of the view that you are so unfit to sit that he made an application for bias.'

'I strongly object to that!'

'Thank you Mr Maxwell, thank you Mr Terracini,' Pat O'Shane said. 'You need not continue. I consider your remarks to be quite impertinent.'

Minutes later Terracini burst out, 'It is readily apparent that you are demonstrating a total unwillingness to listen to any evidence that is in support of Mr Smith's case!'

The packed courthouse looked on, reporters scribbling furiously. Solicitor, David Giddy, tugged at defence counsel's sleeve.

Stroking the back of his hair, Maxwell rose and asked the next witness, Dr Godfrey Oettle, 'What is it you rely on to determine cause of death as drowning?'

The former Director of the Division of Forensic Medicine replied that, among other factors, it is the position of the body, the froth present in the air passages, the appearance of the lungs, an analysis of the blood from the right and left sides of the heart.

'What do you say is the ideal procedure to determine in a case like this whether there is bruising in the neck muscles?'

'The practice at the Division of Forensic Medicine,' Dr Oettle said, 'was to make an incision from each ear down and to reflect the skin away sideways and upwards to expose the front sides of the neck.'

'Was this done, sir?'

'No.'

When Chris Maxwell questioned the procedure carried out by Dr Staraj in the initial post-mortem, of not draining the blood vessels of the deceased's neck prior to examination, Winston Terracini sprang to his feet, his face apoplectic. In heated legal argument, he objected to the attack on Dr Staraj, 'the procedural unfairness to the accused' and demanded an immediate adjournment.

Terracini said he had 'no confidence in the methods employed by this man who appears to carry the brief for the Crown. We will not deal, except in writing, in any shape or form with him, should he remain in the matter!'

'Do I hear a threat?' Pat O'Shane said calmly, 'that the defence will withdraw if Mr Maxwell QC continues to prosecute?'

'We will be here for Mr Smith until these proceedings conclude!'

Professor Bonello, a chiropractic expert, then gave evidence that the snapping noise referrred to by Smith on the listening device tapes was unlikely to have come from the hyoid bone which is surrounded by muscle and fat and well-protected. 'Any hyoid fracture is likely to be inaudible.' He listed a number of different noises that could arise from body tissue under mechanical stress.

Several times Terracini and Maxwell clashed at the bar table: 'My learned friend has indicated that he will not speak to me and it goes without saying that I will not speak to him,' Maxwell said.

'If the Crown wants to paint himself into a corner like a little boy. Get some long trousers—'

'There's only one little boy here!'

'Well I must say I think this behaviour is quite puerile,' Pat O'Shane said. 'When you engage in abuse of the Bench you make a demeaning spectacle of yourself. Indeed when I hear people abuse other people, I start to form the impression that they are losers.'

'I'm not going to be spoken to by *you* in that fashion,' Winston Terracini said. 'Have you got it?'

'You're the one who demeans yourself, Mr Terracini.'

'Don't you dare use comments like that to me!'

At 2 p.m. Winston Terracini made an urgent application that Pat O'Shane disqualify herself from the proceedings. 'It is perceived by those associated with Mr Smith that you cannot dispassionately hear the matter from here on in.'

Chris Maxwell opposed the application. 'This is the most disrespectful behaviour directed towards the Bench that I've heard in over twenty years as a barrister! Your Worship should consider charging my learned friend with contempt.'

'Thank you Mr Maxwell,' Pat O'Shane said. 'Mr Terracini, I can assure you that I have no intention of disqualifying myself. Now I have been abused by the best and the worst in this country, so it doesn't faze me too much, but I must say that I wonder at how your client must feel.'

Wearing a peppermint-striped cardigan and with his white hair sticking up as if he'd just stepped out of a shower, Smith stared straight ahead. He had not uttered a word in the proceedings, apart from whispered consultations with Mr Giddy who would slide over on the wheels of his chair to take instructions.

The witness, Martine Gabby James, then gave evidence that on Thursday, 6 February 1986 she saw Roger Rogerson walk out from a garden in Lang Road, Centennial Park and jump into the passenger's seat of a car that took off immediately. 'Roger drove directly past where I was parked,' Martine James told the court in her marked French accent. 'I think it was the next day that I heard about the death of Sallie-Anne Huckstepp.'

'Can you place a time on this ma'am?' Terracini asked.

'Not exactly. I will say between ten and eleven at night.'

'Are you able to say for certain it was Rogerson?'

'Positive, yes.'

Extracts from the listening device tapes were played by the prosecution. Debra Smith took notes as her husband's rapid aggressive voice echoed around the walls of the court. 'I just snapped her. I just snapped her jugular. She musta been alive when I put her in. Left her floating there. Then dropped the Federal cop's badge right beside her.'

I bowed at Pat O'Shane and walked out for a breath of fresh air. The badge still bothered me. If Smith had murdered Sallie-Anne, why include that false detail? Was it to put investigators off the scent?

Geoff Prentice was standing by the coffee machine, looking uncomfortable in a plaid suit and tie. The former Homicide detective senior sergeant growled and shook my hand until my fingers rang. 'How's it going in there?' He tilted his head.

I told him it was hard to sift the truth from the lies. A number of Smith's details dovetailed with the post-mortem findings but there were parts of his confession that didn't add up.

Geoff Prentice examined me closely. 'I don't know how many blokes you've spoken to in Homicide before?'

'Not many.'

'Well, I've never got anyone yet that's ever told the absolute truth. Even blokes that have confessed,' Prentice said, 'for some reason there's always something they don't tell yer. Like little things. Like you find bloodstains in the kitchen where the murder's taken place. And you'll say did you go into the kitchen? And they'll say, no, no. Yet you know they did. They'll be completely frank with you with everything else, but there's always something they gloss over or they cover up. Some part of their story that they'll lie about or they won't tell you. It always happens with murderers.'

'What about Rogerson?'

Geoff Prentice lowered his voice, one large hand leaning on the coffee machine. 'For a long time Roger was working Neddy with his foot.' The sheriff came out and called, 'Geoffrey Charles Prentice!' And, pulling at his tie, Geoff Prentice followed the sheriff in through the swinging doors.

A line of witnesses waited their turn on the hard wooden benches, leafing through tabloids, staring at their shoes. The railway clocks ticked; a squad of black-jacketed police swept past. One of the witnesses stood out from the rest: a woman in her mid-fifties, dark-haired, quietly dressed. She kept glancing at court no. 2 and shifting her hands around in the bowl of her lap. When the sheriff appeared she gave a little gasp. 'Rosemary Creswell!' he called.

Nervously, Ms Creswell took the oath in the witness box. She told the court that she had acted as 'Neddy's literary agent', visiting him 'twelve to fifteen times at Long Bay' and speaking to him on several occasions about Sallie-Anne Huckstepp. 'Ned disliked her intensely,' Rose Creswell said. 'He made that clear.'

'What did he say?' Chris Maxwell asked.

'He said, "Do you agree that the person who got rid of Huckstepp has done society a great favour?" I did not reply immediately then I said, "I don't think murdering anyone does society a favour."'

On a further visit to Long Bay, Huckstepp's murder came up in conversation and Smith told his literary agent, 'I know what happened because I was there.'

'He made the comment in a quiet voice,' Rose Creswell said, her hands worrying the pleats of her skirt. 'I didn't know whether he was boasting, joking or making the point that he really did know who killed Sallie-Anne Huckstepp so I quickly changed the subject.'

When Winston Terracini rose, Ms Creswell blinked in anticipation. As usual Terracini started in softly. He asked her if she continued to see Mr Smith on a regular basis after *this* conversation.

'Yes,' she said.

'Can I suggest to you, that if you believed he was confessing to murder that would have affected your relationship?'

'Objection!' Chris Maxwell said.

'These objections by the Crown are deliberately meant to keep material from the tribunal.'

'Thank you, Mr Terracini,' Pat O'Shane said. 'It is sheer rubbish from you.'

'Don't speak to me like that!'

'Just move on, sir.'

Twisting a ring on her finger, Rose Creswell admitted to Winston Terracini that she had lied to police in her initial statement because she feared that she would be charged with conspiracy after the fact of murder. Subsequently her house had been broken into, her car stolen and she had received strange phone calls in the night.

The writer, Ian David, had undergone similar harassment since becoming involved with Arthur Stanley Smith. To write the TV docu-drama 'Blue Murder' he interviewed Smith four times at the National Crime Authority offices in Sydney. The Smith family trust was paid $65 000 by the show's producer.

'Did the defendant ever speak to you about Sallie Huckstepp?' Chris Maxwell asked.

'Yes, he did,' David said. 'He had a very low opinion of her.'

'What did he say?'

'That she was a prostitute and a drug taker, a person of the lowest order. He said that she deserved everything that she got.'

When Smith revealed to Ian David that he was 'present with

others when Huckstepp was murdered', David asked, 'Who?'

'With others,' Smith had said.

•

Chris Maxwell conferred with his instructing solicitor, Karen Stafford, who throughout the hearing had impressed the court with her competence and efficiency. Patrician-like, she glided in her long black skirt to check on the next Crown witness.

In his original statement, Detective Senior Sergeant John Ferguson, of the Major Crime Squad, was unable to recall the date that he and Roger Rogerson had attended the Merrylands Bowling Club and, later the same evening, a cheap Assyrian restaurant in the Fairfield area, but one year later Detective Ferguson was able to recall precisely by checking his duty book that the night in question was 6 February 1986.

'Where is this duty book, officer?' Winston Terracini asked.

'I don't know,' Ferguson said.

'You know that there is no record of you and Rogerson ever being at the Merrylands Bowling Club, don't you?'

'No, I don't.'

'So what time did you leave this restaurant whose address you can't tell us and whose name you can't recall?'

'I don't know what time,' Detective Ferguson said.

Over the following weeks a succession of biologists, pathologists, radiologists and a geneticist gave evidence. Photographs of Sallie-Anne Huckstepp's post-mortem and exhumation were passed back and forth between the bar table and the witness box. Hundreds and hundreds of questions were asked concerning her lungs, liver, ligaments, intestines, muscles, skin, ribs, throat, tongue, eyes, fingernails, blood, brain, bones and DNA. Smith's family were nowhere to be seen, the public gallery emptied of the elderly and the curious, and only the hardiest of court reporters continued to sit through the mountain of forensic material.

'Again, dealing with the organs of the body,' Winston Terracini asked, 'The vessels around the heart were inspected, the heart itself, the stomach, the oesophagus and intestines, renal system, the bladder, gall bladder?'

'It would seem,' Professor Hilton of the Institute of Forensic Medicine said in a dry Scottish accent, 'that all the organs were dissected and examined, yes.'

Re-called, the black-bearded Dr Staraj was questioned by Chris Maxwell about the incision he made in the neck from the chin to the sternum.

'Dr Oettle says that because the ear to ear incision wasn't done and because the brain was not removed to allow blood in the vessels of the neck to drain out, then it would make it difficult to find any bruising, if it existed, of the deeper structures of the neck?'

'I disagree,' Dr Staraj said.

The white-bearded Dr Godfrey Oettle took the stand and responded in a confident and careful manner to a probing cross-examination by Winston Terracini.

'Don't answer that question, Doctor,' Pat O'Shane said.

'Can your Worship give a ruling?' Terracini said.

'Yes. The question itself is meaningless.'

'Are you going to give a reason rather than just offering a preposterous statement?'

'I object to this dialogue!' Maxwell said.

'Thank you Mr Maxwell.'

With his own hand against his neck, Winston Terracini demonstrated to the court the process of strangulation. 'Is it possible,' he asked, 'to quantify with what degree of force one could lift a person weighing 57 kilos off the floor?'

'Objection. Dr Oettle is not a qualified engineer.'

'In my submission he should be able to give that evidence because he may have had the experience of certain tests carried out at the OIFM.'

Compared to Terracini, Senior Crown Prosecutor Maxwell's body language was more restrained, his delivery slower. Twirling his gold-rimmed glasses in one hand, he leaned an elbow on the lectern. A corrective services officer in the dock began snoring while Maxwell spoke. Smith turned and went, 'Psst, psst!' Pat O'Shane looked up. Smith gave the guard a friendly nudge with his elbow and the guard's eyes sprang open like he'd been shot.

'Do you think the method of incision used in the first autopsy was adequate?' Chris Maxwell asked.

'No,' Dr Oettle said. 'I don't think the method used was adequate to show the injuries to the soft tissues of the neck.'

Dr Timothy Mark Clayton, a forensic geneticist flown in from London and a world expert on STR profiling, then gave evidence. For the edification of the court he explained what STR profiling entails.

'Let's say I've been given a bloodstain,' Dr Clayton said. 'We remove the DNA from the bloodstain by literally boiling up the stain in some water and this causes the cells to open and release the DNA, then we take a small amount of that DNA and we put it through a chemical copying process. The DNA recovered from a person's blood will be the same as that found in the person's other tissues, such as semen, hair roots, bone marrow. Except for identical twins, each person's DNA is unique.

'If you imagine your DNA as a giant book with millions of pages and the text in the book says everything about you, your DNA governs your hair colour, your eye colour, your genetic traits . . .'

'So the basic text is that you are a human being?' Terracini asked.

'Yes, we've found that at certain pages of the book there's a printing error and we don't know why they're there, or what their function is, but that's exemplified by the same word being tandemly repeated, that is where STR comes from—Short Tandem Repeats. So if we have a sentence on the page, "Mary had a little lamb" and for some reason the word "lamb" keeps getting repeated, but the number of times it's repeated seems to vary between individuals and that's what gives us the variability. Basically the technique involves photocopying out four pages of text. So really it's a printing error in the book of life.'

'My understanding,' Pat O'Shane said, 'is that the DNA is found only in the white blood cells and they break down fairly quickly after the blood has left the body?'

'Yes.'

'How long does it take?'

'If the bloodstain is in a warm and damp environment,' Dr Clayton said, 'the DNA will degrade very very quickly indeed.'

'And the red blood cells,' Terracini continued, 'they don't have any nucleus, is that right?'

'Yes, the red blood cells are practically the only cells in the body which don't contain DNA, the reason being that they have a very short life. We've been thinking of it as a book, but the actual DNA looks like a long thread that's wound into a helix and along the thread there's a code, just like the alphabet, except it's a four-letter alphabet.'

'Now, Dr Clayton, STR is the most sophisticated method that you know of?'

'Yes.'

'Yet DNA can never say positively *that* is the person?'

'That's right. You can positively exclude somebody, but you can never say the DNA positively matches until you've read the whole book and at the moment we are not in a position to read the whole book. It's going to take laboratories around the world 10–20 years to read the entire text. It's that magnitude of a read.'

'And what were the results of your examination?'

'DNA from more than one person was detected on the fingernail clippings of Sallie-Anne Huckstepp. The blood from Arthur Stanley Smith shows that Smith could be the source of some of the DNA not attributed to Ms Huckstepp herself. The blood sample from Warren Richards did not match the STR profile,' Dr Clayton said. 'In my opinion there is weak evidence to support the assertion that some of the cellular material on the fingernails originated from Arthur Stanley Smith.'

'So he's not excluded?' Maxwell asked.

'He's not excluded.'

'That completes the witnesses to be called, your Worship.'

In the corridor Winston Terracini said to me, 'The woman was a prostitute. She was sleeping with ten fellows a day. Of course there'd be DNA from half a dozen blokes under her nails.'

•

On Wednesday morning, Chris Maxwell rose and leaned on the lectern, one hand in the pocket of his immaculate charcoal suit. 'I will open the submission by making some observations,' he said. 'There is no risk that the defendant hated Sallie Huckstepp. He despised her. Smith tells Brown—"Oh look they made a blue, they didn't look under her fingernails for DNA". Well now it's been done, now you get this kind of result. Not conclusive, but would Smith have admitted that if he thought he was being taped. The Crown says no way in the world.

'As to the Federal Police badge the evidence is that a badge, in fact, was found but it wasn't a Federal Police officer's. The reference is a mixture of fact and exaggeration. Just because you get some details that are not consistent doesn't reduce the Crown case. Many of the details on the listening device tapes are completely consistent with the post-mortem findings.

'There is the admission made to Green, the admission made to Creswell and the admission made to Ian David that he was prepared to go "the whole way". The fact that Smith did not give evidence is most significant. There was no attempt by the defendant to explain the tape. It is highly unusual for a person to admit to murder. How did Smith know Sallie-Anne Huckstepp scratched her assailant's face? Not from the inquest, not from the media—no, because the DNA testing wasn't done until *after* Smith had described on the tapes how he strangled this woman with glee.'

Winston Terracini stood up. 'Your Worship will remember the ramblings of Dr Oettle. My submission is that he can't be relied upon to give any reliable evidence. He never saw the insides of her body, he never ever opened the cavities of the deceased. Never. You should completely disregard his evidence as having no weight whatsoever. His rather sad performance does not befit a professional witness.

'Let us turn to motive. There are fingerprints found on Huckstepp's car, but by an absolutely disgraceful performance of the New South Wales Police force, they don't even take Rogerson's fingerprints when he's charged with conspiracy to murder and now they can't compare them!'

'Rogerson's supposed to have been at the Merrylands Bowling Club with some nefarious people, but nobody signs them in, nobody's a member, they just happen to be there and then they go to a restaurant, no times, no notebook, no record of where they were. That's Rogerson's alibi and in my submission—forget about a reasonable jury—nobody believes it!

'So if there is a motive for Mr Smith there's a better motive for Rogerson, because his alibi is a sham and you get a witness who says not that she saw Smith, not that she saw Richards, but she saw Rogerson in close proximity to where the deceased's car was found with fingerprints on it. But the police can't compare the fingerprints of Rogerson because of outrageous neglect! What was the catalyst for bringing down Rogerson? The death of Warren Lanfranchi. Who was in love with him?—Sallie-Anne Huckstepp. Of all the people she feared it was Rogerson.

'There is simply no evidence in relation to Smith other than some weak DNA. No jury is going to be likely to convict on the material that has been presented before this court!'

Winston Terracini sat down. Reporters flipped through notebooks; pens jittered on the page. Smith's daughter conferred in whispers with her wiry boyfriend. Smith leaned forward in the dock and patted the thin shoulders of Mr Giddy. The pugnacious Terracini had put up quite a fight.

•

After 93 sitting days, Pat O'Shane dismissed four other murder charges against Smith because of inconsistencies between his accounts on the tapes and those of key witnesses and forensic and ballistic reports. Debra Smith, wearing a black and white crepe pants-suit, her hair freshly styled and her nails painted red, told the swarm of press mobbing on the steps, 'I've said all along Ned is innocent!'

Three murder charges remained.

In the court vestibule I waylaid the sheriff, a gruff, clean-shaven former military policeman who was privy to the inner workings of

Central Local Court and asked him what the likelihood was of Smith being discharged in the Huckstepp matter.

'Can't tell you that.' The sheriff smiled knowingly. 'But I do have a lot of respect for Pat O'Shane. She's made enemies in high quarters, but she's a very intelligent woman. She'll make the right decision.'

And as he spoke, Pat O'Shane strode past us towards her chambers, a bulging spring-loaded exhibits folder marked *Huckstepp* tucked under her arm.

I went home. No sooner had I opened the door to my apartment than the phone rang. I picked it up and heard W.B.'s voice. 'Got it!' he said. He gave me an address in the city, a time when we could meet and hung up.

The Crown Hotel is a hundred-year-old brick and tile building on the corner of Elizabeth and Goulburn Streets, a short stroll from Federal Police Regional Headquarters and in close proximity to the Downing Centre courts. The top bar was filled with lawyers and law enforcement officers drinking at separate tables. I pulled up a stool by the window and scanned the faces. Most of the lawyers were drinking bottled wine, the cops nursing schooners. Somebody tapped me on the shoulder and I turned to see a lean man in his late forties. He had thick eyebrows, a large bony nose and deep blue eyes.

'W.B.?'

'Call me William,' he said. His hand was as rough as sandpaper. He lowered a black briefcase onto the table between us and popped the catch. There were a lot of questions I had for W.B. but this wasn't the time or the place. He had to drive down to Canberra tonight, he said. Otherwise he'd stay and have a drink. He held out a manila envelope. 'Look, I don't think you should read this.'

'Why not?'

'Take my word.' His eyes locked onto mine.

I stared at the scar tissue at the corner of his cheekbone and prised the envelope from his fingers. 'So what happened to Sallie-Anne?' I said. 'Why her fascination with the underworld?'

W.B. removed his briefcase and rolled the numbers back with a finger. 'When she was fourteen,' he said. 'she was submitted to cross-examination by one of the top silks of the day and copped it full blast. After that Sallie always claimed she lost respect for the law.'

'And the furs? What was in the furs?'

'Photos,' he said.

'What sort of photos?'

'Can't tell you that,' W.B. said. 'I've got to go.' And turning sideways, he squeezed between a table of lawyers and walked out of the Crown Hotel. I watched him climb into a white Ford Fairmont in Elizabeth Street. With a fingernail I slit open the sealed AFP envelope and slid the transcript marked 'Tape Number 5' onto my knee.

WARNING

THIS DOCUMENT CONTAINS SENSITIVE LISTENING DEVICE MATERIAL—IT SHOULD ONLY BE READ WITH THE APPROVAL OF THE TEAM LEADER—ITS CONTENTS SHOULD ONLY BE DISCLOSED TO THOSE INVESTIGATORS WITH A DEMONSTRATED NEED TO KNOW.

V1: Target. Arthur Stanley (Ned) Smith

V2: Gary Trevor T— Prisoner 199

V1: She come down one night to the pub to try and bug me, I was full of drink.

V2: Yeah.

V1: She come and said, 'Can I talk to you, Ned?' I said, 'Yeah.' And she started talking, she started recording me in her bag. I took the fuckin' thing out, I threw it around and jumped on her. Smacked her on the fuckin' jaw.

V2: I remember seeing her on *60 Minutes*. She got on there talking about it.

V1: They were trying to make a martyr out of her. Wrote a song about her and all.

V2: It's called Sallie-Anne.
V1: She reckoned I fucked her so I did, good and proper.
V2: Hah.
V1: That was the most satisfying thing I ever done in me life.
V2: I bet it was.
V1: I waited three weeks for Sallie.
V2: Yeah.
V1: How I got her. She was buying gear off Warren. Warren rang her up at night said, 'Meet me.' She met me the night before I had Abo with me.
V2: Yeah.
V1: We were in a van with the side open. I was going to put her in. 'Oh no, Ned,' she said, 'please don't do it!' She jumped out and took off. Abo knew I was gonna do it.
V2: Yeah.
V1: I got her the next night.
V2: She's a strange lookin' thing, a bit pretty—
V1: She was classy, mate.
V2: Yeah.
V1: I was laying in the grass, she walked in through the big steel gates of Centennial Park, didn't even see me.
V2: Fair dinkum.
V1: I had a black thing on, black balaclava, when she got close I took the bala off, put it down me pants and just walked up behind.
V2: Ooh.
V1: Got her like that and I spun her around.
V2: From behind?
V1: Spun her around, she went aaah, grabbed one hand there like that. 'Know what this is for cunt?' Fuckin' terror in her eyes. I hit her, WHACK, WHACK . . . punched the cunt out of her, I went off me fuckin' head. She put a hand up. BOOM BOOM. I'm giving it to her, I was holding her throat tight. I snapped her jugular just snapped it. She couldn't talk. 'WWAAAAH!' she went. She couldn't breathe, nuthin'. She didn't fuckin' die quick.
V2: Shit.
V1: Six minutes I held her by the throat.

V2: That's a long time, think she would've been dead before that.
V1: I had her by the throat, she was just dangling, she was looking at me, I said, 'You know what this is for cunt?'
V2: What she say?
V1: Couldn't talk or nuthin', she went 'WAARRR' to Warren, help her, he was standing there watching me. Couldn't kill the cunt, I choked her, I put a thing around her.
V2: Fair dink, she's only a slip of a thing too.
V1: About seven stone.
V2: Fuck me dead.
V1: Fuck chokin' mate, takes too long.
V2: Was she on the junk?
V1: Then I put a cord around her neck and garrotted her, didn't fuckin' kill her.
V2: Fuck, she's only a little chick too.
V1: She would've been a nutcase, see I cut off the oxygen to her brain, she would've been a nutcase—
V2: Yeah, she would've been fucked.
V1: Me, me and Warren dragged her and put her in the water and I stood on her in 2 foot of water. Held her under fuckin' water the cunt. Stood on her for five minutes.
V2: Yeah.
V1: They say she had water in her lungs, she must've been alive when I put her in. Left her floating there. Then dropped the Federal cop's badge right beside her.
LAUGHTER
V2: That would've asked a few questions wouldn't it?
V1: Got him the sack, got him pinched and everything.
V2: Yeah.
V1: And he had some stolen mink coats . . . she pinched 'em and sold 'em, oh, that all come out. His name was Smith too, the fuckin' dog.
V2: Did you know him?
V1: No, Roger pinched his badge.
V2: Right.

V1: Roger stole his badge and give it to me, he said drop this beside the body.
V2: To incriminate him.
V1: Yeah. Made headlines, fuckin' Federal Police officer.
V2: I remember the headlines.
V1: And he couldn't explain his badge. You wouldn't believe how they found it.
V2: How?
V1: The SWOS team were running, doing their morning training, they found her floating. They were running past they said, 'What's that?' Pulled her out. The fuckin' SWOS team.
LAUGHTER
V1: Special Weapons Operations.
V2: Fuckin' unbelievable!
V1: Had his fingerprints on it 'cause when Roger give it to me he give it to me in a plastic bag.
V2: Yeah?
V1: Said whatever you do don't touch it. I just shook it out.
V2: Yeah.
V1: I had her ... I took her straight off the ground with sheer strength. Just held her there, I said, 'You know what this is for?' She got me, scratched me down there.
V2: Yeah.
V1: Know the mistake they made?
V2: What?
V1: They never took the stuff from under her fingernails. They would've got my skin from under her nails. She was in there for um, nine hours.
V2: Yeah.
V1: I got her like that, snapped the neck, soon as I got her, snap!
V2: Yeah.
V1: I said 'You fuckin' moll.' Give her a biff. I went WHACK WHACK. She's out like a light, I threw her on the ground.
V2: She would've been—
V1: Then I held her by the throat and her tongue and her eyes come out like that. Tongue swelled up.

V2: Yeah.
V1: When she was gone I put the cord. I had a piece of cord with two wooden broom handles, didn't work so I, I had a knife. I was gonna cut her eyes out but then fuck it, I just drowned her.
V2: Yeah.
V1: I had a mate standing there with a machine gun, he was shaking you could hear him rattling the fuckin' gun.
LAUGHTER
V1: He was standing near a tree. [SOUND EFFECTS] Shut up you cunt. When we was going, he took off like a fuckin' dog.
V2: Yeah.
V1: He's a squarehead, been with me on six murders.
V2: Fair dinkum.
V1: He's a fuckin' top bloke.
V2: He must be staunch.
V1: He won't say a word mate, he's too good.

TAPE CEASED AT 6.05 p.m. 27/9/94 UNIT 7, Cell 19, C Wing, SPECIAL PURPOSE PRISON, LONG BAY.

•

At 10.00 a.m. on Friday, 6 September 1996, Pat O'Shane entered from a side door behind the bench of Central Local Court no. 2. 'All rise!' the sheriff called. The doors were secured and the packed gallery waited for the magistrate to resume her seat. Pat O'Shane bowed, sat down and commenced reading from a laptop computer.

'Considerable emphasis is made by the Crown,' she began, 'on the manner in which the defendant speaks about Sallie-Anne Huckstepp and his killing of her as heard on the listening device tapes as the most satisfying thing he has done in his life. The Crown argues, how did the defendant know she scratched the killer unless he was the perpetrator? What is clear from these tapes is that the topic of killing other human beings is discussed by the defendant in much the same manner as farmers might discuss the weather.

'There were also his comments to Rose Creswell, his literary agent, and in particular his remark to her: "Do you agree that the person who got rid of Sallie-Anne Huckstepp has done society a great favour?"

'Lengthy submissions were made by the defence counsel about the evidence of Roger Rogerson,' Pat O'Shane continued. 'None of that evidence is sufficient to accuse Rogerson and, in any event, does not rule the defendant out of consideration. There is little to be said about Rogerson and his mate Ferguson. They showed their contempt for these proceedings and portrayed themselves as unmitigated liars.

'I acknowledge that there are difficulties with the forensic evidence and note those inconsistencies. I would not go so far as to characterise them as conflicts in the evidence of the forensic pathologists. Otherwise, I accept the Crown submission as to the character, weight and reliability of the Prosecution evidence and I am not of the opinion that a jury, properly instructed, would not be likely to convict.

'Stand up, Arthur Stanley Smith!' Pat O'Shane said.

Wearing a light blue suit, Smith rose in the dock, one tattooed hand resting on the rail, his dark eyes expressionless.

The court went silent.

'Do you wish to say anything in answer to the charges?'

'I'm not guilty your Worship and I reserve my defence.'

'In respect of the matter of Sallie-Anne Huckstepp. You are committed for trial at the Supreme Court at a date to be fixed. Bail formally refused.'

Rolling his head from side to side, Smith was led down to the cells.

In the doorway of Central Local Court, the sheriff exchanged a look with me that didn't need words. There was no doubt what had happened to Sallie-Anne when she was 31, but I still wanted to find out what had happened to her when she was 14.

14

Bondi

Ramsgate Avenue runs at a forty-five degree angle through North Bondi down to Ben Buckler Point, where you can stand on the rocks and gaze across the bay at the splendour of Bondi beach. Waves thrash at the mouth of the hundred-year-old ocean outfall which branches back to the city in a labyrinth of sewer lines. Divided into four apartments, 9 Ramsgate Avenue is a two-storey white stucco building formerly owned by Naum and Judith Krivoshow, Russian Jews who migrated to Sydney from Azerbaijan via Palestine in 1926. Described as 'hard workers', Naum and Judith Krivoshow had three children, Rose, Isaac and Jack. To support his family, Naum Krivoshow travelled around the State selling things out of a suitcase.

'He knocked on my door in Muswellbrook,' a friend, Ronnie Eagleton, recalled, 'and asked if I wanted to buy some clothes. I said what have you got? I think I bought some trousers. Then Jack, the youngest, came back to deliver them. When I came down to Sydney I ran into Jack again. The mother never spoke a word of English. She used to get my dinner and talk to me in Russian and I didn't understand a word she was saying. The older brother Ike—he was mentally retarded. He wasn't over bright, a lovely big fat boy. Mrs Krivoshow used to dote on him. Then there was the sister,

Rose. It was always a mystery about her. I only met her once. She was walking down the passageway. I thought, "Hey! Here's the sister that no-one wants to talk about." The youngest, Jack, was into a few businesses. He's very clever, self-taught. He was wild, a very attractive man. No problem with the female side of things.'

'We used to go to the Sheraton in Double Bay for dinner dances,' a friend from the 1950s, Lee Shields-Rossit, remembered. 'I was going out with a Jewish boy. It was Christmas and I said could I bring a girlfriend along. I can't remember how I met Pat, but I introduced her to Jack Krivoshow. Patricia was sixteen, very thin, long blond hair with a distinct English accent, but it wasn't cockney and it wasn't lah de da. She was living in Bayswater Road in a block of flats with her mother. I remember she wore a black and white check dress, long petticoats. She wasn't too good in the foot department. It might've been that first night, or the next, anyway she got pregnant damn quick.'

Twelve days before her seventeenth birthday, Patricia Anne Merbach, the daughter of an Australian father and English mother, visited a terrace in Rushcutters Bay. A roly poly man with soft pudgy hands led her down to a small dark room that smelled of disinfectant. He gestured for her to climb up onto a metal table covered with a white cotton sheet. Patricia took off her petticoat and stockings. The man explained that 'the treatment' was £60 with anaesthetic, or £40 without. Wearing rubber gloves he pressed lightly around the edges of her abdomen. Patricia stared at the steel instruments soaking in a jar of cloudy liquid on the chipped sideboard. She shut her eyes and felt the sharp tip of a glass syringe probe between her legs. Terrified, she jumped off the table, grabbed her hat and underwear and ran sobbing out the door. Seven months later, she moved into Ramsgate Avenue with her husband and new baby daughter.

From the beginning Judith Krivoshow made no secret of her feelings towards 'the English girl'. Patricia was not Jewish, she had no money of her own, and she was more sophisticated than the Krivoshows. According to a neighbour, the mother-in-law was a tyrant who ran the block of flats in Ramsgate Avenue like an army camp: 'She used to ask you how much money you had in your bank account!'

But Jack Krivoshow disagreed. 'My mother was very severe but a caring person,' he said. 'My parents worked like two dogs to bring their kids up. They knew what Pat was like. My mother was fastidiously clean, a person of great hygiene, there was not a speck of dust in our house, she resented people if they weren't clean. You didn't walk into our house with your shoes on. My wife was an emotionally unstable woman. Promiscuous.'

'She was pretty loose,' Lee Shields-Rossit agreed. 'Very irresponsible. Patricia played up while Jack was working. She was far too young to be a mother. She just hit the town.'

Several of Jack's friends suspected that Sallie-Anne might not be his biological daughter, but as soon as they saw the child they changed their minds. Sallie-Anne was the spitting image of her father.

'She was an absolutely adorable baby with big blue eyes and long lashes,' Lee Shields-Rossit said. 'Sallie-Anne was a gift.'

A keen photographer, Jack Krivoshow would set up his tripod, camera and lights and take stylish black and white photos of his baby daughter. He dressed her in expensive outfits from Double Bay, read her nursery rhymes and rocked her to sleep. For eighteen months Jack worked as a salesman for Remington, struggling to pay the bills. After the birth of a second child, Debra Jane, Jack decided to emigrate to Canada with the idea of sending for his wife and daughters once he got established. 'No sooner was I on the boat,' Jack said, 'than *she* was in someone else's bed.' Pat fell pregnant and wired him asking for money for 'medical treatment'. Jack sent it. When she brought the children over to Canada, Jack caught her in bed with a sailor. Then a month later she walked out on him leaving him alone in a strange country with two baby girls. Debra remembers snow piling up around the front door, her father going off to work in a brown trenchcoat.

'Being in Canada with two kids on your own was not fun,' Jack Krivoshow said. He was selling office equipment, selling anything he could to get by. There was a recession on. When he returned to Sydney he stepped off the boat with four shillings left in his pocket, caught a cab to Bondi. For a brief period he was re-united with Patricia, but six months later she was gone again. This time for good.

Left to cope with two children under the age of five, Jack sold cars at City Ford and drove taxis on the weekends. In 1959 there were no support services. His mother helped out in the daytime; friends chipped in at night.

'When Jack came back from Canada,' Lee Shields-Rossit recalled, 'he turned up on my doorstep with Sallie and Debra, one in each arm. They had big saucer eyes and blond hair. Little pink coats with these little pink hoods. They were absolutely beautiful children. Gorgeous. I adored them.' Lee was a TV producer at Channel 7 and one day she took Sallie and Debra along with her to work. 'I got them on the Johnny O'Keefe show,' Lee said. 'They were on "Sing Sing Sing" on the Christmas special, Johnny singing to them. I got them on Reg Quarterly's kids' show. Sallie was very clever. I looked after her and Debra like they were my own children.'

Sallie's appearance on the Johnny O'Keefe show met with such success that she was invited back. A young apple-cheeked boy sang a love song to her with Johnny O'Keefe sitting in the middle, the choir behind. Johnny was impressed with the six-year-old. He asked her what she wanted to be when she grew up and Sallie said, 'a dancer or an actress'.

For months afterwards all Sallie could talk about was JOK. Being on TV was an enormous thrill and she quickly acquired the taste for it. The television industry needed kids. Her appearance on 'Sing Sing Sing' led to offers by advertisers for Sallie and Debra to model kids' clothing, appear in ads for Omo, floating soap, powdered milk, detergent and David Jones specials. The money was welcome and helped pay for Sallie's schooling at Moriah College in North Bondi where she had two Hebrew lessons a day. 'At primary school Sallie was very popular,' Debra said. 'She was doing well, she was on the right track, she wanted to achieve.'

'Very grown-up,' a Moriah College teacher remembered, 'a little bit rebellious, but always had fabulous report cards.'

Jack Krivoshow was extremely proud of his daughters and when he was home he spoiled them. 'C'mon little ladies,' he'd say. 'We're going to a restaurant.' He'd do their hair, put flowers in it and tell them how beautiful they were. 'There's not many good-looking Jewish girls,' he'd say to them. 'You two can have anyone you want.'

For a man to raise two girls on his own in 1961 deserved respect. Jack did well financially and bought property in Dover Heights, but was rarely at home. After school hours Sallie and Debra were minded by their obsessively clean grandmother. All her towels and sheets were white and she bathed the children until they were red raw.

'Grandma used to give Sallie-Anne some beltings,' Debra said. 'We had to eat boiled rice and milk and it was horrible.' For lighting matches under her bed, Sallie-Anne was dragged into the bathroom and Judith Krivoshow beat the backs of the seven-year-old's legs with a wooden spoon. 'You're turning into another Sushanna!' she yelled, referring to her eldest Rose, who came and went at Ramsgate Avenue in an air of mystery.

One day Judith threw the children out into the street in their underwear, cursing them in Russian for tramping sand into the house. Sallie learned to avoid her grandmother. She adored her Uncle Ike who lived in the same block of flats and would sit on his unmade bed while he read her stories from the Pentateuch and the Talmud, stories about great Jewish heroes. Sallie's favourite was baby Moses being hidden in the bullrushes on the banks of the Nile. With her blue eyes wide open, Sallie would ask Ike to read that one again, biting her nails while she listened. Uncle Ike was her best friend. She confided to him about the other girls at Moriah, how they said she was different because she had blond hair and no mother.

At nights, while grandma lay snoring on the couch, Sallie and Debbie would sneak into Aunt Rose's room and slide the heavy drawers open on her mirrored dresser. In the darkness they touched velvet and silk and ran small curious fingers over her fox fur with its white-streaked tail and hard tiny clawed feet. Once, Aunt Rose caught Sallie behind her wardrobe, trying on her cinch-waisted

Christian Dior dress. Rose tore the garment from Sallie's hands. 'You fucking little cunt!'

A dark, stunningly beautiful woman, Rose Krivoshow worked at two jobs and spent her money on designer clothes. The children were forbidden to enter her room. Neighbours recall slamming their windows shut when the aunt 'came out with filth, absolute filth'. A famous European artist had painted Rose when she was fifteen and had wanted to take her to America, but her mother wouldn't let her go. 'It wasn't a good scene,' a family member revealed. 'Ike used to bolt his door because Rose threatened to gas him.'

Despite clashes with her aunt and grandmother, Sallie enjoyed the freedom of her childhood. In the late afternoons she walked down to Ben Buckler Point holding her baby sister's hand and stood on the headland staring at the two fibreglass mermaids that graced the giant rock on the tip of the headland. She went barefoot and played with the other Jewish kids by the sea. She loved Bondi and for the rest of her life she would never stray far from the Eastern Suburbs.

For a short period Aunt Rose cared for the two girls when they moved into 40 Eastern Avenue, Dover Heights. 'They irritated me a lot,' Rose said. 'Raiding my underwear. Sallie-Anne was an adventurous child. She always wanted to test her wings and fly. She thought she had nine lives.'

Jack's friend, Ronnie Eagleton, then arranged to receive the two girls after school. 'Sallie grew up quickly,' Ronnie Eagleton said. 'Their father thought the sun shone out of them. Sallie-Anne was a little rogue, a ringleader, she led Debbie round by the nose.'

Physically, Sallie was over-developed for her age. Compared to other girls she was also far more sophisticated. She knew how to order in restaurants, she'd been on television, she modelled clothes. She went swimming and dancing, played basketball and excelled at running. Even as a nine-year-old, Sallie saw how some older men on the beach looked at her. She was tanned, her hair bleached by the sun and her legs were muscular.

'She was terribly adult for her age,' her father said. 'An emotional person, very strong-willed.' When she got home from school, Sallie did the housework. Along with the cat, Sallie and Debra would climb through a missing pane of glass in the bottom of the back door. As they grew older Sallie and Debra were left more and more on their own. Neighbourhood kids used their house as a secret meeting-place and played 'spin the bottle' and 'doctors and nurses'. At the age of ten, Sallie put on childish strip shows, serving milk and cookies at interval.

'I guess you could say she was a Lolita,' a close friend of the family said. 'She was a cunning little girl. Fascinated with sex and with her body. The whole family were bizarre.'

One evening, Lee Shields-Rossit and the singer, Al Lane, came over to babysit. Lee cooked dinner and Sallie-Anne refused to eat her spinach. Al Lane said, 'You're not leaving this table until you eat that.' Sallie stood up and went down the hall. A door slammed. Minutes passed then Lee got up to look for her. Sallie had disappeared. 'We searched the house,' Lee said. 'We called the police in. Al and me and two uniformed constables combed the hills of Dover Heights. We looked everywhere.' At three o'clock in the morning Jack arrived home from driving cabs. 'Sallie's run away,' Lee told him. The three of them went out calling her name in the dark. 'We thought she'd gone over a cliff,' Lee said. 'The next morning at dawn we found her. Sallie was sitting in a cupboard inside the house. She'd stayed there perfectly still all night.'

Several of Jack's friends now believed that Sallie-Anne needed discipline; others felt that she needed love. Jack was seeing a Jewish woman who lived across the road in Dover Heights. Instead of sneaking back and forth at dawn each morning, the woman suggested to Jack that they get married. It was a quick courtship. The woman had a daughter from a previous marriage and Jack was looking for a mother for his girls. 'We were married for two years,' Jack said. 'Naïvely I thought she'd be good for the kids.'

According to Debra Krivoshow, when the stepmother moved in she perceived the ten-year-old Sallie as a threat. 'Estelle was very cruel to Sallie-Anne,' Debra said. 'She wasn't allowed out of her bedroom until 7 a.m. and if she wanted to go to the toilet she'd have to wee out the window. Once Sallie wet her panties and Estelle made her wear them around her neck. Dad turned his eye to a lot of that. Another time Sallie ate some cherries out of a tin and Estelle punished her by making her eat a cold chop with Ajax on it.'

When the rest of the family went on outings, Sallie-Anne would be locked in her bedroom 'sitting within a circle chalked on a piece of paper'. The stepmother cropped Sallie's hair, forced her to wear ugly dresses and took her own daughter, instead of Sallie, to modelling. She accused Sallie-Anne of being in love with her father 'in a sick way'. When she caught the two sisters in bed one morning she called them lesbians. 'I didn't even know what a lesbian was,' Debra said.

Sallie-Anne told friends that her stepmother often struck her across the face with the heavy gold rings on her hands.

Thirty years later, Sallie's stepmother denied that any of these events occurred. She admits to striking the child, but only on the legs and the backside. 'It wasn't a good marriage,' Estelle said. 'There was a lot of friction. Sallie-Anne was impossible. I remember having an argument with her in the bathroom and I was hyperventilating. The only time in my life that has happened to me. Sallie ran wild. She was clever. I never won an argument with her. I just couldn't deal with her. I said to Jack, what will I do about Sallie? "Oh, let her do what she likes," Jack used to say.

'Sallie was ten years of age!' Estelle said. 'She was the only person that's ever frightened me. She could look at you and lie. As she got older she grew more manipulative. Nobody has the right to tell me what to do, she'd say. I do what I want.'

A few months after she moved in, Estelle discovered Sallie, Debra and her own daughter, sorting through a box of pornographic photos Jack had developed in his North Sydney studio. 'Dad lets me look at them,' Sallie said. But another girlfriend of Jack's recalls the photographs as being simply 'artistic nudes'. Estelle decided quickly that she didn't want her daughter, Marion, growing up in this household. On another occasion she found Sallie hiding her wet underwear behind a dresser. Estelle and Jack took the child to a psychiatrist.

'I don't know one psychiatrist I've been to since I was eleven,'

Sallie told a reporter years later, 'who has really done anything for me except screw me up more.'

Estelle's daughter, Marion, remembers Sallie-Anne as a daredevil. 'She had no fear of anybody. When she hated, she really hated. She'd look at you like an evil cat; give you that stare.'

'Estelle did a lot of damage to the kid,' one of Jack's girlfriends said. 'But I don't think it was Estelle's fault quite frankly. It was Jack's. He was cold, withdrawn, always working.'

On Saturdays Sallie-Anne dressed in her best clothes and went to the synagogue. She was proud of being Jewish and had a bat mitzvah at the age of twelve. 'She was right into hanging with the Jewish kids,' Debra Krivoshow said, 'Jewish families would take us home for lunch.' During her final year of primary, Jack removed Sallie-Anne from Moriah College because of the high cost of the fees and enrolled her in Rose Bay Public School.

Many years later, when Sallie-Anne had achieved notoriety in the Sydney underworld, one of her classmates would write to the *National Times*:

> SIR, Any endeavour to associate Moriah College with Mrs Huckstepp and her lifestyle is entirely erroneous and ill-founded and can only be described as an attempt to further sensationalise the already sordid details of Mrs Huckstepp's life at the expense of a school which consciously instils community mindedness and personal integrity and also has an excellent academic record.
>
> Barbara Oser,
> Double Bay, NSW

At the age of twelve, Sallie-Anne enrolled at Dover Heights Girls High School. Her teacher, Val Scanlon, remembers her as a beautiful girl. 'I think Sallie's trouble was that she was too pretty,' Ms Scanlon said. 'She wasn't a bad girl, she just grew up physically very early. I used to see all the men watching her. She was too attractive. At thirteen she could pass for eighteen and in many ways that is a burden for a young woman.'

Three months after Estelle left, Sallie-Anne was walking home from Dover Heights when a red MG pulled up alongside. A man with silver hair and a trimmed moustache asked her if she needed a lift. Sallie-Anne glanced at the soft bucket seats and the man's black leather driving gloves and shook her head. The man leaned a corduroy-jacketed arm over his roll-bar, offering her a cigarette.

Sallie took the Salem from between the man's fingers and inhaled, shifting the strap of her schoolbag. The school bus rumbled up Military Road, girls' noses pressed against the back windows. 'Can I buy you a coffee?' the man asked.

'I don't think so,' Sallie said.

'Don't be alarmed, I'm a psychologist and perfectly respectable.'

Sallie smiled.

'You know what gapped teeth signify, don't you?' the man asked.

'No.'

'They're a sign of a highly-developed sexuality.'

Laughing, Sallie turned on her heels and strode up the pavement in her navy tunic and blouse, the red MG following her as far as Eastern Avenue where the man tooted and waved. She slipped through the missing pane in the back door and locked herself in the bathroom. In the mirror she touched her gapped teeth with a finger. Was he really a psychologist? He looked older than her father. The following afternoon a dozen red roses arrived on her front doorstep. 'From Rex', the note said, 'with affection'. Older men, Sallie-Anne quickly discovered, were attracted to her like flies. Whenever she walked along the beach they came up alongside, wanting to talk, to flirt, to reassure her of their good intentions. Once a cassocked priest approached her at dusk, gripping her wrist so tightly that she carried a bruise there for days. Did she know it was wrong before God to parade about in such a short skirt? 'Well, don't do it!' Sallie said and pushed him off.

At Dover Heights High she grew more rebellious. On the surface she was the school outlaw, but secretly she dreamed of becoming a great actress and marrying her leading man. She wanted to have five children. She was artistic, popular and she loved attention. 'Would Sallie-Anne Krivoshow please come to the office!' the PA system crackled at least once a week. And with a weary sigh and a dramatic shrug of her shoulders Sallie would get up from her desk and stroll down the corridor to Miss Peacock's office, lean against her open door as if to say, 'What now?' At lunch times she smoked outside the fence and skipped class. 'Everybody liked her at school,' Debra Krivoshow said. 'Sallie had a way about her.'

The singer Renée Geyer recalls going to a high-school party at the Krivoshows' house in Dover Heights. 'Sallie was very sweet,' Renée said. 'A bit lonely, a bit sad. She had this smiling face and big blue eyes. The party was just for Jewish kids.'

With Estelle gone, Sallie resumed the adult's role in the household, getting dinner ready, washing, ironing, looking after her sister. She started hanging around Vinny's milkbar in Bondi. She was thirteen years old but, according to Debra, Sallie-Anne carried herself like a twenty-year-old. 'You couldn't expect her to still be a child after all she'd been through with Estelle, and she wasn't. She was a grown woman.'

According to a friend, it was from watching 1960s' television that Sallie-Anne learned how to be a woman. She loved to wear make-up. One night she came home wearing a new black top she'd bought from Gasworks in the Junction. It was tight and groovy and did up with two straps. 'Sallie-Anne was quite big-busted,' Debra said, 'you couldn't see anything, but Dad started going mad at her. He ripped her top, saying, "What are you doing going out dressed like a slut?" I walked over and hit him on the head with a frypan.'

'We could go for six to twelve months without talking to each other,' Jack Krivoshow admitted. 'Sallie had an explosive temperament, just like her aunt.' He had high hopes for his elder daughter, because she was so intelligent. He wanted her to marry well. 'If you girls play your cards right,' he used to say, 'you'll have them lining up at the door.'

A good-looking Jewish boy from a prominent Bellevue Hill family started to call around to Eastern Avenue. The boy was madly in love with Sallie-Anne, but she wouldn't come out of her bedroom. Her father begged her to go out with him. 'Please, this boy is from a very good Jewish family!' No-one could understand her reluctance. 'Why don't you like him?' Debra whispered in the bedroom.

'Because,' Sallie said, 'he's too straight.'

'Sallie could have had any man she wanted, wealthy or not, if she'd put her mind to it,' Debra said years later, 'but she was attracted to bad boys.'

At fourteen she still mixed with the Jewish crowd, but she was branching out. She played basketball with Hakoah Ladies' Basketball Club and made new friends at Bill's Surf Shop. One Saturday she ran into three boys down at the south end of Bondi and they asked her to come up to their flat and have a smoke. Sallie thought they meant cigarettes. She walked up Bondi Road with two other girls to the boys' flat and everyone sat down. There were records playing and one of the boys rolled a joint, then they passed it around and Sallie had about two hits out of it. It relaxed her and made her feel slightly drowsy.

A week later, on Sunday morning, she met a friend, Mick Kiggins, down at Bondi beach. Mick asked her to come for a ride with him. 'We went to a place at 14 Taylor Street, Darlinghurst,' Sallie said, 'and we knocked on the door and a fairly tall university guy answered and Mick said something that I didn't hear and we went upstairs and one of the guys, I don't know his name, but he had a slight accent and wore glasses, he pulled out a whole bag full of grass from behind a wardrobe and divided it in half and Mick paid him $225 and the guy put the grass in a shoe box and Mick and I caught a cab back to Bondi and sat on the beach near the rocks and Mick gave me about two matchboxes in a plastic bag.' Sallie took it home and had a couple of joints with a girlfriend and then she hid the matchboxes in the bathroom. At least once a month, depending on how upset she got, Sallie smoked a joint with the 20 or 30 young people who gathered at the southern end of Bondi beach.

On Thursday, 18 August 1969, her father drove her to the Great Synagogue dance where an older boy introduced himself. His name was Danny Freilich and he was in sixth form at Vaucluse Boys High.

'How old are you, Sallie-Anne?'

'Fourteen,' she said.

Sallie wore eye-shadow and a white mini skirt with a French-style striped top, and when Jack Krivoshow picked his daughter up later that night he gave the young man a lift home in his taxi to a big rambling house in Bellevue Hill. 'What a nice Jewish boy,' Jack said.

The next day, Danny called around to Eastern Avenue and Sallie and the eighteen-year-old had coffee and talked about a newspaper article on drugs. Danny liked his kicks and asked Sallie if she'd ever tried marijuana. Sallie said she had. He asked her if she'd tried acid and Sallie said no. Danny said he could get her 'a ticket', because he liked to have something different. Each time they went out to the pictures or a dance Danny picked Sallie-Anne up and then afterwards he would escort her home. Two weeks after they started dating, Danny came over about three o'clock in the afternoon and watched TV. Jack Krivoshow was out driving his cab and Debra was at a girlfriend's place. Sallie hung out the washing and when she came inside she sat on the floor beside Danny and started to tickle him under the arms.

'We ended rolling around the floor and Danny kissed me,' Sallie told police. 'I was lying on the floor and he touched me on the breasts and then his hands moved down to my pants and he undid the zipper in my trousers. He took my trousers right off, also the pants I had underneath. Then he took his own trousers, underpants, shoes and sox, and coat off and threw them on the floor. He continued to kiss and cuddle me and he got on top of me between my legs and put his penis in my vagina and moved up and down on top of me for about fifteen minutes and then he rolled over and pulled me on top of him. He put his penis in my vagina again and we were like that, I was on top of him, when I heard the key in the front door. I jumped up and ran into the bathroom. Then I heard a knock on the door and Dad said, "Come out as soon as possible, Sallie-Anne." I had another pair of trousers in the bathroom so I put them on and when I went out into the lounge room, Danny was gone but all his clothes were still in a pile on the lounge room floor.'

'Whose trousers are these?' Jack Krivoshow said.

Sallie did not reply. She watched her father storm outside to see what he could find. He strode around the back yard, but found nothing, so he came back in and bundled up the pair of men's rubber-soled boots, blue trousers and jacket and put them in the boot of his car. 'Who's been here and what have you been doing?'

'I don't know,' Sallie said.

Her father went out again and searched underneath the house. He came back with Danny, who had a towel wrapped around the lower part of his body. Sallie recognised the towel from their clothes-line.

'You've been having relations with my daughter!' Jack said.

'No sir.' Danny sat on the couch.

'Give me an explanation then!'

Danny said that he didn't want any trouble, that this could break up his parents' marriage. He said he was receiving treatment from a psychologist. 'Please, Mr Krivoshow, give me a break.'

Sallie's father picked up the phone. He told his daughter he was going to ring Bondi police. Sallie argued with him. 'No Dad, don't.' She went into the kitchen, from where she heard her father talking on the phone. Danny stayed in the lounge room.

Two uniformed policemen arrived at the house. Minutes later Danny's parents rushed over and then two plainclothes detectives appeared on the doorstep. There was barely enough room for all the adults inside, everyone arguing at once.

'I was sitting there on the couch with a dirty red dick, because she had her periods,' Danny remembered 30 years later. 'The cops wouldn't let me get dressed. They said do you know how old she is? I said, "sixteen." They took me down to the station and then next day my father got a phone call. One of the detectives said to him, "Maybe if you pay X amount it'll be over." They were asking for thousands.'

Danny's father refused to pay.

'She wasn't a virgin,' Danny said. 'She wasn't my first and I wasn't hers. A lot of guys had made love to her before I got there.

She was a pretty intelligent girl and we were smoking and dropping acid. I thought I'd found nirvana, because I'd found a Jewish girl who fucked. They charged me with two counts of carnal knowledge.'

'That's when the troubles started,' Debra Krivoshow remembered. 'Word spread through the Jewish community. Sallie was branded and that's when she started to go bad. In the Jewish community the woman is always blamed, the woman is a slut. Sallie got a shocking deal. They were two healthy young people.'

'What would you do if you walked in on your teenage daughter having sex on the floor?' Danny Freilich asked. 'Would you call the police?'

'It was wrong to call them,' Jack Krivoshow admitted years later. 'I had a moralistic attitude.' He denied trying to blackmail the Freilichs, who had a large property portfolio. But Julia Deal, Jack's girlfriend from those days, recalls Jack saying to her that he was going to get compensation from the boy's family 'for ruining his daughter'.

According to Estelle Krivoshow, Theo Freilich came to her father's furniture factory one morning and begged her for help. He said his son was going to go to gaol and that Jack Krivoshow had phoned him after hiding the boy's clothes and demanded $10 000. 'This will hurt you more than me!' he had apparently said when Theo Freilich refused to pay.

But police records indicate that Jack Krivoshow rang the Freilichs after he rang Bondi station.

With the committal hearing set down for October, Jack sold the house at Dover Heights and moved his daughters back into Ramsgate Avenue so that Rose and Ike could supervise the girls at night. Three of the flats were rented out and Jack, Ike and Rose shared the fourth. Sallie and Debra slept in bunks in the same bedroom as their father.

One morning Sallie was late for school. Her uniform was on the line and her father stood at the top of the stairs and screamed at her to hurry up. 'Fuck you,' Sallie said.

'Well, when she got upstairs,' Debra recalled, 'Dad lost it. We were sleeping in Grandma's old room. He took to her with an electric cord, she was in a corner and she was screaming and he wouldn't stop, and I was standing there and I couldn't believe the beating he was giving her. He lost control. He went that bad on her. Whipping her around the face, the head, welts on her cheeks. An hour later he went near her and she started crying, freaking out. This was just after Danny Freilich.'

Two detectives visited Sallie-Anne at home and told her that the accused's family had engaged a prominent Queen's Counsel. 'Do I have to be a witness?' Sallie said. 'There's nothing to worry about,' the detective sergeant assured her. 'Just tell the magistrate the truth.' Embarrassed by her ordeal, Sallie stayed away from school; she avoided the beach crowd. With her father and a friend, Julie Pearce, who was also a witness for the prosecution, Sallie arrived at Redfern Courthouse wearing pancake make-up and a white mini skirt and top.

'My name is Sallie-Anne Krivoshow,' she told the closed court. 'I am fourteen years old and I go to Dover Heights Girls' High.'

'Tell me exactly in detail what was done,' the police prosecutor said.

'Danny inserted his penis in my vagina.'

'Did he keep still or move?'

'He moved.'

'Did you notice anything about yourself. Your private parts were they dry or wet?'

'Wet,' Sallie said.

At 11.55 a.m., Mr Laurence Gruzman QC, assisted by two instructing solicitors appeared for the defendant. Gruzman stared at the fourteen-year-old girl. 'I would like to have it noted how Miss Krivoshow is dressed today—I can't think of a word to describe it.'

'À la mode?' the Magistrate suggested.

'You take drugs, don't you?' Gruzman began.

'I used to,' Sallie said.

'It's been part of your life for a considerable time to have sexual intercourse with fellows who've provided you with drugs, isn't that right?'

'No.'

'Did Danny Freilich provide you with drugs?'

'Yes.'

'And on each occasion he provided you with drugs, you had sexual intercourse with him?'

'No.'

'When did you first have sexual intercourse?'

Sallie turned to the Bench. 'Do I have to answer this?'

'Yes,' the Magistrate said.

'At the beginning of this year,' Sallie told the court.

'How many boys have you had sexual intercourse with?'

'Two.'

'Who are they?'

'Do I have to answer this question?' Sallie asked.

'You have to answer it,' the Magistrate said.

'Danny Freilich. And a boy ... ah ... named ... ah ... Paul.'

'Paul Hedley?'

'Yes.'

'How many times did you have intercourse with him?'

'Twice.'

'Do you swear you were a virgin when Paul Hedley first had intercourse with you?'

'Yes,' Sallie said.

'You know a boy called Mick Kiggins?'

'Yes.'

'And you had intercourse with him?'

'No, I did not.'

'Any boy can undress you, can't he?'

'No.'

'Provided he has drugs in his possession?'

'No,' Sallie said.

'Your pants are showing.'

'They are not!' Sallie said.

'We at the bar table,' Mr Gruzman QC said, 'are of the opinion that this witness ostentatiously shows her underclothing.'

'When a young woman wears short skirts,' the Magistrate ruled, 'every time she crosses her legs, she must show some part of her underclothes, I'm afraid.'

'Might Mick Kiggins be called into court,' Gruzman continued. MICK KIGGINS IS CALLED AND ENTERS COURT. 'Is this Mick Kiggins?'

'Yes,' Sallie said. MICK KIGGINS LEAVES COURTROOM.

'You were in that boy's bed on Saturday night?'

'No,' Sallie said.

'You got undressed?'

'No,' Sallie said.

'All except your panties?'

'No,' Sallie said.

'You told him you would have intercourse with him but you were having your periods?'

'No, I didn't.'

'Madam, you let it be known to everybody that you would have sexual intercourse with anyone who provided you with marijuana?'

'I did not,' Sallie said.

'Mick Kiggins provided you with marijuana?'

'Yes.'

'And you had sexual intercourse with him?'

'Not at all.'

'I put it squarely to you that boys have given you marijuana in return for sexual intercourse!'

'No.' Sallie clutched her arms to her breast.

'Are you distressed?' the Magistrate asked.

'I'm very cold, sir.'

Warned not to discuss this case with anyone, Sallie was stood down. In the corridor she passed Danny and his three legal advisers huddled together. With a flick of her head Sallie-Anne gave them a contemptuous stare and strode out into Redfern Street in her knee-high boots and white vinyl skirt accompanied by her friend, Julie Pearce, who had also given evidence for the prosecution. Hunching into the wind, Sallie lit a cigarette and quizzed Julie on what Gruzman had asked her. The two girls had been separated while giving evidence.

Julie said he asked her if Danny knew Sallie was fourteen; Julie told him that Danny *knew* Sallie was in third form. Then the man asked Julie how many boys she had made love to, except he called it *intercourse*. He wanted to know if Julie had had *intercourse* with Jeffrey Williams and she said yes, Michael Williams and she said yes, Harry Nightingale and she said no, Robert Candy and she said no, Ross McDonnell, yes, Wayne Blighton, no, Phillip Greathead, no, Paul Hynes, no, Robert Cottrell, no, and Greg Heath, yes. He asked her if she liked having *intercourse* with a number of boys one after the other. 'You have done that haven't you?' Julie said yes. 'You're known as "The Case" aren't you?' And she said yes. 'That means that you're known as the girl who will sleep with anyone?'

'Bastards.' Sallie glanced over her shoulder at two men wearing grey felt hats right behind them. Sallie grabbed Julie's arm and ducked into a women's shoe shop. The men hung about outside, jotting in notebooks. When the two fourteen-year-olds left the shop the men tailed them to South Sydney Leagues Club where they shouted abuse at Sallie.

Sallie informed her father who spoke to the Prosecutor who then raised the matter in court. He warned that if this intimidation continued he would instruct detectives to take action under the Crimes Act. In response, Mr L. Gruzman QC complained that it was not fair that these two girls should be allowed to talk together when one of them was under cross-examination. He asked Sallie if she had discussed any matters connected with this case with her friend.

'No,' Sallie said. 'We talked about my exams.'

'You've always had a keen interest in sex, haven't you?'

'No.'

'You used to go out with the boys at Moriah College and take your pants off?'

'I did not.'

'When you were eight years old there was an inquiry into your conduct at the college?'

'I was ten or eleven,' Sallie said.

'Part of that inquiry was about you going into the bush with boys and exposing yourself?'

The Prosecutor stood up. 'Objection.'

'We're showing that this girl is a prostitute and an associate of same,' Mr Gruzman said. 'I can carry it through in an unbroken chain to this time.' ESTELLE KRIVOSHOW ENTERS COURTROOM. 'This is Mrs Krivoshow, is it not?'

Sallie started to cry. MRS KRIVOSHOW LEAVES COURTROOM.

'Is the witness alright?' the Magistrate asked.

'Yes.' Sallie blew her nose.

Gruzman continued his cross-examination.

'Were you in the habit of deliberately wetting your pants with urine?'

'I had a weak bladder,' Sallie told him.

'And you used to store up all the soiled panties in the wardrobe, didn't you?'

'No.'

'I can't see what the personal habits of a young child have to do with it,' the Magistrate interrupted.

'A matter of credence, your Worship. I'll go further. Did you take money from Marion's and Debbie's money boxes?'

'No,' she said.

'Do you remember an occasion when your mother—I refer to Mrs Krivoshow—saw you sitting with your legs apart and your pants showing?'

'I saw my mother once and I walked past her in the last two years.'

'I put it to you that your mother saw you at Kings Cross at ten to one in the morning with an older man with a beard?'

'A moustache,' Sallie said.

'You were dressed in hippy gear, weren't you?'

'No.'

'You were wearing a hippy blouse and an Indian braid around your head?'

'No!'

'Do you tell lies?'

'Everyone tells lies.'

'The real reason is that you act as a prostitute?'

'No, it is not.'

'You know what a prostitute is, don't you?'

'Yes.'

'Did your Aunt Rose give you a pair of tiger-striped pyjamas?'

'Yes.'

'And they were torn where the breasts and the sexual organs were?'

'No they weren't.'

'Your mother objected to you wearing these pyjamas, did she not?'

'Not that I remember.'

'Did she tell you they were cheap and nasty?'

'No.'

'That you shouldn't be wearing pyjamas that a prostitute had worn?'

'No, she did not.'

'Your Aunt Rose is a prostitute isn't she?'

'Objection!'

The Magistrate stood Sallie down while legal argument ensued. Mr L. Gruzman QC reminded the Bench that one of the statutory defences of carnal knowledge in New South Wales was that the witness 'was a prostitute or an associate of prostitutes'. He then called for a warrant requiring the Commissioner of Police, Mr Allen, to produce the criminal record plus fingerprints of Rose Krivoshow.

After a lengthy adjournment, police records revealed that Rose Krivoshow—aka Rene Khan, aka Rene Lane—had eleven convictions in New South Wales and Western Australia for 'Offensive Behaviour Stopping Men' and 'Assist to Keep Brothel'.

When Sallie was re-sworn, Gruzman confronted her with a police mug shot, SPL PH 61/2984: 'This is your Aunt Rose isn't it?'

'Yes,' Sallie said.

'Did your father ever say to his brother at the table, "Who are you trying to kid, Ike, you know Rose is a prostitute, she has been one since she was sixteen?" '

'I've never heard my father say that. Never.'

'Did Ike say, "Look Jack, you don't have to worry, Rose has always been booked under different names." '

'No, he did not.'

'Have you ever heard your aunt referred to as a prostitute?'

'Never.'

Gruzman asked Sallie if she had any obscene photographs. Sallie admitted to looking at some B&W photos of nude women from her father's wardrobe. She had his permission to look at them. 'Were these women standing or sitting?' Gruzman wanted to know. 'Just sitting,' Sallie replied. Gruzman put it to the fourteen-year-old that these photographs, in fact, showed two men and one woman having *intercourse* with the 'woman sucking the other man's penis'.

'No, that's not true!' Sallie said.

'And you showed them to the girl next door?'

'I didn't even see them to show her,' Sallie told the court.

For 35 minutes, Gruzman cross-examined Sallie-Anne about her Aunt Rose. 'Did you say "Rose says why break your back when you can earn a fortune lying on it?" '

'No, I didn't,' Sallie said.

'You know she is a prostitute, don't you?'

Sallie denied it. She denied telling her classmate, Edwina Bauman, that she was going to be a prostitute if she failed her fourth-year exams. She denied kissing Danny Freilich's penis in the back of a 1956 motor car.

'Are you prepared to swear on your oath?'

'Yes, I am,' Sallie said.

In his final submission, Mr L. Gruzman QC told the court that this innocent young man, Danny Freilich, needed protection far more than this unfortunate girl. 'Frequently seen at a wine bar, she was prepared to have intercourse with boys who gave her marijuana,' Mr Gruzman said. 'It is our submission that this makes her a prostitute. It is a difference between sexual intercourse for love as opposed to intercourse for some material reward.'

There was also evidence that Sallie-Anne was associating with 'a common prostitute'. Association between A and B could not be stronger than to show A lived under the same roof as B. 'Also the "see-through pyjamas" was the sort of thing you would expect a prostitute to give to a young girl,' Mr Gruzman said. 'That is why girls who are an associate of prostitutes don't need protection.' This young girl was no virgin. She associated with a girlfriend who admitted to having intercourse with three boys at once, 'an extremely perverted type of sexual intercourse'. It was perfectly obvious that this girl fell outside the class of persons to whom the criminal law gives its protection.

'That being so,' Mr Gruzman concluded, 'we ask your Worship to take the bold step and discharge my client.'

'Stand up, Daniel Aaron Freilich,' the Magistrate said. 'You are charged that on the 25th day of August you did unlawfully and carnally know Sallie-Anne Krivoshow, a girl above the age of ten years of age and under the age of sixteen, to wit the age of fourteen years. Do you wish to say anything in answer to the charges?'

'I am not guilty, your Worship,' Danny said.

'You are committed for trial at the Court of Quarter Sessions,' the Magistrate said. 'Bail $50.'

Sallie-Anne strode out of Redfern courtroom. She had liked Danny, but he was her blood enemy now. She could never forgive him for recruiting her stepmother.

Sallie stood in the foyer with Julie Pearce, biting her fingernails. Her head reeling with the eminent QC's questions. Did she use a contraceptive? Did she take the pill? Had she ever fallen pregnant?

She was so glad it was over. She wasn't giving evidence at the trial. She'd run away first. Julie squeezed her arm and, sharing their last cigarette together, the two girls hurried down the steps towards the trains. A woman and two men approached them in the street. 'Is your name Sallie-Anne Krivoshow?'

'Yes.' Sallie dropped her fag underfoot.

'This is Sergeant Fricker and Detective Bannister. I'm Detective Sergeant Phillips attached to the Drug Squad. We'd like to ask you some questions at CIB.'

Sallie climbed into the rear of the black police car and waved goodbye to Julie. At the station, she told the two male detectives and the undercover policewoman that her father was working until midnight. There was no other adult she could ring. Detective Phillips informed Sallie that it did not matter. She need not answer nor say anything unless she wished, but what she did say would be recorded and may be used in evidence. 'Do you understand that?'

'Yes, I do,' Sallie said. Detective Phillips switched on his recorder. It was 5 p.m. 'What drugs have you been using, Sallie?'

'Just grass,' she said.

'When you say grass, do you mean Indian Hemp?'

'Yes.'

'What form did you smoke it in?'

'In a joint.'

'When you say a joint do you mean that the Indian Hemp is rolled in a cigarette form?'

'Yes.'

'How many times have you smoked this Indian Hemp?'

Sallie said that she had smoked it down on Bondi beach six or seven times. She smoked it with other young people.

'Do you have any idea where these young people are obtaining this drug from?' Detective Phillips moved his chair closer.

'Lots of places,' Sallie said. 'Some go to Maitland, some go to Noosa. I believe it's growing up there. Others buy it from places like Taylor Square and they are getting a lot of acid from university guys.'

'Have you ever tried the drug LSD?'

'I tried it once,' Sallie said.

'What effect did it have?'

'I had a real nightmare. I saw things that were not there. I thought I was six inches tall and people were miles high!'

'Where were you?' Detective Phillips asked.

'Down the beach.'

At 7.15 p.m., the three detectives adjourned for Sallie to have her dinner in the cells and then the questioning continued from 8.15 p.m. in the interview room until Sallie was charged on her own admissions at 10.10 p.m. Detective Phillips asked Sallie if she could remember the names of any other young people that she had smoked Indian Hemp with.

'Danny Freilich.'

'Where does this person live?'

'Victoria Road, Bellevue Hill, I think his phone number is 381526, if you have a telephone book,' Sallie said, 'I will look it up for you.' She took the directory from the detective, ran her finger down the page. 'Yes, there—184 Victoria Road and that is the correct telephone number.'

'Any other names that you recall?'

'No.'

'Is there anything further that you wish to tell us about your use of drugs?'

'What can I say,' Sallie said, 'except I will try never to take them again.'

15

The trial

Thirteen years, eight months and five days after Sallie-Anne Huckstepp's murder, the trial of Arthur Stanley (Ned) Smith begins in Darlinghurst. When the Crown Prosecutor, Patrick Power, a late replacement for Chris Maxwell, reads extracts from the listening device tapes to the jury, the 54-year-old Smith busies himself tapping at the keys of his silver laptop. With the exception of one elderly woman and a middle-aged man, this is a young jury—eight men, four women—carrying yellow notepads and dressed in jeans and bright T-shirts as if on excursion. Sascha Huckstepp, the first of the Crown's 67 witnesses, tells the Supreme court that her mother was 'buying drugs off Warren Richards' and that her mother's solicitor, Val Bellamy, also acted for Roger Rogerson.

'Did your mother ever discuss with you selling information?' Winston Terracini SC asks.

'She wasn't selling it,' the 26-year-old Sascha says, 'she was trading information to help Dave Kelleher.'

'Was it a common practice for your mother to tape people?'

'With the police,' Sascha replies, ' yes.'

•

For an hour, former Federal Police constable Peter Smith gives evidence of his brief relationship with Sallie-Anne. 'She was psychologically dependent on me,' he explains.

'Sometimes you had to have sexual intercourse with someone to get information?' Winston Terracini suggests.

'Yes,' Smith says.

'Now, why did you want the fur coats?'

'They belonged to Assistant Commissioner McCabe.'

'But why did this concern Federal Police?' Justice Abadee interjects.

'Because they were being stored in a Federal safe house.'

'But *why* were they being stored in the Federal safe house?' the Judge wants to know.

'You'll have to ask Assistant Commissioner McCabe.'

'You were aware that certain New South Wales Police at this time were being targeted by the AFP?' Winston Terracini continues.

'There was a particular [drug] operation in which various New South Wales Police popped up.'

'Did Ms Huckstepp tell you that Roger Rogerson had tried to murder her with a "hottie" [contaminated needle]?'

'That's correct.'

'She also told you she had taped Detective Gary Spencer?'

'Yes.'

'Did you ever have any dealings with Gary Spencer?'

'He contacted me after her death and wanted an informal meeting. He wanted to know what was on the tapes.'

'He was concerned?'

'Yes, he was most concerned.'

'How did he know these tapes existed?'

'I don't know,' the barrel-chested Smith replies. 'She used to call him "Gucci".'

'Ms Huckstepp had a penchant for nicknames,' Terracini remarks to the jury. 'Did Spencer give you the impression he knew where Ms Huckstepp's tapes existed?'

'No.'

'But he was desperate to get hold of them?'

'He was keen to find out their contents.'

'Did you tell New South Wales Police that Sallie-Anne Huckstepp had told you Roger Rogerson was trying to kill her?'

'Yes.'

'In your police diary,' Terracini continues, 'you don't refer to Ms Huckstepp in endearing terms?'

'No.'

'In fact you refer to her as "Smackie"?'

'That's correct,' Smith says.

•

It becomes apparent that the new Crown Prosecutor is struggling with the complexity of this brief. He stumbles over dates and fails to alert the jury to the fact that Sallie-Anne had told Peter Smith she also feared for her life from Neddy Smith. By contrast, Winston Terracini and Mr Giddy know their material inside out. The names of corrupt New South Wales Police officers roll off Terracini's tongue and, when Ian David enters the witness box, he wastes no time in inquiring what the writer of 'Blue Murder' thought of Rogerson's alibi for the night of 6 February 1986.

'I found Mr Rogerson's alibi to be worthless.'

'Mr Smith told you that Warren Richards was present at the death with others?'

'That's right,' David says. 'Smith was able to relate the manner in which she died in a very detailed way.'

Literary agent, Rose Creswell, follows David into the box. She informs the court that Sallie-Anne's murder always struck her as a crime Smith knew something about.

'Do you recall telling the police that Smith said to you he knew what happened because he was there?' Terracini asks.

'Yes, I did,' Rose Creswell replies, and in a surprising development she adds that what Smith actually said was, '*I know I never done it. I oughta know because I was there.*'

The inclusion of the preceding sentence in her evidence has weakened the Crown case. I ring Creswell at her office the following morning and ask why—after four years—she has chosen to modify her story. 'I've always known that's what Neddy Smith said,' she tells me. 'Whatever the consequences I decided that I had to tell the entire truth.'

•

In the corridors of Darlinghurst Court I find Debra Krivoshow talking to detectives. Tanned and wearing a black trouser suit, Debra bears a striking resemblance to Sallie-Anne. She has the same blue-green eyes and gapped teeth; her hair is dyed blond. Other witnesses are staring at her. An old man and a young man wearing identical suits approach us. The old man's collar is a size too large, his neck freshly barbered. 'You're Sallie's daughter?'

'Sister,' Debra says.

'This is my son.' The young man smiles.

'And you are?' Debra asks.

'I knew Sallie-Anne before all this business.' The old man waves at court no. 2. 'A long long time ago. You're very much like her.'

Debra laughs. 'Should I take that as a compliment?'

'Oh yes,' the younger man interjects.

'I was in the drug squad in the early seventies.' The old man leans forward. 'I always liked Sallie. A lovely girl.'

Debra watches the old man totter down the steps, gripping his son's forearm. She glances at me and then, shielding her face with a newspaper, strides out into the street through the posse of waiting photographers. Later, in a Darlinghurst cafe, she tells me that she has no doubt Neddy Smith, with the assistance of Warren Richards, murdered her sister. 'Neddy tried to get her in the car a month or so before,' Debra says. 'I think Sallie-Anne worked out where her smack was coming from, that it was police smack. Both Richards and Smith were working for Rogerson. Because she had caused so much trouble before, Rogerson said let's get rid of her.

'One evening,' Debra continues, 'not long after Sallie's murder I met this detective in a nightclub. A little short guy. I was with a group of girls and one of them said to me, "That's Billy Duff." He didn't look like a cop. I went over to him at the bar and said, "Gee, you look really tired."

'He said, "I've been in court all day."

'And I said, "I know what that's like."

' "How would you know?" he said.

'I told him my sister was murdered.

' "Who's your sister?" he asked

' "Sallie-Anne Huckstepp."

'And Billy Duff went white, he turned his eyes away.

'I said, "What is it?"

'He pulled me aside and he talked to me for an hour. "Listen, I'm Bill Duff," he said. "I can't tell you right now who killed your sister, but I know it's going to come out. I promise you, no matter what happens it's going to come out who killed her." '

•

Detective Starling is being cross-examined. He responds directly and frankly to the questions, turning to face the jury. The jurors seem relieved to encounter an honest detective.

'You went to Berrima Gaol to see convict Rogerson?' Terracini asks.

'Yes, sir.'

'Rogerson volunteered Malcom Spence as an alibi. Is Spence still in the lunatic asylum?'

'No idea, sir.'

At the time of Sallie-Anne Huckstepp's death, investigators were closing in on Rogerson's activities?'

'Yes, sir.'

'You've spoken to Martine James and she provided police with a statement that she saw Roger Rogerson on the night of Sallie-Anne Huckstepp's death near the entrance to Centennial Park?'

'Yes, sir, along those lines.'

'She swore on oath it was Rogerson she had seen.'

'Martine James is not only ill,' Starling reveals, 'but concerned. She doesn't want to give evidence in this matter.'

•

Dr Godfrey Oettle has conducted 15 000 post-mortems. The former Director of the Division of Forensic Medicine guides the jury through their blown-up colour photostats of Sallie-Anne's post-mortem, pointing out the petechial haemorrhages in the whites of her eyes and the lining of her eyelids. He indicates bruising on her neck consistent with manual strangulation and marks on her skin consistent with the application of a ligature. He pinpoints scrape abrasions on her back which are consistent with Sallie-Anne having been dragged into the water.

'You're aware that the accused said he stood on her back,' the Prosecutor asks. 'Were there any marks consistent with that?'

'There was no evidence of any shoe imprints.'

While the jurors, in pairs, study the exhibits, Dr Oettle continues his evidence: 'Yes, I think it is quite possible for a strong man to lift a person weighing 53 kilos off the ground and hold her there.'

The defence team have their heads down. Dr Oettle is a major obstacle to the claim that Smith's confessions on the tapes were wildly inaccurate.

'What does the word consistent mean?' Terracini asks.

'A situation that is probably caused by a certain action,' Dr Oettle replies.

'You give evidence for over an hour and yet you never saw one internal organ of the deceased. Correct?'

'Only after the exhumation.'

'Let's forget about that,' Terracini snaps. Much of his cross-examination concerns the alleged ineptitude of Dr Staraj and is lost on the jury who continue to stare down at their colour photocopies. The marks on Sallie-Anne's throat provide the more compelling narrative.

At the conclusion of Dr Oettle's evidence, the prosecutor suggests chirpily that it might be time for lunch. Mr Giddy rocks in his chair and Terracini resumes his seat. This has not been a good session for the defence.

•

Gwen Beecroft is sitting outside the court reading her statement. Gwen only knew Sallie-Anne for five weeks, yet here she is, fourteen years later, still living under Sallie's shadow. After Gwen gives evidence I bump into her in Oxford Street. Fluttering her small hands, she asks me how she went. Good, I say. Like so many witnesses in this case, Gwen is delighted that her part is over. Now she can get on with her life.

Glenn Stone has flown in from Darwin. He walks with the aid of a stick and tells the court that Sallie-Anne told him that Neddy Smith had raped her. In the absence of the jury, Terracini makes an urgent application that his Honour tell the jury that there has been no corroboration that his client had any sexual connection with the deceased. Justice Abadee instructs the jury that the allegation of rape is no more than an allegation of rape; that there will be no evidence called to support such allegation. In the court vestibule Glenn Stone shows me the jagged bullet wound in his leg. The surgeon had to extract large pieces of bone after Glenn was shot from behind with a high-powered rifle. 'I know who did it,' Glenn says.

•

Fifteen kilos lighter, Mr Brown is unrecognisable from the man who gave evidence three years ago. His face is lean and pinched; his complexion sallow. No longer in witness protection, Mr Brown is said to have recovered from a serious illness. He explains to the court that there were two switches at the back of his computer, one to switch on the tape and one to start the recording from the hidden microphones. He describes in detail how Smith demonstrated strangling Sallie-Anne with his bare hands. 'Ned got pretty excited. His mannerisms and his voice. Like he would speak quicker.'

Smith fixes his eyes on his former cellmate.

'Warren Richards was present when Ned strangled Sallie-Anne,' Mr Brown says. 'She scratched him down his cheek like this.' He demonstrates to the jury with a raking motion of his fingernails.

The prosecution has provided members of the jury with individual headphones. Justice Abadee and the three barristers remove their horsehair wigs to listen to the six DAT tapes. Sascha Huckstepp, sitting beside Detective Starling at the rear of the court, also listens to what Smith boasts he did to her mother.

'Know what happened when I got home?' Smith tells Brown.

'What?'

'Got Michelle [Richards] to meet me down the pub. She come in and said ... "You fuckin' cunt you want to ..." WHACK, WHACK, WHACK and scratched me and all.'

'Good one.'

'Had about 50 witnesses.'

'Yeah, good stuff.'

'I said, "Look what you did", and I give her a clip. Roger ran over and said, "Cut it out, Ned, oh look what she's done to your head."'

•

It is clear from these transcripts that Smith had no idea he was being taped. The impression which lingers is of a man who derived personal and emotional satisfaction from revisiting Sallie-Anne's murder.

'I couldn't get her for a while, she was too smart for me.'

'Yeah,' says Mr Brown.

'Avoided me all the time you know.'

The tapes roll on. The clearest indication that Smith was acting under instructions occurs when he describes how Sallie turned up in the middle of Centennial Park.

'If it's got to be done,' Smith says, 'it's got to be done.'

'Yeah.'

'Nothing you can do about it.'

I stare at the accused hunched in the dock, a pair of black headphones clamped to his head. In his autobiography Smith had written that among those who celebrated after Sallie-Anne's murder were 'several police officers'.

•

At 6.50 a.m. the next day Martine James is arrested at her home on a bench warrant prepared by the defence team and signed by Justice Abadee. Fingerprinted and detained for four hours she is conveyed in a police wagon to the cells beneath Darlinghurst Supreme Court and brought up into the dock next to Neddy Smith. Suffering from pancreatic malabsorption and denied her medication, Martine's hands are trembling.

'I sent them a medical certificate,' she tells me in the interval. 'I didn't expect to be treated like this.' She repeats her story that she saw Roger Rogerson come out of a garden in Centennial Park on the night of Sallie-Anne's murder. She remembers it was between nine and ten o'clock.

'What day was it?' I ask.

'A Sunday,' Martine says.

I tell her that Sallie-Anne was murdered on a Thursday.

Martine admits she is not sure of the day. She made a note in her diary at the time and later supplied the diary to detectives who were investigating the murder. Martine has not seen her diary since.

•

Former Detective Sergeant James (Jimmy) Waddell was in charge of the original investigation at Centennial Park. He admits under cross-examination that he knew Roger Rogerson well.

'He was a mate of yours, wasn't he?' Terracini asks.

'I regard him as such, yes.'

'Did you ring Rogerson on the day Sallie-Anne was found dead?'

'I can't recall,' Waddell says.

Former Detective Sergeant Conrad (Con) Moores was in charge

of the re-investigation pertaining to Sallie-Anne as part of Task Force Snowy. He admits under cross-examination that he is due to stand trial on a charge of conspiracy to pervert the course of justice.

•

The cost of this fourteen-year-old investigation has run into the millions. Smith's legal aid team comprises two barristers as opposed to the Crown's one. Flown out from England for the second time, Dr Timothy Clayton tells the court that he tested the DNA extracts from the fingernail clippings taken from the left-hand of Sallie-Anne together with Smith's blood samples. He found weak evidence to support the assertion that some of the cellular material on the fingernails had originated from Smith.

For reasons of law the jury are not informed that Rogerson's palm prints have now been taken and do not match the prints found on the boot of Sallie-Anne's car. The defence team will not risk Smith giving evidence in this trial. Instead, they rely on his wife to provide him with an alibi.

Debra Joy Smith tells the court that 7 February is their wedding anniversary but on 6 February 1986 she and Ned had celebrated it early at the Phoenician restaurant in Newcastle, arriving home at 11.30 p.m. The next morning Ned received a phone call from Rogerson. Ned left to go and use the public phone. When he came back she packed his bag for him and he drove to Sydney around lunchtime.

'Was there some reason why you chose to go out the night *before* you actual anniversary?' the Prosecutor asks.

'Ned knew it meant a lot to me, to wake up Friday morning and have him there.'

The Prosecutor tenders a draft copy of Smith's book *Catch and Kill Your Own* in which Smith had written that he was in the Iron Duke Hotel with Rogerson on the Friday when Rogerson received a phone call from the detective in charge of the Huckstepp investigation.

'Yes, but that doesn't state a time,' Debra Smith says, 'and it doesn't really say Ned wasn't home.'

Under cross-examination she admits that she has lied on oath for her husband before.

'I put it to you that you lied here in this court today?' the Prosecutor says.

'No.'

'I put it to you that when you saw your husband on that weekend he had scratches on his face?'

'No.'

Smith's elderly mother-in-law, Gloria McHale, confirms that she always minded the grandchildren on her daughter's wedding anniversary. She tells the court that in 1986 Debra rang and said Ned had to go to Sydney because there was a murder. When questioned as to the date she minded the children, Mrs McHale says it was a Friday. 'Seventh, yes, that's right.'

'Were you at their home on the evening before?'

'No.'

In the dock Smith holds his head in his hands.

•

Day after day forensic experts trail in and out of the box. Professor Hilton confirms that Sallie-Anne was strangled until she was unconscious and then drowned; that a number of small bruises on her face, jaw and the inside of her mouth were caused by an application of force; that marks on her neck were consistent with the edge of a belt being applied.

The defence team have hired their own forensic pathologist who claims that the injuries to Sallie's face were not consistent with Smith's confessional material in terms of blows described, that he saw no evidence of the deceased being lifted by the throat and held in the air for some minutes. When Terracini reads aloud from the transcript details of the attempted garrotting, Smith's wife, seated at the rear of the court, turns her face to the wall.

•

Word among the court reporters now is that Smith will be acquitted. The consensus is that the Crown's case lacks vigour. In his closing address, Patrick Power tells the jury that Smith chose to exaggerate some aspects of his involvement and add things to his story. 'There are questions that will always remain about the death of Sallie-Anne Huckstepp,' Power says. 'She was one of the great whistle-blowers about police corruption in New South Wales, certainly the one who gained the greatest notoriety. It is clear that she had a deep dislike for Mr Smith. It is also clear that Smith worked very closely with Roger Rogerson and also knew Warren Richards. Whether these two people were involved in the death of Sallie-Anne Huckstepp we will never never know.'

For reasons known only to Power and his instructing solicitor, not only are Rogerson and Richards not called to give evidence, but neither is Mr Green, the former seaman who told the committal hearing that Smith had rung him in February 1986 and said that, 'I'm going to get rid of that Sallie. I want you to bury her for me.' The jury never learn that Smith and Richards were seen together just five weeks after the murder. What is most disconcerting is that the rape allegation is not pursued in court.

The defence assert that Smith only became aware of the deceased at the Lanfranchi inquest, rejecting any suggestion that Smith and Sallie-Anne had a sexual connection in the past. Yet a simple investigation reveals that Sallie-Anne had told half a dozen people, including Debra Krivoshow, Wendy Bacon and Scott McCrae, that Smith had raped her. She told her barrister, Ian Barker QC, in a taped interview that the rape took place in early 1981—months before Lanfranchi was shot—and that she had kept her distance from Neddy Smith ever since.

'You don't have to like him,' Terracini tells the jury, pointing at the accused. 'There is a presumption of innocence. If you don't give Mr Smith a fair hearing then eventually *no-one* will get a fair hearing!' Cleverly, Terracini works his audience, raising and lowering his voice. In the space of half an hour, he manages to weave into his closing address the Wallabies' world cup victory, Shane Warne's leg break, the Athenians, the Romans and the Norman coat of arms. Members of the jury take notes. Mr Giddy rocks approvingly in his chair as Terracini refers to a conspiracy of corrupt police. 'Are you scared? Well, you don't have to be. But there are evil, evil people in this case and the stakes are very very high!'

One by one Terracini spells out the inconsistencies on the tapes. ' "Roger stole his badge and give it to me." We know this a lie. Absolute rubbish! We go on: "Had his fingerprints on it. Roger give it to me in a plastic bag." This is not an exaggeration! Every single piece of this is false. It is nonsense! Smith didn't drop a badge at the scene. It is rubbish! Uncontradicted rubbish!'

Smith sits as quiet as a statue in the dock. Watching him, I remember the words former Homicide detective Geoff Prentice had used at the committal, 'Murderers never tell the whole truth. There's always something they gloss over or they lie about.'

•

In the lunchtime adjournment I roam the grounds of the Supreme court complex, down past the old convict jail and back up Bourke street to the brick and stone former Darlinghurst police station where Sallie-Anne accrued 31 arrests. One of the jurors has fallen ill and the court adjourns for the remainder of the afternoon. At home there is a message for me. 'Thought you might like to hear this,' W.B. says when I ring him back. He reads out a statement from the former manager of the Iron Duke Hotel, William James Duff, in which Duff told police that Neddy Smith came into the Iron Duke at 11 a.m. on Friday, 7 February 1986.

'Listen to this bit,' W.B. says: ' "It was unusual for Ned to come into the hotel on a Friday morning. He came up to me and we had a conversation. I also noticed something about him. I do not wish to enter into the contents of the conversation I had with Smith at this stage." '

'So why haven't the prosecution called him?' I ask.

'The DPP have a policy of not using the testimony of convicted criminals,' W.B. says. 'Apparently Smith walked into the Iron Duke with blood on his face.'

•

When W.B. hangs up, I ring Michelle Richards and ask if Warren Richards will speak to me. Michelle promises to get a message through to her husband in Long Bay.

According to Mr Brown, Neddy Smith strangled Sallie-Anne because Roger Rogerson had said she was taping police who were supplying heroin to the drug trade. The only New South Wales policeman Sallie was known to have taped was Gary Spencer. At dusk I drive out to Rose Bay police station to talk to Spencer. Ever since Sallie's inquest, Gary Spencer's name had been linked with her death.

A tall, lean man wearing an inspector's uniform, Spencer greets me in the foyer and leads me downstairs to his office. The walls are covered with maps of the Eastern Suburbs and fuzzy posters of missing persons. A police radio crackles in the background. The first thing Gary Spencer does is read through the documents I have brought him from the trial. He denies ringing Peter Smith to find out the contents of Sallie's tapes. 'Why would I ring that idiot?' Spencer says. 'I'm not stupid.' He tells me that he didn't discover Sallie-Anne had taped him until the inquest.

'You must admit that your association with her doesn't look good?'

'You want to know the truth?' he says.

'Yes.'

'I met Sallie-Anne Huckstepp twice.' Spencer leans back in his chair. 'The first time when we executed a search warrant on 17/2 Eastbourne Road in Darling Point. We were searching for heroin and arrested another woman in possession of a small quantity. I had a conversation with Sallie-Anne about the activities of a major drug dealer we were targeting.'

'Who?'

'Warren Richards. When she came back to the Drug Bureau I gave her my number. "If you want to talk about Richards," I said, "ring me." In December 1985 we arrested one of Sallie's runners, a woman called Jennifer Bain, in the Cross. Bain was taken to Waverley station and charged with possession of ten foils. That afternoon I received a phone call from Sallie-Anne who wanted to meet. "I'll tell you about Warren Richards," she said. I was the youngest guy in the Drug Squad in those days and here was the possibility of nailing a prime target. I had to find out what she had to offer. I went to the Golden Sheaf and it was a set-up.'

'You had no idea she was taping you?'

'Sallie-Anne was a chameleon, she could play people off the break. She was very clever. She wanted to have something over me.'

'Why?'

'So she could get her foils back. I didn't realise what she was doing. I wish I'd never gone there.'

'And that was the last time you saw her?'

Spencer nodded in his chair. 'At 4 p.m. on the day she was murdered she rang me at the Drug Bureau and wanted to see me. I was busy and told her to ring back. At the inquest I found out that she had taped me. Then Henderson and Kiely manufactured that tape in Parklea Prison which had Rogerson, Richards and me supposedly planning her death. They even rattled dice in a glass to make it sound like we were drinking.'

'Why go to so much trouble?'

'Revenge,' Spencer says. 'I put Henderson away. My boss identified the voice as mine. I was cautioned by Task Force Alpha. At one stage I thought, I'm gone. They're going to charge me with Huckstepp's murder.'

'But it was all coincidence?'

'That's the truth,' Spencer says. 'It hurt my career. I still get "How's Roger going?" or "How's Richards?" from other police. I have to laugh it off. The whole story is too bizarre for words.'

•

Reporters are gathering outside Darlinghurst Court. Justice Abadee finishes his summary and gives the jury their final instructions: 'You are not here to play the role of sleuths.' They are sent out with half the pieces. One of the regulars has brought along a bottle of wine to present to Smith. He has wrapped it in coloured paper. I ring Michelle Richards and she says her husband won't talk. I don't tell her that Gary Spencer has told me that he believes Richards killed Sallie-Anne because she was seeing Federal Police. I don't tell her that I have heard from a source within Smith's camp that Richards was the killer. I am introduced to an ex-Fed who went through the academy with Peter Smith and Terry Muir. 'It was common knowledge what was in those fur coats,' he tells me. 'Photos.'

'What sort of photos?'

'Let's just say a very senior officer had to get them back at all costs.'

•

Former detective sergeant Bill Duff has recently been paroled after a three-year-sentence for supplying 57 grams of rock heroin. I meet him in a city hotel. Duff is wearing a floral shirt, slacks, trainers and carrying a mobile phone and an electronic diary. A short stocky man with a grin which reveals his two lower incisors, he chain-smokes while I talk. 'Geoff Prentice told me that you rang him when he had Warren Richards in custody and asked, "Have you got my little mate there?"'

'Didn't happen,' Duff says.

'What about Smith?'

'Neddy Smith is a skunk,' Duff says. 'I saved his life, dragged him into the Iron Duke and locked the hotel door when this bloke in a car was going to back over him. When the cops were going to off Neddy in my beer garden, I warned him. Then he makes up all these lies about me.'

'Did Smith come into your hotel at 11 a.m. on Friday, 7 February 1986 with blood on his face?'

'It wasn't blood,' Duff says. 'He had scratch marks down the side of his face. He was shitting himself.'

'What did he say?'

'He wanted to know certain things.'

'Like what?'

'He wanted to know how long a body stays underwater. I told him from experience what I knew. Then at twelve o'clock it's on the news about Huckstepp. I rang a mate of mine in the police force, I said, "Get surveillance to take a few snaps of Neddy. He's walking around Sydney with these deep gouges in his face."

'On Saturday Ned comes in early and says, "Bill, that conversation we had yesterday it didn't happen." I said, "Righto."

'I got a message to Geoff Prentice to come and see me, but he never did. Geoff's a nice bloke, but he wasn't the right man for the Huckstepp investigation. He was dealing with first graders. They should've knocked that brief over in three days. Soon as Huckstepp was dead you pull the file on her, you find out who was offside and then you go and have a mag to them. Dead set, that was an easy brief. I let them know, I said come and see me, but Geoff never came near the Iron Duke. He was too scared because I was under surveillance.

'I just hope Smith gets some terrible disease for killing her,' Duff says. 'It was a low act. I can't think of a word for him.'

•

The jury have been out for less than five hours when the message spreads through the corridors that they have reached a decision. Within minutes reporters and hangers-on pack the benches of courtroom no. 2. The Prosecutor arrives, clutching his wig. Members of the media check their watches. Terracini paces in front of the dock.

At 2.11 p.m. the foreman, wearing a blinding yellow shirt, leads the jurors in through a side door. Smith stands.

The judge's associate asks if they have reached a verdict. 'Not guilty,' the foreman says.

For a moment the court is silent. Smith leans over and shakes the hands of his defence team. Reporters file out into the foyer. Dressed in black, Sascha Huckstepp has sat at the rear of the court every day for five weeks and listened to what Smith did to her mother. Now she ventures through the doors and out to the street, pursued by photographers.

I wait until everyone is gone and walk out onto Darlinghurst Road. It is Friday afternoon. The sky is blue and clear. A bunch of women sweep past, laughing, well-groomed. I have lost count of the number of times people have told me their Sallie Huckstepp story. Like the reporter who met her once for a drink in Glebe. 'She was supposed to go and meet Channel Nine lawyers at 7.30 p.m. sharp,' he said, 'but at 9.30 we were still drinking. She cost me a fortune in bourbons. It was a night to remember.' Or the brother of the famous rock star who went around to her apartment to buy a hundred dollar deal on the day of her murder. 'Sallie was a bubbly, beautiful lady,' he said. 'The first time I saw her she answered the door with her arm in plaster, wearing a yellow bikini. I remember staring at her body the whole time.'

And there was the former vice-squad detective who came up to me outside the old Darlinghurst Court and told me that Sallie-Anne Huckstepp was a lot of things. 'She was a flirt, a drug-addict, a part-time whistleblower and a full-time underworld figure,' he said. 'But she had guts, I'll give her that.'

16

Warrant for the arrest

Three months shy of her fifteenth birthday, Sallie-Anne appeared in Metropolitan Children's Court to face the charge of smoking Indian Hemp. A psychiatric report prepared by Brisbane Street Child Guidance Clinic described her as an attractive girl with an IQ of 123.

'Sallie has been kept in an adult role by her father since her stepmother left,' the psychiatrist wrote. 'Mr Krivoshow keeps the family together and does not realise his own subconscious problems which cause Sallie to behave in a non-conforming fashion. Besides, there are the uncle and aunt who all play their part in this unusual family circle.'

The District Officer from the Department of Child Welfare visited Sallie at home. 'I saw the lass on about three occasions and some improvement was effected in her behaviour,' he wrote. 'It is obvious that too much domestic responsibility falls upon Sallie and that the father's working hours (afternoon to midnight) are unsuitable. Miss Rose Krivoshow, aged about 40, has no employment, deriving income from property, and impresses favourably. Accommodation is somewhat overtaxed in her rather shabby, but adequately furnished three-bedroom Bondi flat. The family appears to be a close-knit one with the Jewish sense of responsibility towards its members. Although Sallie is inclined to be hostile towards her aunt, and still maintains that there is nothing wrong with smoking marijuana, she is terrified of being sent to an institution, as she wishes to go on to sixth year and become an actress.'

The Magistrate perused the official documents and peered down from the bench. 'You're a bit young for the drugs, aren't you?'

'Yes,' Sallie said.

'Do you always wear eye-shadow and make-up like that?'

'Yes.'

'Don't you think it's a bit overdone for a fourteen-year-old?'

'No.'

'Well, I do,' the Magistrate said. 'Are you going to give the crowd away or am I going to lock you up?'

'I'll keep out of trouble,' Sallie said.

'That is not what I asked you. Are you going to give the crowd away, all the boys and all the girls?'

'Yes,' Sallie said.

'What do you know about marijuana?'

'Nothing, I suppose.'

'Ever made a study of it?'

'No,' Sallie said.

'Do you know it is fairly well used along the seaports from Egypt to South East Asia?'

'Yes.'

'Do you know that this area has the highest rates of disease and deformity in the world?'

'Yes.'

'It seems to be one of the chief solaces of the have-nots. It is a known fact that if you have enough you go mad. There is no need to qualify that.' The Magistrate turned to Rose. 'What is your opinion of Sallie?'

'I think she should be made to realise she's in serious trouble,' Rose Krivoshow said.

'You take "pot" and you're not getting too much out of it so the people who are pushing hard drugs say, well, we'll give you a shot of heroin. This is why we are worried about you young people who sneak down the beach to have a few puffs. How long have you been with your aunt?'

'A couple of weeks now,' Sallie said.

'When you go down to the beach in future you'd better swim.'

Released on probation for twelve months, Sallie travelled home with Rose who was wearing a red designer dress she'd picked up in a Paddington op shop. Sallie admired her aunt's taste, the way older men glanced at her sideways on the bus. It was the first time she'd been alone with her since the Freilich case and Sallie asked her aunt why she had got involved in prostitution.

'I didn't do it for fun,' Rose said, 'I did it to save myself from a life of drudgery.'

'I couldn't do it,' Sallie said. 'I just couldn't.'

'Forget about it, Sallie,' Rose said. 'It's not for you.'

When Rose was fourteen she'd had to leave school and get work because her father couldn't afford to keep her on. For two years she gave her mother her pay envelope unopened. One pound seven and sixpence. 'It was hard,' Rose said, 'I had nothing.' Her father, Naum, wouldn't let her wear slacks. Trousers were for men, he used to say. She had a very restrictive upbringing and she rebelled against it.

'How did you get started?' Sallie asked.

'I was struggling to make ends meet,' Rose said. 'One night a girlfriend told me how much she was earning at a private residence in Kings Cross. My ears pricked up. I was tired of scrimping and saving, so I thought, why not?' Rose said. 'Lots of women do it for free. I told your grandmother I was a ground hostess for Ansett.'

Sallie laughed, biting at a nail. 'Weren't you scared when you went into the bedroom with them?'

'I'm a good talker,' Rose said. 'I used to get out of everything I could.'

That evening Sallie sat on the edge of her uncle's unmade bed and told him about the girls she had met at the courthouse, some of whom were lesbians and prostitutes. Sallie said that if she was ever locked up or sent to a shelter she would come out ten times worse because she would probably succumb to their advances. She denied that she would be weak enough to accept, but 'like dripping water,' Sallie said, 'if you are there long enough and so many girls approach you, it does wear away your resistance in the end.'

Nodding his head Uncle Ike shuffled around the room in his big baggy trousers and singlet. Her uncle never passed judgment. What's more, he listened. Sallie said that even though it was a condition of her probation that she attend school and be of good behaviour, she wasn't going back to fourth form. Everyone knew about her carnal knowledge case. Friends, parents, the entire Jewish community. She had met this boy called Steve who was in a band. They were going to be huge just as soon as they started performing their own material. 'I'm going to run away,' Sallie said.

'What about money?' Ike asked her.

Sallie slipped a hand beneath his mattress and pulled out a glossy magazine, started thumbing through the pages. 'I'll get a job. The Whiskey Au-Go-Go is looking for waitresses.'

Uncle Ike retrieved his adult magazine from her grip and dropped it into a drawer. 'Where will you live?'

'A girlfriend has this flat,' Sallie said, 'in Bourke Street. I'll have my own room.' With a flick of her head Sallie indicated the doorway. 'Anyway he doesn't want me here. All he cares about is *her*.'

'Your father works very hard,' Ike said.

Sallie took out a small tobacco tin and papers and rolled a cigarette in her lap. 'He's sending Debra down to SCEGGS in Moss Vale. He wants to get rid of us so he can have Maggie all to himself.' Sallie struck a match and blew smoke at the window. 'He treats me like a child. I'm not going through another Estelle.' Sallie held out the joint. 'You want some, Uncle Ike?'

Ike shook his head, emptying his wallet out on the bed. He handed Sallie three $20 bills. 'Pay me back when you get on your feet.'

Sallie hugged her big soft uncle. Years later, when she was working in Darlinghurst, she would hide the money she earned on the street with Uncle Ike. When the Vice Squad raided the dirty bookshop Ike worked in, looking for Sallie's money, he refused to give it to them.

After the block of flats in Ramsgate Avenue was sold, Ike shouted all his friends to expensive restaurants in the Cross, hired a Rolls-Royce and gave Sallie $2000. In six months, he blew his inheritance on good-time girls. 'If things get really bad,' Sallie would often tell friends, 'I can always go to Uncle Ike's.'

She folded the money he gave her into the pocket of her tunic and walked up the stairs to no. 4. She lay on the bunk beside her sleeping sister. Her father was out driving cabs. They slept in the same bedroom but didn't say a word to each other. By the faint light through the window Sallie wrote in her journal, 'I don't get on with my father, he resents me, he's not really my father.'

Conditions between Sallie and Jack were so intolerable that Jack phoned the Children's Court requesting the removal of his daughter from the family home. He told her district officer, Miss Montague, that Sallie often stayed out until 3 a.m. and that she was not conforming to any of the court's conditions. In reply, Sallie said that she was well-behaved but had come out in a nervous rash because of the tension and her dislike of her father and his 'new friend'. She said that every time her father told her not to do a thing she deliberately went out and did it, just to prove her independence.

The following evening Jack removed the front door key to prevent Sallie from taking her clothes and walking out. 'I've lost control of her,' Jack told Miss Montague. 'I don't know what it is. Maybe I've been too strict. We don't get on.'

'Sallie has many good points,' Miss Montague reported to the Child Welfare Department. 'She is an extremely pleasant girl, well-mannered and honest with money, but she does not accept the moral standards imposed by society. She feels that she is entitled to as much sexual freedom as any adult.'

'I don't want Sallie to remain with me any longer,' Jack told the Children's Court.

'What are we going to do with you, Sallie?' the Special Magistrate asked. 'From what I understand you and your father are fighting so much you would be both prepared to see the last of each other for a long while.'

'Yes,' Sallie said. 'Could I go and live with my uncle?'

'I think she needs some sort of discipline,' Jack said. 'He wouldn't be able to control her.'

'I can get on well with him,' Sallie said. 'He understands me, when he says something he gives a reason.'

'He has moved into a small two-bedroom flat,' Jack told the magistrate, 'which he shares with my sister at the moment, but she won't have Sallie in the place.'

'You mean there would be just you and your uncle?'

Sallie nodded.

'No,' the Magistrate said.

'Perhaps a further remand period in custody might be considered,' Miss Montague suggested, 'while inquiries are made with the Methodist Christian Fellowship.'

'What do you think of the idea of a hostel, Sallie?'

'I don't want to go to a hostel,' Sallie said. 'I couldn't live with those sort of girls.'

'What makes you think you are so different?'

'I don't know, but I just couldn't live with them.'

'What would you do if I let you go home?'

'I would get a job,' Sallie said.

'What sort of job?'

'In a pharmacy. I would be trained as a beautician.'

'Sallie thinks she is a lot older than she really is,' Jack said. 'Perhaps she can explain to you why she is getting presents from a 45-year-old man.'

'She will have to go to Minda,' the Magistrate ruled.

'I don't want to go to Minda,' Sallie said.

'Well, you have to, it's for your own health's sake.'

Detained for two weeks in the hospital section of Minda Remand Centre in Lidcombe, opposite Rookwood Cemetery, Sallie was examined by a physician who found no evidence of venereal infection and no sign of pregnancy. On her file he scribbled, 'intelligence—high; moral sense—poor'. Allowed to go home temporarily with her father and his new girlfriend, while inquiries were made to provide her with alternative accommodation, Sallie told Miss Montague that if she was sent to Parramatta Training School or to any institution she would go mad.

'I want to set up my own flat,' Sallie said. 'I am completely capable of managing my own affairs.'

'There is a definite personality clash between this girl and her father, who is threatened to an extent by his teenage daughter in his new relationship,' Miss Montague wrote in her report. 'Committal to a convent for a period might assist.'

A constable from Bondi Station visited Sallie and informed her that both charges of carnal knowledge against Danny Freilich had been dropped.

'Why?' Sallie said.

'Don't know, miss,' the constable said. Perhaps the officer was unaware that the Crown Prosecutor had written to the Attorney General a week earlier recommending that a bill not be filed.

'I have suppressed as far as possible the disgust I feel,' the Crown Prosecutor wrote confidentially, 'for the manner and extent to which Counsel for the accused attacked the character of the complainant who was only fourteen years of age. Much of the material used in cross-examination emanates from the complainant's stepmother. This attack was carried to the point of suggesting that the child, at some unspecified time, had stolen from the money boxes of other children. Sallie has acted in a sophisticated manner, by applying make-up and her previous sexual experience. In my opinion, the case ought not to be prosecuted.'

Sallie welcomed the news. She was relieved she didn't have to go through that again. She had no faith in the courts. No faith in the law.

Shortly before dusk the following evening, while her father was out driving cabs and Debra was visiting a schoolfriend, Sallie-Anne went into her grandmother's old bedroom and borrowed a suitcase. She packed her giraffe-print dress, her knee-high boots from Raymond Castles, her black top from Gasworks and the long white linen dress she'd bought on her fifteenth birthday. On top of her clothes she laid out a six-month supply of the pill, her make-up bag and her little black journal.

On the pavement, Sallie turned and glanced back at the white stucco block of flats where she had spent so much of her childhood. The idea that Aunt Rose's money had helped grandma pay off the mortgage made her laugh.

Sallie walked down to the south end of Bondi where she rested on a rock, her back to the low concrete wall and her bare heels cooling in the wet sand. She smoked a joint listening to the waves roll in, watching the sky turn dark blue. Tonight she would catch a taxi to her small bed-sitter, sleep on the smelly spare mattress on the floor and early tomorrow morning she would ring Steve and he would drive over on his Triumph and help her find work. She was going to show her father, her friends—everyone—what she was capable of. She had always known she was cut out for something special, that one day people would remember her name. She had to be strong. 'I know I've got talent inside me somewhere,' Sallie wrote in her journal. 'I just don't know where it lies.'

She picked up her suitcase and shoes and strode across the sand, climbed the grassy slope to where the white and yellow lights were burning on Campbell Parade. A few stars were out and a derelict was begging near the bus shelter. Sallie dug in her purse for loose change; she only had enough for her fare. Her father always used to say, whenever they saw someone down on their luck, 'there but for the grace of God go I'.

Sallie waved at the traffic and a taxi skidded alongside. The driver took her case, slung it in the boot and, staring at her bare brown legs asked, 'Where to sweetie?' 'Darlinghurst,' Sallie told him. She slid into the back seat, her heart beating with excitement. She knew that in the weeks ahead the police would come searching for her, but she was not afraid. She had no regrets. She leaned towards the rear-view mirror and brushed her eyelashes with a mascara wand. She fixed her lipstick and let out her hair. The taxi accelerated up the hill. Tonight she was young and beautiful and she had never felt so alive.

WARRANT

To all Police Constables in the State of New South Wales

WHEREAS information on oath hath this day been laid before the undersigned by an officer of the Department of Child Welfare that having made due inquiry, he believes that

SALLIE-ANNE KRIVOSHOW,

a child under sixteen years of age, to wit, of the age of fifteen years, born 12.12.54, has committed a breach of the conditions of her probation in that she has not been of good behaviour.

I therefore command you, in Her Majesty's name, forthwith to apprehend and take the said child (young person) to a Shelter, there to be detained pending the determination of a Court constituted under the Act.

CHILD: Left home at 4/9 Ramsgate Avenue, Bondi. May be with young man known as 'Steve' belonging to group 'Clearwaters'.

Build—slight with solid muscular legs.
Complexion—fair to light olive.
Hair—Light brown curly, worn usually in small pony tail.
Eyes—Deep bluish-green
rather large mouth, good teeth.

Acknowledgements

This book does its best to be a factual account of the life and death of Sallie-Anne Huckstepp. It is based on over 90 interviews, hundreds of transcripts of court proceedings, New South Wales and Federal Police files, archival material and original documents by and about Sallie-Anne Huckstepp that were discovered during the research. Acknowledgement is made to the following published sources: '60 Minutes', 'The Last Days of Warren Lanfranchi', 5 July 1981; Elisabeth Wynhausen, 'On the Run—Life of a Crim's Girlfriend', *National Times*, 12 July 1981; A Willesee documentary, 'Sallie-Anne', 1982; *Penthouse Magazine*, 'The View from Hay Street', May 1982 and 'Amateur Night', March 1983; Background Briefing, ABC Radio, 'Sallie-Anne', 29 June 1986.

The author is especially grateful to Debra Krivoshow, Scott McCrae, W.B., and Gwen Beecroft. He would also like to thank Wendy Bacon, Julie Clarke, Andrew Cowell, Dennis Cruse, Helen F, Andrew Haesler, Judy Johnston, Jack Krivoshow, Margaret Krivoshow, Rose Krivoshow, Darrell Lanfranchi, Roz Nelson, Richard Neville, Godfrey Oettle, David Oliver, Geoff Prentice, Greg Ryan, Martin Sharp, Lee Shields-Rossit, Glenn Stone and a number of other people who for personal or professional reasons wished to remain anonymous.

The author is particularly indebted to Ann Dombroski for her careful reading of the manuscript, her encouragement and helpful suggestions over the six years it took to complete the work. Special thanks go to Noel King, Lyn Tranter and Sophie Cunningham. Part of this book was written with the assistance of the Australia Council.